The
rea

CP/494

Escape From Kabul

Also by Levison Wood

Walking the Nile
Walking the Himalayas
Walking the Americas
Eastern Horizons
Arabia
Incredible Journeys
The Last Giants
Encounters
The Art of Exploration
Endurance

Also by Geraint Jones

NON–FICTION
Brothers in Arms

FICTION
Ambush (Blood Forest)
Siege
Legion
Traitor
Rebel

Escape From Kabul

The Inside Story

Levison Wood &
Geraint Jones

HODDER &
STOUGHTON

First published in Great Britain in 2023 by Hodder & Stoughton
An Hachette UK company

1

Copyright © Levison Wood & Geraint Jones 2023

A CIP catalogue record for this title is available from the British Library

Hardback ISBN 9781399718127
Trade Paperback ISBN 9781399718141
eBook ISBN 9781399718110

Typeset in Bembo by Hewer Text UK Ltd, Edinburgh
Printed and bound in Great Britain by Clays Ltd, Elcograf S.p.A.

Hodder & Stoughton policy is to use papers that are natural, renewable
and recyclable products and made from wood grown in sustainable forests.
The logging and manufacturing processes are expected to conform
to the environmental regulations of the country of origin.

Hodder & Stoughton Ltd
Carmelite House
50 Victoria Embankment
London EC4Y 0DZ

www.hodder.co.uk

For those who never came home

Contents

Timeline

11 September 2001	World Trade Center attacked in New York.
October 2001	Operation Enduring Freedom begins.
December 2001	UN authorises ISAF (International Security Assistance Force).
20 June 2002	Operation Herrick begins.
August 2003	NATO assumes ISAF command.
March 2006	16 Air Assault Brigade deploy to Helmand Province.
June 2006	ISAF mandate expanded.
2009	Counterinsurgency operations begin.
2011–2014	Three-year transition to Afghan-led security operations.
October 2014	End of UK combat operations.
December 2014	End of US and NATO combat operations, withdrawal of ISAF. Operation Herrick ends.
1 January 2015	Afghan forces assume security responsibility. NATO establishes Resolute Support Mission. Operation Toral begins.
February 2020	Doha peace agreement signed by the US and the Taliban.
April 2021	US and NATO announce revised withdrawal plan.

1 May 2021	Coalition forces begin withdrawing, to be completed by 11 September 2021.
8 July 2021	Operation Toral ends.
13 August 2021	Operation Pitting begins.
15 August 2021	Afghan Government falls.
28 August 2021	Operation Pitting ends.
30 August 2021	The final US troops leave Afghanistan.

Glossary

2 Para – 2nd Battalion, The Parachute Regiment

3 Para – 3rd Battalion, The Parachute Regiment

82nd – 82nd Airborne Division, United States Army

9 Squadron – 9 Squadron, The Corps of Royal Engineers

23 Engineer Regiment – 23 Engineer Regiment, The Corps of Royal Engineers

1/8 Marines – 1st Battalion, 8th Marine Regiment, United States Marine Corps

A400M – Transport aircraft used by the Royal Air Force

A/B/C Coy – Designations of rifle companies: an infantry company being a subdivision of a battalion, typically made up of 100–150 personnel

Ally – Slang used by Paratroopers to describe something as good looking/cool/exciting/fun

Al-Qaeda – Islamic terrorist organisation headed by Osama Bin Laden

ANA – Afghan National Army

ANP – Afghan National Police

ANSDF – Afghan National Security and Defence Forces

ARAP – Afghan Relocations and Assistance Policy

ATF 444/333 – Afghan Commando Unit

Buckshee – British Army slang used to describe either something easy to do or something free/gratis/complimentary (or possibly stolen)

C-130 and C-17 – Transport aircraft types

Card Alpha – A category of British military Rules of Engagement

Casevac – Evacuate a battlefield casualty

CENTCOM – Central Command, the US military command responsible for the region which included Afghanistan

Chevron – Named for its shape, this was a combat engineer-installed structure of shipping containers to enable the processing of evacuees between the Baron Hotel and Abbey Gate

CIA – Central Intelligence Agency

CO – Commanding Officer

COC – Combat Operations Centre

Cpl – Corporal

C-RAM – Counter Rocket, Artillery, and Mortar: C-RAM is a weapons system designed for intercepting incoming fire

CS gas – A form of tear gas

CSM – Company Sergeant Major

DAB – Da Afghanistan Bank, the central bank of Afghanistan.

Daesh – Derogatory term for the Islamic State

Doha Agreement – Peace agreement signed by the United States and the Taliban on 29 February 2020 in Doha, Qatar

DShK – Soviet heavy machine gun

DZ Flash – Coloured insignia worn on the sleeve of a Parachute Regiment soldier to denote their battalion

EOD – Explosive Ordnance Disposal

FCDO – Foreign, Commonwealth & Development Office

FIFA – Fédération Internationale de Football Association, the governing body of international football (soccer)

GRO – Graduated Response Option

HKIA – Hamid Karzai International Airport, Kabul, which became the hub of the evacuation efforts

Humvee – High Mobility Multipurpose Wheeled Vehicle (HMMWV)

IDF – Indirect Fire

IED – Improvised Explosive Device

IOC – Infantry Officers Course: specialisation training for United States Marine Corps infantry officers once they have graduated from The Basic School (TBS)

IS – Islamic State, a militant Islamic group

ISAF – International Security Assistance Force

IS-K – Islamic State of Khorosan, an affiliate group of Islamic State operating in Afghanistan

JFHQ – Standing Joint Force Headquarters

JIC – Joint Intelligence Committee

Jihad – Islamic principle of the struggle, often used to describe violence and warfare against non-believers

JOC – Joint Operations Centre

JTAC – Joint Terminal Attack Controller

LES – Locally Employed Staff

LO – Liaison Officer

M4 – 5.56mm carbine weapon

MATTs – Mandatory Annual Training Tests

MEU – Marine Expeditionary Unit

MOD – Ministry of Defence

MP – Military Police or Member of Parliament

MQ-9 – Reaper Drone, a type of unmanned aerial vehicle used for surveillance and missile strikes

MRAPS – Mine-Resistant Ambush Protected vehicles

NATO – North Atlantic Treaty Organisation

NEO – Noncombatant Evacuation Operation

NGO – Non-Governmental Organisation

NCO – Non-Commissioned Officer

No. 7 Squadron – a unit of the Royal Air Force

NPR – National Public Radio, an American privately and state-funded nonprofit media organisation

NSC – National Security Council, an HM Government department

NVA – North Vietnamese Army, People's Army of Vietnam

OC – Officer Commanding

Op Fingal – Codename for the deployment to Afghanistan in 2002 that included 2 Para

Op Herrick – Codename under which all British operations in the war in Afghanistan were conducted from 2002 to the end of combat operations in 2014

Op Pitting – Codename given to the British military element of the Afghanistan evacuation

OPTEMPO – Operational Tempo

Op Toral – Codename for the British presence within Afghanistan post-2014 as part of NATO's Resolute Support Mission.

PBA – Post Blast Analysis

PJ – Pararescue Jumpers

PTSD – Post-Traumatic Stress Disorder

QRF – Quick Reaction Force

RAF – Royal Air Force

RMAS – Royal Military Academy Sandhurst

ROE – Rules Of Engagement

RoKit Foundation – Charitable organisation within RoKit group

RSM – Regimental Sergeant Major

SAS – Special Air Service

SEALs – Sea, Air, and Land Teams, the US Navy's primary special operation force

Sgt – Sergeant

SIVs – Special Immigrant Visas

SNCO – Senior Non-Commissioned Officer

SOP – Standard Operating Procedure

SPMAGTAF – Special Purpose Marine Air-Ground Task Force

Stagging – On guard, guarding

TBS – The Basic School, US Marine Corps Officer Training

TF444 – Afghan Commando Force

TF Polar Bear – A task force in Kabul made up of soldiers from the US's 10th Mountain Division

TOC –Tactical Operations Centre

TRIM – Trauma Risk Incident Management

UN – United Nations

UNHCR – United Nations High Commissioner for Refugees

UNICEF – Agency of the United Nations responsible for providing humanitarian and developmental aid to children.

USAF – United States Air Force

USMC – United States Marine Corps

USMC EOD – United States Marine Corps Explosive Ordnance Disposal

USS – United States Ship

US SOF – United States Special Operations Forces

USSR – Union of Soviet Socialist Republics

VBIED –Vehicle-Borne Improvised Explosive Device

WFP – United Nations World Food Programme

Authors' note

For security and safety purposes the names of some interviewees have been changed. The interviews have been transcribed accurately and dialogue has not been altered in any way other than to protect the identities of vulnerable people or for operational security purposes. Any opinions held within the book are those held by the authors and those quoted and are not the official stance of HM Government or the UK Ministry of Defence. The spelling of words alternates between British English and American depending on the nationality of the user. All facts contained within the book have been verified or substantiated, and citations are provided where necessary.

Introduction

On 13 August 2021, I received a hastily written WhatsApp message from a friend in Afghanistan detailing a supposedly agreed 'peace deal' that the Afghan government had made with the Taliban. It stated that the president had effectively given up his power and would flee the country, and that the Taliban leadership would enter Kabul within two days.

I could hardly believe what I was reading. None of this was in the news, not yet. Even the British government didn't seem to be aware of the imminent collapse, and even if they did, it didn't seem to be a priority. Most of them were on holiday.

This had to be wrong. Surely the capital would not fall to the Taliban? Not after twenty years of war that claimed the lives of over 150,000 Afghans and 457 British service personnel. After all the blood, sweat and tears of a war that seemed to go on forever, we couldn't actually lose? Surely we weren't about to surrender all of whatever it was that we were supposed to have gained? The world's superpower, the United States, was not really going to retreat and capitulate to an enemy of sandal-wearing tribesmen?

This cognitive dissonance came crashing down two days later, when a victorious Taliban entered Kabul. The twenty-year war was over.

That day – 15 August 2021 – I received another message, this time from a British member of parliament. He asked if I could help him to extract one of his former colleagues from the country: a former Afghan special forces operative, now in hiding in Kabul.

I said that I would try to help. Using the power of social media and what is colloquially known as 'the reg net', I asked my own former colleagues in the Parachute Regiment if anyone could assist.

The same day, another old friend, Geraint 'Gez' Jones, contacted me to see if I had any way of assisting another Afghan special forces soldier who had worked with the Americans. As the country crumbled, thousands of veterans were scrambling to pull out their allies.

All roads pointed towards an old comrade: Mike Pratt, currently working for CNN as a security advisor, and presently on paternity leave in London. Mike became the centre of a web of veterans, politicians, civilians, and soldiers on the ground. He worked tirelessly for two weeks, barely sleeping, and managed to coordinate the rescue of more than seventy Afghan allies out of Kabul, including the ones mentioned above.

Mike was but one of many veterans lending a hand in what became known as the 'Digital Dunkirk': the Herculean effort to extract as many of our Afghan friends from the clutches of the Taliban as possible, before it was too late. For some, help did not come quickly enough.

Afghanistan has a dear place in my heart. I first visited the country in 2004 as a young aspiring writer, hiking across the central mountain passes and staying with local families. I was enamoured with the kindness and hospitality that I received, and it was a country that I revisited many times. A few years later I served as an officer in the Parachute Regiment, and returned to Afghanistan in 2008, this time to fight the Taliban on Operation Herrick, the British Army's mission to Helmand

Province. My co-author Geraint Jones was a decorated soldier in the Royal Welsh, also serving in Afghanistan in 2009/10.

Neither of us were present for the fall of Kabul, and yet, thanks to the generosity of the military network and the Ministry of Defence, we were able to secure access to speak with a great many of those who were. This book is the net result of interviews with over forty people, ranging from soldiers of the Parachute Regiment, members of the Civil Service, the British ambassador, politicians, generals, charity workers, journalists, US military members, Afghan civilians, and even the Taliban themselves.

It hopes to provide a glimpse into the chaos of that frantic fortnight that led up to complete allied withdrawal from Afghanistan by the end of August 2021. It is not, of course, a comprehensive account of every perspective, but it does try to give a balanced viewpoint from a number of often conflicting positions.

For some, the escape from Kabul was an unbridled tragedy. For others, it was a heroic achievement against all odds. Either way, for good or ill, it deserves a place in our nation's military and political history.

This book serves to remind us of the bravery and service of our Armed Forces, of the sacrifices made in Afghanistan, and of the mistakes that were made in underestimating a determined enemy. The Fall of Kabul will be remembered by history, and this book hopes to see that the people who were there will be remembered too. Not least, the Afghans who were left behind. The US-led mission may have ended when the last aircraft left the runway, but the plight of the Afghan people has not.

Major Levison Wood
London, October 2022

I

The Forever War

Blood cannot be washed out with blood.

– Afghan proverb

Few wars began and ended with such tragic, televised drama. The events of September 2001 and August 2021 held the attention of global news audiences, who stared agape at the unfolding horror. Bodies fell from the sky in America on 9/11. They did again twenty years later, over the skies of Afghanistan. It was the absence of hope that made people jump from the burning towers of New York. It was the absence of hope that made people cling to the landing gear of aircraft leaving Kabul.

Following the al-Qaeda attacks on the World Trade Center, a tide of conflict had flooded Afghanistan, but twenty years later the deluge of foreign interference was ebbing, leaving behind the skeletal remains of a democracy already picked clean by those who chose corruption and greed over their own people. Unlike 9/11, the death of Afghanistan's fledgling democracy was not a single, violent moment. Rather, the events in Kabul were the country's last gasping breath. Any patient hope by those who had fought bravely against the odds was, by the hot and dusty August of 2021, all but gone.

There is no doubt that the events of that month were nothing less than a tragedy, but it is often amongst such suffering and despair that we find a glimmer of the very best of human-kind. Look to any warzone and you will find people who have traded their safety for service. War often brings to the fore such protectors; those who would risk their lives so that strangers may live.

Operation Pitting – the British code name for the evacuation of Kabul – was no different. From those who manned the barri-cades and flew the aircraft to those who fought 'the WhatsApp War' in their homes, there was no shortage of heroes that stepped up to the plate.

That being said, this book does not seek to glorify or justify what has happened in Afghanistan. That many of the military personnel and civilians who served there had good intentions does not mitigate the human cost. However one feels about the twenty years of war, there is no question that its final few months were a disaster for the international community, and more importantly, for Afghans. The deck of cards that had been the Afghan Security Forces fell more quickly than generals and politicians had ever imagined; at least, in public. Many Afghans who had bought into the American-led vision were left behind, and at the mercy of the victorious Taliban.

Hundreds of British military personnel, thousands of Americans, and troops from several other NATO countries took part in the evacuation of their own people and of those Afghans who had helped them during the occupation, but for every family rescued, many more were left behind. At the beginning of August, around 18,000 Afghans had started the application process for America's resettlement programme, a number that does not include family members and dependants.[1] According to the organisation No One Left Behind, some 300 Afghans were murdered because of their ties to the US-led mission.[2] Despite a heroic effort by those on the ground, a report by Wartime Allies estimated that out of the 81,000 applications to America's programme by 15 August 2021, 78,000 were left behind.[3]

'Due to my services for the U.S forces/gov[ernment], my family and I are living in a terrible situation with fear and frustration,' one Afghan told Wartime Allies. 'We are under Taliban direct threat and right now hiding somewhere in Kabul. Please help us, save our life and evacuate us from this terrible situation.'[4]

'I am under serious threat because Taliban have been searching for those who have worked for the US government, especially linguists. Taliban targets people who had affiliations with US government [...] and find different excuses for their killings and then make it seem as [if] they were not involved in the killings,' said another.[5]

The same threat exists for many of those who had applied to the UK's relocation scheme. 'We've got a hundred thousand applicants at the moment,' said Ben Wallace MP in the autumn of 2022.

Those left behind after the evacuation included a wide range of Afghans who had held positions such as interpreters, members of the Afghan special forces, members and employees of the government, and even Western passport holders.

'It was madness,' said one Afghan-born British national. 'There were thousands of people gathered there, pushing each other backwards and forwards. Most of them didn't have any documents. We waited there for thirteen hours, but my name was never called. They didn't make a line, or try to separate British citizens from the others. If I was born in London, I wouldn't have been treated like this. The Foreign Office has to answer that question.'[6]

'Making a line' was exactly how Western militaries had planned to process civilians, but what emerged on the ground was total chaos, out of which the service personnel managed to pull off the impossible.

An unrealistic timeline – set for political reasons – doomed many Afghans to be left behind. After twenty years of NATO presence in the country, such a rushed exit was not only sorrowful but shameful, and this book will not shy from documenting the reality of the situation, supported by accounts of those who were there.

Set against the backdrop of this impossible mission we will hear from the soldiers, sailors, airmen, Marines, and civilians who did everything in their power to rescue strangers from the other side of the world. Some of these service personnel would pay with their lives; everyone, with a part of their soul. The war at large had already taken a large mental and physical toll on those who were there, but the retreat from Kabul, and the moral injuries that followed, are likely to have caused as much, if not more, mental anguish than the poppy fields of Helmand.

Soldiers are trained to fight. What that small task force of international troops did in Kabul was over and above the call of duty. Many that went there had little training and no experience for what they would be asked to do. It was a unique and defining moment in military history.

On the one hand, it was a proud moment for the members of our armed forces, but on the other a dark stain on our government's commitment to our allies. It was not, of course, the first time that those on the sharp end have been asked to do the impossible because of a failure of leadership at the highest levels, nor will it be the last. Soldiers exist for war, which means that they exist to act in times of failed diplomacy. Kabul 2021 was no different.

In 2001, following the attacks of 9/11, teams of Western special forces began to arrive in Afghanistan to search for Osama bin Laden and to kill or capture the residual Taliban fighters that were thought to be protecting him. Before long, the British and Americans had committed thousands of troops to this hunt, and there seemed to be no end in sight. It is important to note that the Taliban was not considered a terrorist group in 2001, nor was it designated as one during the entire twenty-year war. Still, that would not stop American-led forces from fighting it with increasing numbers of troops and materials. To understand Op Pitting, it should be remembered that what began as counter-terrorism operations morphed into a massive counterinsurgency effort far more akin to the Soviet occupation of Afghanistan than the Western special forces actions of the early days of the war.

Allying themselves with the Northern Alliance, US-led forces initially made quick and impressive gains against al-Qaeda. Only a few months after 9/11, Osama Bin Laden was nearly cornered in the caves of Tora Bora. Then, for reasons that left many scratching their heads, the US command decided against deploying the US Marine Corps reserve that could have sealed the iron noose around the terrorist leader's neck. One sector was devoid of any Western military, and it was through this route that Bin Laden escaped into Pakistan. He would remain at large for another ten years.

The chance to quickly avenge the attacks of 9/11 – and destroy the organisation that had carried them out – had slipped through NATO's fingers. Worse, the mishandling of Iraq in 2003 onwards provided al-Qaeda with a huge pool of recruits. Close to death in 2001, the organisation began a rapid expansion. Twenty years after Tora Bora, it is still one of the largest terrorist groups in the world, with affiliates across the globe.

Despite the escape of Bin Laden, and even as Iraq was descending into a bloodbath, things in Afghanistan were seemingly more positive. The al-Qaeda camps and presence were largely gone. The Northern Alliance had triumphed over the Taliban, bringing large swathes of the country under their control. Kabul was in Western hands and, for the time being, peaceful. The Taliban had withdrawn to the Pashtun-dominated provinces of Helmand and Kandahar, or over the border into Pakistan. They had been routed in the early fighting, and were doing what people are apt to do in such a defeat: blaming each other, and going through an internal power struggle. Attacks on NATO troops were rare, in part because of the small numbers, but that was not to remain the case. In December 2001, there were only 2500 US military personnel in Afghanistan. Three years later there were 20,000. Five years after that, 67,000.[7]

By the end of 2001 the Taliban had been driven from their seat of power, and al-Qaeda in Afghanistan had been smashed to pieces. How was it then, that eight years later, the number of American troops in the country had increased thirty-fold? And, even with the help of their NATO allies, they could not keep a lid on the Taliban insurgency?

NATO had gone in, routed the enemy responsible for 9/11, and punished the government that had allowed them to use the country for terrorist training. Save for the capture or killing of Bin Laden, who was now in Pakistan, many felt that the mission was accomplished. Time to go home?

As we all know, that isn't what happened.

Instead, Western soldiers arrived in Afghanistan in ever-increasing numbers, and with them came NGOs (non-governmental organisations), private military contractors and businesses. It is up to the individual Afghan to tell you if this was a good thing or not, but one thing is clear: NATO's deployment started to look less like an anti-terrorism task force, and far more like an occupying army with a vested interest in staying put.

Alongside the Vietnamese, who have successfully ousted several armies from their country, the Afghans have one of the most impressive histories when it comes to defeating invading empires. Afghans forced Alexander the Great into a bloody stale-mate, they caused the Mongols and Sikhs no end of grief and in the 1800s they had driven out two British armies, the first of which was almost slaughtered to a man.

In 1842, a British and East India Company force was driven out of Kabul by an armed uprising, and marched to join the British garrison in the town of Jalalabad. Most never made it. The column was hampered by winter snows in the mountain passes, and from the heights came enemy fire, and vicious ambushes. The British column was not wiped out in a single moment, but suffered the death of a thousand cuts. The British lost 4500 troops and 12,000 camp followers. It was, without doubt, one of the greatest disasters in the history of the British Empire.

And they were not the last superpower to be humbled in the 'graveyard of empires'. In more recent times it was the Afghans (with a bit of CIA assistance) who defeated the might of the Soviet Union in the 1980s. Given this record, is it any wonder that many Afghans felt confident in taking on the might of NATO, and challenging 'American hegemony'?

Afghans think of former military victories in the same way that the English think about the 1966 football World Cup.

7

Fighting against invaders is a generational pastime in Afghanistan. It's expected. It is what their father did. Their grandfather. Their ancestors. The Taliban, who consider themselves the rightful heirs of the Mujahideen, became the enemy in the longest-running front in the Global War on Terror. NATO's decision to oust them from power, and the subsequent twenty-year war, was to prove deadly for more than 150,000 Afghans, as a new generation of warriors took up arms on both sides.

'How would you feel if I went to your homeland and started recruiting your countrymen to fight its own people?' asked Suhail Shaheen, a Taliban spokesman. 'Wouldn't you want to fight us back?'[8]

Britain was involved in the response to 9/11 from the outset. This began with a predominantly special forces mission with the help of RAF aircraft. Then, in spring 2006, 16 Air Assault Brigade was deployed to Helmand Province in Southern Afghanistan, where British troops saw combat that was more akin to a full-scale war than a peacekeeping mission. It was a bloody fight that lasted for years, with British casualties peaking in 2009/10.

Between 2006 and 2014, British soldiers fired 46 million rounds of small arms ammunition in Helmand Province, and at least 80,000 105mm artillery shells.[9] Considering that the British Army fired 1.5 million shells on the Somme – one of the most horrific battles in history, which lasted for five months – the 80,000 British shells fired in Helmand Province is a massive number when one considers that this battlefield was populated by civilians.

Atop this artillery was the close air support that saved so many allied lives. In 2006, in Musa Qala, it took continuous 'danger close' air strikes to keep the Taliban from overrunning the thinly stretched British outpost. Such airstrikes were made necessary by the exposed positions that units were placed in, but they came at a dreadful price. The year 2009 was a bloody one for British troops, but the same was true for civilians in what is euphemistically known as 'collateral damage'. By August that year, the UN estimated that some 350 civilians had been killed in coalition airstrikes. It is worth noting that, by this point in the war, the use of such firepower had been severely tightened.

During the eight years that British troops were 'on the front-line', if you had asked a British soldier why he was in a dusty, rural patrol base, he probably would have answered with one of the following:

'To fight the Taliban.'

'To stop terrorism.'

'So that Afghanistan can be a democracy.'

'So that girls can go to school.'

Many British soldiers are young parents themselves, and often the toughest amongst them would soften around the Afghan children. To risk one's life for the education of others seemed like a risk worth taking, but was NATO really waging a war of trillions of dollars so that girls could go to school?

There are many countries around the world that have liter-acy as low as Afghanistan, including many that are regularly visited by war, such as South Sudan, Burkina Faso, and Niger. There is no large NATO mission in any of these countries. Enabling girls to go to school, and raising the literacy level of the country as a whole, was a noble effort, but it was not *the* effort.

Was it so that Afghanistan could become a democracy? How

one felt about the success of this aim will likely largely depend on what part of the country they visited. In Kabul, one could see that individualism was on the rise, albeit caught in the sticky web of tribal, racial, and religious sectarianism. In the villages of Afghanistan, tribal alliances meant more than democracy. A country of warlords and religious leaders does not abandon strongmen and tradition while their home is in turmoil. In the West we often vote for the safe bet in politics: 'better the devil you know'. It is naive, and rather condescending, to think that all Afghans would drop centuries of tradition to embrace a Western idea, at a time when democracy seemed to be stumbling in the West.

A British soldier could often find himself unable to persuade his friendly interpreter about the merits of the Western way. It was not as if our own political leaders were beyond reproach, or that democracy had made us immune from war. Afghans value tribe, and family. Some of them saw our society, with its small number of children, and high rates of divorce, and decided that they preferred what they had. Many did not want the Taliban's harsh interpretation of Sharia law, but neither did they want to be moulded into the West's step-child, with 'democracy' at the forefront of that cultural push. Western countries had come to democracy on their own winding paths over hundreds of years. None had it installed at gunpoint.

To be clear, attempting to lay the grounds for democracy is no bad thing. Showing a people that a system can work is very different to insisting that it *must* work. NATO's presence in Afghanistan, and the elections that followed, have opened the minds of many Afghans to a new possibility. Some will reject it. Others will embrace it in full. Perhaps some will find a way to tailor it to suit Afghanistan. It is a problem that must be solved by the people who know the culture and place as intimately as they know themselves. It is a problem that can only be solved by the Afghan people.

The longer NATO stayed in Afghanistan, the more credit was given to the Taliban's claim that it was an invading, occupying force. The longer fighting went on, and the higher the civilian casualties mounted, the more Afghans would prefer peace under a harsh government than under a more moderate one. In 2001, the West had the chance to be a friendly and generous big brother to the new government in Kabul, and do it from a distance, limiting our military involvement to special forces missions and air power.

Instead we stayed to fight the Taliban, who had not been responsible for 9/11, and as was previously mentioned, were never designated a terrorist group. Rather than let the Taliban fly their flag over a town, NATO bombed and fought over that town for years, and then left it. After the suffering of the local population, the Taliban flag went up anyway.

Even President Joe Biden, who had been part of the administration responsible for the continued presence in the country, stated that 'our mission in Afghanistan was never supposed to be nation building'. This begs the question as to why – if the Taliban was not a terror group – the war was allowed to go on for two decades.

If NATO's twenty-year mission was to eliminate terrorism, then it failed. Al-Qaeda are still present in Afghanistan. So too are the Islamic State Khorasan (IS-K), who grew to their strongest not before, but during the war on terror.

'A lot of them are disaffected Taliban,' said Tony, a United Nations security advisor who saw out most of the war and stayed on in Afghanistan after the Taliban takeover. 'They felt they were selling out the Taliban ideals.'

If defeating terrorism was the objective, then the NATO mission was a failure. The idea that 'if we weren't fighting them over there, we'd be fighting them over here' is demonstrably false. Most of the Taliban were Afghan locals who were picking up a rifle for the duration of the occupation, or as often as money was put into their hands. These were not global jihadists.

It is true that there has not been another terrorist attack on the scale of 9/11, but was this achieved because Western militaries were dropping bombs on Afghan villages, or because of better intelligence and targeted special forces raids against the heads of organisations like Daesh and al-Qaeda? The West and NATO have the scalpels necessary to deal with the cancer of terrorism. But for some reason in Afghanistan, we tried to treat it with a mallet. In 2022, the successful drone strike in Kabul against al-Qaeda's leader, Ayman al-Zawahiri, undermined the claim that NATO ever needed boots on the ground to take out the people who plotted mass murder.

Since 9/11, which claimed close to 3000 innocent lives, more than 7000 US military personnel have died in Iraq and Afghanistan. Another 179 British servicemen and women were killed in Iraq, and 457 in Afghanistan. A 2021 study by Brown University estimated that the Afghan security forces lost 69,095 personnel, and their enemy lost close to 53,000. Civilian deaths were put at 46,319. When all other groups are considered, such as foreign workers killed, Brown's total death toll for NATO's Afghan war was 176,000.[10] Excluding the enemy dead, this is the equivalent loss of life of two 9/11s a year, every year, for twenty years.

Such a cost demands a clear and precise goal, but what would a NATO win have looked like? No one knew. By contrast, the Taliban's aim was simple, and unequivocal.

Drive the invader out.

This need not necessarily be done in the conventional way. The Allies had driven the Axis out of occupied Europe with great formations of troops supported by masses of artillery, armour, air power and infantry. The Taliban had neither the training, the equipment, nor the will for such mass operations. When they tried to overrun coalition positions held by Western troops, they had come away battered, leaving the ground littered with their dead. They were simply no match for the marksmanship and fire discipline of first-grade NATO troops, or the air power and artillery that they could bring to bear, and their ability to take this punishment won them a certain estimation from many British soldiers who fought against them.

Major Adam Jowett of the Parachute Regiment recalled the aftermath of one fight in Musa Qala, 2006, when the Taliban had tried and failed to overrun his position. 'Perhaps it was the feared desecration by dogs that pushed the Taliban into action, but soon, unarmed men began appearing from the growing shadows. They made themselves known, walking in the open, their hands visible and manner unthreatening. Sentries settled in behind their guns, but I made no move to stand the company to. Everything about the men's demeanour spoke to their intention – they had come to recover their dead. I did not even have to speak the order for my men to hold their fire. Every one of them understood that, and I expect they felt some grudging respect that a man would risk himself so brazenly to recover the body of a friend.'[11]

In British army doctrine, the rule of thumb when attacking defensive positions is that the attacker should outnumber the defender by 3 to 1. The Taliban often had this numerical superiority. In the early days of Operation Herrick, the Taliban would frequently conduct 'human wave assaults', but the waves would break against British marksmanship, and Allied airpower. Not only were these tactics depleting their manpower, but the failures sapped the morale of the fighters. No matter how strong one's religious faith, a fighter knows when they come off worst. By contrast, the morale of British and American troops was high: they were facing down these attacks and killing the enemy in their thousands.

Thanks to their training, and the incredible skill and bravery of the NATO medical teams, the casualties inflicted upon the Taliban came with relatively few deaths in their own ranks. NATO forces were not unscathed, but the casualty figures in some of these sustained battles were nothing short of miraculous, and a testament to the training standards that the Western armies had continued to hone over hundreds of years. That most men walked away from the massive firefights of Helmand was down to the lessons learned on the Somme, in the Normandy Bocage, and in the ruins of countless European towns and cities. They were lessons learned in blood, and those past sacrifices continued to save the lives of British soldiers many decades later.

The Taliban had their own history and doctrine, some of it imported from the insurgency of Iraq. Taliban leaders such as Mullah Dadullah followed al-Qaeda's playbook, making gruesome DVDs of the murders of those who supported the regime in Kabul. Members of the two groups met, and exchanged tactics. Suicide bombings, never a Taliban tactic of the past, began to rise in Afghanistan. Just before 9/11, al-Qaeda had killed the Northern Alliance leader, Ahmad Shah Massoud, 'the Lion of Panjshir', in such an attack. Several years later, Dadullah began to recruit and deploy his own suicide bombers. One of the Taliban's most extreme leaders, he was killed in a raid by special forces in 2007.

Mercifully, suicide bombings in Afghanistan were not as frequent as they were in Iraq, but the infamous 'roadside bombs' were soon the biggest killer in both theatres of war. In Afghanistan, where most of the tracks were dirt, these devices tended to be buried in the road rather than hidden alongside them. Some were designed to target soldiers on foot. Others, armoured vehicles. They could even be found in compound walls, or trees. Their use resulted in a steady stream of maimed and dead coalition soldiers.

The sites of these devices were often overlooked by Taliban fighters armed with AK-47 rifles and RPGs. In the confusion that followed an exploding IED, when the troops were trying to reach their dead and wounded comrades, the Taliban would open fire. They would also harass patrols and patrol bases with anything from a single shot, to a withering hail of fire. Where NATO troops were pushing into Taliban-held areas – such as during Operation Panther's Claw, in 2009 – the Taliban would fight within grenade throwing distance. Such tactics negated the use of the coalition's greatest strength: airpower and artillery. Instead, Western soldiers would have to clear ditch by ditch, wall by wall, and often at the point of a bayonet. When the Taliban felt that the fight was lost, they would withdraw, regularly leaving their weapons and equipment behind so that they could pass as civilians.

For most British soldiers, their tours became deadly games of cat and mouse. Given an area of 'ground' to 'hold', the troops would spend six months patrolling, seeking out IEDs and the enemy. Rarely would they catch the Taliban off-guard. Almost always it was the enemy who opened fire first, and it was them who decided when the fight was over. This was invariably when the British gained the upper hand, either through superior small arms fire, or the arrival of air power above them. There were instances of the Taliban standing and fighting, but there was no need for them to fight to the death. They simply had to bleed the occupying forces, and to show the populace that they were defending the soil of Afghanistan.

This could be incredibly frustrating for British forces, who were hampered in their efforts to follow through on success because of the belts of IEDs that lay in their way. Whether moving on foot or in vehicles, it is incredibly difficult to push deeper into enemy territory without taking casualties from IEDs. Having spoken to hundreds of veterans of the campaign, there was the will amongst the ranks to take that risk if it meant defeating the Taliban and winning the war, but by then the British public and politicians had lost the stomach for casualties, if they ever had it in the first place. Despite having effectively withdrawn in 2007 from fighting in Iraq, in 2009 there was only one British Brigade deployed to Helmand. This, at the time, represented about a tenth of Britain's available infantry.

British units deployed for six-month tours. This was a legacy of the conflict in Northern Ireland. Soldiers deployed to the Far East in the Second World War knew that they'd come home when the war was won. For US soldiers in Vietnam, a deployment was twelve months. The US Army continued this tour length for Iraq and Afghanistan. Extending the length of British tours would not have changed the fate of Afghanistan, but it may have allowed British troops to have the upper hand during their years of deployment.

Newspapers often bemoan the lack of equipment given to the 'Poor Bloody Infantry' on the frontline, but it is lack of time, lack of numbers and a lack of real consistency that really dooms a conventional force to being on the receiving end of guerrilla tactics. There is a case to be made for no boots on the ground, or for many. What Britain deployed instead was enough to stir the hornet's nest, but never enough to pacify it. In Helmand, young Brits lived in conditions that were almost unthinkable to their friends and family back home in a First World country: no electricity, no water, and an enemy who could appear at any time, from anywhere.

Another downfall of the six-month tour was that a new Commander meant a new plan. And so, as regular as the seasons, there would be a change of strategy in the British sector. Rather than finding one strategy that worked, and sticking with its architect, brigadier after brigadier was given a bite at the cherry. Frank Ledwidge and Simon Akam have both written compellingly about the British Army rank structure being top heavy, and the repeated change of commands meant that the Afghan people of Helmand were constantly on the end of one different British plan after another. Imagine, after the battle of El Alamein, if General Montgomery had been relieved because it was 'someone else's turn'. Apply this to other leading wartime generals – Slim, Patton or Eisenhower, or Major General Jeremy Moore of the Falklands Campaign.

General officers failing in their jobs should certainly be fired, but the tragedy of the six month policy is that several of the brigadiers' strategies showed real promise. It wasn't that any of them were incompetent: it's that without continuity, there could never be more than six months of real progress in any direction. 'It was obvious to a civvy outsider that a Para Commander was different from someone with a special forces background, who was different from a marine,' said a member of the FCDO (Foreign, Commonwealth & Development Office) in Kabul. 'And it would have been obvious to Afghans too – friends, foes and fence-sitters alike.'[12]

And yet, despite all of the issues and all of the casualties, the British forces fought the Taliban to a standstill, and more. The enemy were driven from many towns, and forced to rely on hit-and-run tactics. Because of the sacrifice made by the coalition, Afghans were able to vote in elections, and girls were allowed to attend newly opened schools. There was positive change, particularly in the larger population centres. Life expectancy increased by a massive twenty years. Afghanistan's population was triple what it had been in 1998. Literacy rates doubled, and infrastructure such as hospitals and schools were put in place. Women could hold positions in government, and elsewhere. Things that we take for granted in the West – such as sports, and music – began to thrive in parts of the country. Human rights, and the human experience, was opened up for millions of Afghans.

In the British sector, where the combat mission ended in 2014, the locals of Helmand were shown that there was another way to live, and that it did not have to involve the Taliban, and their violent interpretation of Sharia law. That being said, it would be naive to think that because the opportunity was there to change tradition, all Afghans wished to embrace it. Many were happy with the way things were. Some were too scared of the Taliban to change. Others just wanted one side or the other to prevail so that their home would no longer be a front line. An

insurgency, no matter how brutal, does not work without sufficient support from the populace.

As well as the sacrifice of tens of thousands of Afghan security
forces, civilians, and NATO troops, 457 British service personnel
gave their lives for the military mission to make this a reality. For
every dead soldier, there was a family torn apart. For many
parents, their own life ends with the death of their child.

Johnny Mercer MP, former Minister for Veteran Affairs,
described the effects of the death of a British officer on the
man's parents. 'When he died, his parents never recovered. His
father and mother both died early too. The impact is huge.'

Asked if he regrets going to Afghanistan himself, Mercer said,
'I don't feel bitter about my time in Afghanistan ... I think there
were a lot of bad people in Afghanistan, and we killed a lot of
bad people. And that's not wrong. But also, I saw the huge toll it
took on other people, and you couldn't come away from that
without any regret, because you don't want to see families go
through that. So, do I regret it? It's not an easy question to
answer. I don't regret what had to be done, but I do think we
could have done it differently, and better.'

This sentiment is often echoed by other British personnel,
who believed that their cause was just and their enemy wicked,
but lament the suffering of the families: Afghan and British. It is
a struggle to reconcile that cost with the outcome.

As well as the 457 fallen, a further 616 British service personnel were seriously, or very seriously injured.[13] This could mean
anything from missing limbs to destroyed hearing and loss of
eyesight. Problems that would plague them and their families for
life. And that figure does not include PTSD (post-traumatic
stress disorder) or other mental health issues. During the years of

British military operations, there were more than 7000 medical air evacuations. More than 2000 British troops were wounded in action.[14] Every one of them was a volunteer. Most had joined the forces knowing they might go to Afghanistan. They did so willingly and sometimes eagerly. Some wanted to see action and adventure, others because they believed in the dream of a better Afghanistan.

In the summer of 2021 that dream fell to pieces, and now, perhaps for the first time in the twenty-year Afghan mission, the priorities of soldiers, politicians and civilians all aligned onto a single outcome: *to escape from Kabul.*

2

Pandora's Box

If Iraq and Afghanistan have taught us anything in recent history, it is the unpredictability of war and that these things are easier to get into than to get out of.

— Robert Gates, former US Secretary of Defense

Very few wars end in the total annihilation of one side or the other. Most come to a close with negotiations, one side or both recognising that further fighting is futile. There is, more often than not, a plan for peace.

What makes Afghanistan different is that the plan for peace was spoken about years before the end of the war, and not in the way that the West was accustomed to. In the Second World War, nothing short of 'unconditional surrender' would suffice for the Allies. But, in 2010, President Barack Obama announced a planned withdrawal of American troops from Afghanistan. This was at a time when battle was still raging across the country. Obama hadn't quite thrown the towel into the ring, but he had told the enemy that America would do so within the next couple of rounds. All the Taliban had to do was hold out.

And they did. First up to the Doha Agreement in 2020, and then until NATO had withdrawn military assistance to the Afghan security forces. America and NATO had a plan, of course. But so did the Taliban, and theirs was better.

Few members of the Western public had even heard of the Taliban until that fateful September in 2001. After the fall of the Twin Towers, however, these bearded militants became a household name for their part in harbouring Osama bin Laden. For a time, as they dissolved into the mountains and caves of the Afghan–Pakistan border, they were assumed to have been defeated. Then in 2006, when the British Paras were sent into Helmand, they resurfaced like a phoenix from the ashes. Over the next few bloody years, the Taliban and their fierce resistance dominated news cycles in London and Washington.

The superficial image of a Taliban fighter is well ingrained into our national psyche. A dark and swarthy warrior in a brown or black shirt wearing a military waistcoat and a dusty turban. In his hand a Soviet-era AK-47 or rocket-propelled grenade. His face half hidden by a black beard and with kohl round his eyes, he cuts a sinister figure. The beaten sandals on his feet and long curly hair are testament to a hard life of religious fundamentalism lived on the fringes of society. To the Western eye he is a brutal, misogynistic barbarian, more suited to the middle ages than the twenty-first century.

And that is where the knowledge about the Talibs often ends: even among the people who were sent to fight them.

'I didn't really know anything about the Taliban except that we were there to kill them,' said Joe, a soldier in 3 Para. It's a common answer from veterans of the conflict.

A research paper, written at the University of California in 1997, defined the Taliban as: a movement of Islamic students, mullahs, Pushtun tribesmen, and ex-mujahideen with the backing of Pakistan.[1]

It is beyond the scope of this book to offer a comprehensive look into the Taliban's history, hierarchy, and strategies, but we must have some idea, in order to understand their goals, and how it was they came back to power after twenty years of fighting the world's most powerful military.

The Soviet invasion and aftermath

To know the Taliban, one must know about the state of Afghanistan in the years that preceded its creation. In the spring of 1978, the country's moderate government was overthrown in a Soviet-backed coup by officers with communist leanings.

The new Marxist government was quick to try to remove any opposition from its largely uneducated populace and it dealt with its detractors in the most brutal manner, including the executions of 27,000 political prisoners in under two years. This was a major factor for the beginnings of the insurgency. Another was religion.

Afghanistan has long been proud of its Islamic heritage, which was often at odds with the new Communist regime. Marxism raises 'the state' above God. It raises communist theory above the Quran. This was, of course, blasphemy to the devout. Afghanistan is also a deeply tribal country, where military forces could be raised in the same way that kings in England would call upon the fyrd – the freemen of the land – to come and stand against an invading army. In countries like Afghanistan, when your tribal leader calls, you must answer. A people with such a long history of invasion and conflict relies upon such an honour system. Without it, they would have been swept away with the sands of time.

These separate groups of Mujahideen – 'those who engage in jihad', which means a struggle or fight against enemies of Islam – began insurgencies across the country. This, combined with

23

the internal disputes of the ineffective government, was the trigger for the Soviet Union to invade at the end of the year. The 'proletariat' of Afghanistan had rejected communism, and that was not something that could be tolerated.

The following extracts by the Minister of Foreign Affairs, Andrei Gromyko, are taken from a Top Secret meeting of the Soviet Politburo in March 1979:

> The situation in Afghanistan has deteriorated sharply, the centre of the disturbance at this time being the town of Herat. There, as we know from previous cables, the 17th division of the Afghan Army was stationed, and had restored order, but now we have received news that this division has essentially collapsed. An artillery regiment and one infantry regiment comprising that division have gone over to the side of the insurgents.
>
> Bands of saboteurs and terrorists, having infiltrated from the territory of Pakistan, trained and armed not only with the participation of Pakistani forces but also of China, the United States of America, and Iran, are committing atrocities in Herat. The insurgents infiltrating into the territory of Herat Province from Pakistan and Iran have joined forces with a domestic counter-revolution. The latter is especially comprised by religious fanatics. The leaders of the reactionary masses are also linked in large part with the religious figures. The number of insurgents is difficult to determine, but our comrades tell us that they are thousands, literally thousands.
>
> In my opinion, we must proceed from a fundamental proposition in considering the question of aid to Afghanistan, namely: under no circumstances may we lose Afghanistan. For sixty years now we have lived with Afghanistan in peace and friendship. And if we lose Afghanistan now and it turns against the Soviet

Union, this will result in a sharp setback to our foreign policy. Of course, it is one thing to apply extreme measures if the Afghan Army is on the side of the people, and an entirely different matter, if the army does not support the lawful government. And finally, third, if the army is against the government and, as a result, against our forces, then the matter will be complicated indeed.[2]

'Complicated indeed' would serve to summarise the next four decades of Afghanistan's history, every year of which would be marred with bloody tragedy.

In December 1979, more than 25,000 Soviet Union soldiers entered Afghanistan. A total of 620,000 would serve there in nearly ten years of occupation. Almost 10,000 would die in combat, 4000 would die of wounds, and another 1000 from disease and illness. Like the NATO mission that was to follow, the Soviets would prop up a central government and hope that spreading troops across the towns and countryside would work. Many of these former defences could be seen by British soldiers twenty years later. Some were even occupied by them.

As the Soviet presence grew, so did the will and the numbers of the Mujahideen guerrillas. They came from all over the world to fight the jihad. One among them was a young man from a wealthy family in Saudi Arabia. His name was Osama Bin Laden.

The Afghan mujahideen were a hard and determined enemy, ambushing the Russians, and terrorising them through the gruesome treatment of prisoners. Almost thirty years before Islamic State were releasing videos of the most extravagant and barbaric deaths of their captives, grainy footage was released of the Mujahideen murdering their prisoners. Some were buried up to their heads in the sand, then kicked until decapitated (a practice once used by the British on the natives of Australia). Others were tied to horses that were whipped in different directions, literally pulling prisoners apart. Nothing had changed in the hundred years since Rudyard Kipling had written:

> *When you're wounded and left on Afghanistan's plains,*
> *and the women come out to cut up what remains,*
> *jest roll to your rifle and blow out your brains*
> *and go to your gawd like a soldier.*

With such atrocities, Russian soldiers were never under the impression that they could surrender. To fall into the hands of such an enemy was a fate worse than death, but many of the Soviet soldiers were conscripts with the most rudimentary training. Lest the impression be given that they were lambs fed to the wolves of Afghanistan, it is worth remembering that the Soviets inflicted some 90,000 casualties on the Mujahideen, including 56,000 deaths. As seen in Vietnam, Iraq, and NATO's own war in Afghanistan, it was proved that a higher body count did not equate to winning. Insurgents pay a high price for their victory, but it is a victory nonetheless. Occupying forces leave wondering what was achieved through the deaths of their friends.

Between these two warring factions there are the civilians, who pay the highest cost in every war. Afghan women were abducted, raped, and murdered. There were massacres of civilians, and every imaginable form of death. Estimates of the civilian dead range from around 500,000 to 2,000,000. Likely, more than 5,000,000 fled the fighting as refugees. All this from a country that had a population of 13.4 million in 1979. By 1989, as many as half of Afghanistan's civilians had been killed, or become refugees. This unquantifiable tragedy is something that we must remember when looking at the origins of the Taliban.

'When I was a child, the USSR invaded our country,' said Mujahid, who would later take up arms against the American-led forces. 'They had their headquarters in our area. My family was encouraging us to defend our land and religion. I was also one of those suffering from bombardment.'[3]

Those who would fight in the Forever War grew up around the violence of an occupation. Their lives have been defined by war. Even when the Soviet Union withdrew from the country at the beginning of 1989, the war between the Afghan government and the Mujahideen went on for another three years. America was supplying one side with arms, the Soviets the other. In 1990, there were talks about withdrawing this support so that a diplomatic solution would need to be found, but the super-powers could not agree on terms, and so the civilians of Afghanistan were subjected to more suffering. A further 400,000 Afghans perished during the civil war years of the 1990s.

It is against this bloody backdrop that the Taliban rose to power. In the early 1990s, local warlords exploited the chaos for their own power. Extortion, on a dirt poor populace, was rife. Rape and murder were commonplace. Drugs produced in the poppy fields ended up in the veins of Afghans looking for an escape.

In 1994, a group of religious students took matters into their own hands and subdued a local warlord. Rather than replacing one extortion racket with another, these new fighters were perceived as fair, and just. Their influence and support quickly spread, drawing many former Mujahideen to their cause. Within two years they had become what we now know as the Taliban, and in 1996, they seized Kabul. For more than fifteen years there had been nothing but instability and death. In such times, people often turn to religion, and Afghanistan was already a devout country. That the Mujahideen had driven out the godless invader was seen by some as proof of the righteousness of their cause. It follows that, in the wake of such loss, and with holy warriors the victors, the architects of jihad would now become embedded in the ruling of the state.

Though the Pashtun-dominated group were strict, and often brutal, this was accepted by many in the population as preferable to what had been the norm for more than ten years. Public flog-gings and executions established a medieval kind of order, but it was order nonetheless. It is easy for us in the West to tut at such methods, but it is worth asking ourselves what we would be willing to accept if it meant bringing an end to a war that was claiming hundreds of thousands of lives in our homeland.

In the north of the country, the mostly Tajik population continued to resist Taliban control, but by 2001 it was clear that the Taliban were in power in most of the country. The finger is always pointed at their interpretation of religion, but this hard-line faith was born out of, and tolerated because of, almost twenty years of continuous war. Given that NATO's mission in Afghanistan lasted for two decades, we should not be surprised that hardline groups such as IS-K are gaining support.

The Soviet war in the country gave birth to these religious extremists in an earlier guise. These groups – often international in make-up and funding – found a willing host in Afghanistan's Taliban, and among the groups to set up training camps there was al-Qaeda, led by the former Mujahideen, Osama Bin Laden.

Attack on America

The 9/11 attacks, masterminded by Osama Bin Laden, were the reason that the Taliban became a household name. Though the Afghan civil war had made the news, it was one conflict among many and had taken a backseat to what was happening elsewhere, particularly British Army deployments to the first Gulf War (1990), Bosnia (1992), Kosovo (1999), and Sierra Leone (2000). The scale of death in the Balkans was dwarfed by what was happening in Afghanistan, but there was no appetite in the West to follow on the heels of the Soviet occupation, and to act as a UN peacekeeping force there, as they were in Bosnia and Kosovo.

This quite undermines the idea of later Western intervention in Afghanistan as a humanitarian endeavour. Hundreds of thousands of Afghans were dying in the early 1990s, and the Taliban of the late 90s were just as brutal and oppressive as the Taliban of 2001. It was only when America suffered their own attack that the West came to Afghanistan.

Ten days after 9/11, Mullah Omar, credited as being the leader of the Taliban, was interviewed and asked if he would give up Osama Bin Laden to America. He replied, 'No. We cannot do that. If we did, it means we are not Muslims, that Islam is finished. If we were afraid of attack, we could have surrendered him the last time we were threatened.'[4]

It is reported that he told Taliban commanders: 'Islam says that when a Muslim asks for shelter, give the shelter and never hand him over to the enemy. And our Afghan tradition says that, even if your enemy asks for shelter, forgive him and give him shelter. Osama has helped the jihad in Afghanistan, he was with us in bad days and I am not going to give him to anyone.'[5]

In an interview with a Pakistani journalist, Omar said, 'I don't want to go down in history as someone who betrayed his guest. I am willing to give my life, my regime. Since we have given him refuge, I cannot throw him out now.'[6]

It was a decision that would affect the lives of millions and lead to twenty years of war, but in the end, the Taliban's regime would only be given up temporarily.

Nation building is a term often used to describe what became of NATO's mission in Afghanistan, but for all of the arms, the training and the publicly stated confidence, the Western-backed nation was a castle made of sand. Without NATO soldiers to hold patrol bases, Western air power to smash Taliban attacks, and Western promises to continue to do so, everything that had taken twenty years to build quickly crumpled beneath the rising tide of Taliban fighters. When the country fell to them in 2021, the Taliban were strong, but the Afghan Security Forces, on paper, were stronger.

Anti-war sentiment for Iraq was strong in the West from the get go. By contrast, there was broad support for action in Afghanistan. Unsurprisingly, given that 9/11 had occurred on US soil, 88 per cent of Americans polled in October 2001 favoured military action. In April 2021, a poll conducted by the hawkish Fox News found that 50 per cent of those polled wanted some kind of US presence to remain in Afghanistan for counterterrorism purposes[7] (given the previous twenty years, this could mean anything from special forces working with the indigenous population, to tens of thousands of conventional forces scattered across the country). What had changed?

It is perhaps safe to assume that very few people expected the military action in Afghanistan to last for one decade, let alone two. The Great War was over in four years. The Second World

War in six. The Falklands and Gulf War were over in less than a year, and British offensive military action in Kosovo and Sierra Leone was done in weeks. The British public – Western publics – had largely come to expect quick, decisive victories. The decades of struggle in Northern Ireland, the brutal years of Vietnam, and the countless lingering sores of civil war around the world were conveniently forgotten. Two decades came as a shock to most.

It shouldn't have. The War on Terror is, by definition, a war against a tactic, rather than a defined enemy. Even if it could be agreed that it was a war against terrorists – they, whoever they might be, are an unconventional enemy. It is, therefore, not a war that can be won by conventional means, or in a conventional timeframe. The Taliban knew this. There was no need to stand and trade blows until one side was on the canvas. They only needed the stamina to keep going. To outlast, and out-distance their enemy.

By 2009 this was clearly their tactic, and yet the West continued to insist on playing by their conventional rules. It is reasonable to suggest that Afghanistan did not fall in 2021, but a decade earlier in December 2010, when President Obama announced that the US would withdraw. From that day forth, the result of the war was perhaps already decided.

The Afghan government did not help the chances of its own survival. Corruption and nepotism were rife, giving the Taliban ample opportunity to point score with the local population, particularly in rural areas, which were not seeing the development that was happening in Kabul. (One imagines that the Taliban would leave out the fact that it was their presence and attacks which made such development impossible. The transport of turbines to the Kajaki dam, a major infrastructure project in Helmand, required the involvement of 5000 British troops.)[8]

Mujahid, who had grown up during the Soviet invasion, studied for a degree in Social Care, then worked with NGOs in the country. He wanted 'to help those who are in prison and help those who are addicted to drugs in different ways. Our youths' lives were destroyed, when I saw that I chose this field.'

But his path became a bloody one. In 2009, when his brother was killed fighting for the Taliban, Mujahid volunteered to take up arms against 'the invaders'.

'I was forced to leave my home and go to the mountains to defend our rights. If I stayed, it was clear that I would've been killed, so it's better to stand against the invaders.'[9]

Civilian casualties also fed into support for the Taliban – or, at least, support for an end to the war. Much of the toll was paid by people in rural areas, who saw little of the improvements that residents of Kabul could enjoy. The country was becoming fractured, and a common opinion was that the Taliban would dominate the rural parts of the country, while the government held the population centres. How a country divided in this way could be expected to function is not clear.

'I thought the country would probably split and the Taliban would stay out in the country,' said Johnny Mercer, pointing to the stiff resistance that the Afghan special forces units had put up in the south of the country.

'It all changed really when the technical support left. They woke up one morning at Bagram airbase and the technicians had just left, and so they had no air support. It became clear to them that they were going to get massacred. I don't really buy this stuff that you heard from Biden and other people about "they just ran away" ... I think that's a load of bollocks. They don't really understand how warfare works in that part of the world. I think they fought fucking bravely, and they lost a lot of people. Your president's left the country . . . what would we do in that position? Obviously, you'd like to think you'd just fight to the last man and die wrapped in the flag. But I think you've got to be realistic.'

In an interview with NPR (National Public Radio), Suhail Shaheen, a Taliban spokesman, was asked how he believed the end of the twenty-year war came so quickly. 'Well, I think it showed the support of the people. It showed our movement for liberation of the country was a popular uprising. And it showed that those who were working for the Kabul administration, they were bigger and stronger and sustaining themselves only because of the bombardment and cruise missiles and air strikes, drone attacks of the pilots. Otherwise, when they started withdrawing from the country, the people rejected them and they had no support from the security forces.'[10]

America and her allies had come to Afghanistan first to destroy al-Qaeda, but as reporter Hollie McKay wrote: 'It is often lost that Afghans themselves were not part of the September 11 attacks. It was Saudi operatives who drove planes into the Twin Towers more than two decades ago, and it was the financier himself who was found and killed on Pakistani turf almost a decade later.'[11]

In the twenty years that followed 9/11, it was Afghans who paid in blood for that attack. Many of them were oblivious to what had happened in New York. When McKay asked a young 21-year-old university student if he had heard of Osama Bin Laden, the young man looked at her with a puzzled expression.

'No. Who is this?'[12]

Negotiating with 'terrorists'

'We don't negotiate with terrorists' is a slogan that has been around since the Nixon administration, and there are examples that lend a very strong credence to it: the Iranian Embassy siege, and the assault by the SAS, perhaps being the most famous example of all.

It was likely a heavy dose of realism that led to talks being opened with the Taliban. NATO had put great effort into killing more than 50,000 of them, and they ranked with ISIS, al-Qaeda, and the Jaysh al-Mahdi (JAM) as the most prominent foes in the Global War on Terror. And yet, according to NATO itself, the Taliban are not terrorists now, and nor were they at any time during the twenty-year war in Afghanistan.

Terrorists or not, many in the West were shocked to learn that there were negotiations being held with the Taliban. After all, there was no such option for Nazi Germany, or Imperial Japan, and they were both major powers. Unconditional surrender or war were their choices. With the Taliban, it would be different.

'On the basis of the Doha Agreement, the Americans should leave peacefully and they withdraw from Afghanistan peacefully,' said the Taliban's Shaheen. 'So during their withdrawal from Afghanistan, we will not attack them. That was written in the Doha Agreement. But as you see, the Americans violated that agreement. It was until the first of May that they should have withdrawn all their forces and then President Biden said that we will withdraw until September 11. But still, we restrained our forces not to attack American troops because they are withdrawing from our country. And so we expect them that they withdraw until September 11. And if they continue to station furthermore in the country, that could be considered, of course, occupation, continuation of the occupation.'[13]

The Taliban had set the date as a final insult – to evict the Americans on the twentieth anniversary of 9/11. In the end, perhaps to save face, America decided to leave a few days earlier: a decision that would strand more than 100,000 refugees.

Doha was not the first time that deals had been struck with the Taliban, and the idea that NATO countries were talking with their long-time enemy did not come as a surprise to many British veterans. The Good Friday agreement had involved negotiating with terrorists in Northern Ireland, and the Global War on Terror has its own examples.

In 2006, a deal was brokered by tribal elders to allow the British garrison to evacuate their makeshift base in Musa Qala, Afghanistan. The combined force of Paras and Royal Irish had fought the Taliban tooth and nail for weeks, inflicting massive casualties on the enemy. However, to prevent themselves from being overrun, and to evacuate casualties by air, it required a huge amount of ordnance to be dropped on the town. These decisions were never taken lightly, but there was no getting away from the fact that the coalition was destroying the town they had come to protect. Once the tribal leaders asked them to go, it was time to listen.

In the days that followed, and in a strange twist of fate, Paras found themselves shopping for fruit and veg in the same bazaar as Taliban fighters. It wasn't easy for either group, but under the leadership of Major Adam Jowett, the British soldiers showed that they were as disciplined out of fire as they were under it. Easy Company put the fate of the town ahead of their personal grievances, and were eventually transported by cattle trucks to the desert west of the city, suspecting ambush and treachery at every point.

They were eventually collected by Chinook helicopter, and for a time the Taliban kept to their word, and stayed out of the town. However, Musa Qala would eventually be fought over again, and again. It finally fell to the Taliban in 2015, after the British withdrawal from Helmand. At least twenty-three British soldiers were killed in Musa Qala between 2006 and 2010. The story of that town is indicative of what happened in much of the province: the use of airpower to avoid being overrun, a push to retake it with stronger forces, an insurgency of ambushes and IEDs, British withdrawal, the crumbling of local forces, and eventual recapture by the Taliban.

In 2007, in Basra, Iraq, another deal was struck with the enemy. This time, with the Shia militias with whom the British had been fighting heavily. The British hierarchy agreed that they would withdraw from Basra and release militia detainees in return for a halt to attacks on British forces. The city had to be retaken by the Iraqi and US militaries in Operation Charge of the Knights, which involved heavy fighting. After the final prisoners had been released from British custody, the Shia militias launched a massive rocket attack on the British base outside of Basra. It was a surprise to no one who had been fighting them, but somehow the idea that 'Britain does not negotiate with terrorists' persisted.

It should be noted that – like Kabul – the deal in Basra left those who had cooperated with the coalition at the mercy of the militias. In light of the fact that Iraqis working for the British forces were routinely tortured and murdered, this is quite unforgiveable, and should have served as a warning of what would happen in Kabul.

It did not.

Doha and beyond

What the Democrat president Obama started in 2010, the Republican president Trump sealed in 2020 with the Doha agreement. The deal, signed in February of that year, committed to all NATO forces being withdrawn from Afghanistan by May 2021. This was not a deal done with the sitting government, such as had taken place in Iraq, but with the Taliban. The enemy.

Ben Wallace, himself a British Army veteran, was the UK's defence secretary at the time. 'The die was cast with this Taliban deal. And if someone had taken a cold examination of each measure in this deal, then I think people would have recognised that this deal was going to lead to rapid success of the Afghan Taliban, because the measures in it were really straightforward. So, forcing the release of 4000 Taliban prisoners, which of course included some of the nastiest and most capable leaders in it.'

Wallace cites the cessation of special forces missions and air support as being instrumental to the collapse.

'You removed from the table the two things that the Taliban feared most,' he said. 'It was a *fait accompli*. There was not a political maturity that was in parallel with our military capability. And then . . . you had different people with different views as you got towards the end of "is the game up?" and I said in one meeting, "The game is up."'

There was some optimism however that the Taliban of 2021 would be different to that who had been ousted in 2001.

'There's been a lot of discussion about whether we were dealing with Taliban 2.0,' said Dominic Raab, the UK's foreign secretary. 'There was, I think, a lot of optimism bias about that, and frankly a lot of wishful thinking. And that did not come from me. And it did not come from the diplomatic assessment. When you've been in a conflict for close to twenty years, and you've invested so much blood, sweat, tears and treasure, I think there is a natural human instinct to want to believe it's had more of a positive impact than it has in reality, both on the Taliban, but also on our ability to get the Afghan security forces resilient enough to see off anything that the Taliban might do. I feel there was a lot of optimism bias.'

It was an optimism not claimed by Raab:

There was probably somewhere between a 50 to 75 per cent chance of a Taliban takeover, as a result of the Doha Agreement, and a 25 to 50 per cent chance of civil war. I think there was a lot of wishful thinking from those that had engaged with the Taliban, about Taliban 2.0. It was mostly from the military side.

When the Doha Agreement was in place, and when you have a timeline-based approach, I felt that we were at risk of a rushed departure. I think the military assessment in the UK, and possibly amongst what you'd call the professionals rather than politicians in the US, were more optimistic that the Taliban would wait it out, and would only really begin the slow choking of the Afghan forces from May and then when it was extended, from September. I couldn't see anything that meant that was realistic. At every available opportunity I challenged what I thought was an optimism bias, that the Taliban would wait until September, and it was in my view, wishful thinking that the Taliban takeover, which was more than likely, wouldn't happen until 2022 at the earliest.

Agreeing to withdraw all of NATO forces assisting the Afghan government according to a political timeframe was tantamount to announcing that you will throw your child into the swimming pool on a set date. NATO's attitude seemed less like the International Security Assistance Force it had proclaimed itself to be, and more like Ivan Drago (the Russian boxer from *Rocky IV*) declaring, 'If he dies, he dies.'

'Operation Pitting was run by the MOD [Ministry of Defence]. It was not run by the Foreign Office,' explained Dominic Raab:

> But it seemed to me that the scale of the task, under the pressures that they faced, was always going to lead to something which was, let's say, somewhere between unstable, uncertain and chaotic. And the big failure, in my view, was a strategic failure. First of all, not understanding how during the US presidential election, the Doha Agreement, and the sense that America was no longer going to commit to 'forever wars' was baked into a bipartisan approach on both sides of Capitol Hill in the US. It just was. And I think the idea that President Biden would backtrack, was just a huge amount of optimism bias, frankly, and a lack of cold, hard, realistic thinking.
>
> I think the truth is, there's a much bigger question. We'd been in Afghanistan for so long. What were the benchmarks for success in Afghanistan? Was it absence of terrorism? In which case, actually, we had a very good record of absence of a terrorist attack outside of Afghanistan by al-Qaeda, or any other of those groups. Was it bringing forward a more consensus based politics in Afghanistan? That had clearly not happened. Protecting women and girls? Yeah, I think we did a pretty good job. Drugs? Big question mark.

In terms of the scale and timeframe for UK commitments, I don't think there was ever a clear, coherent argument. I constantly pressed for at least some benchmarks, because then we will be able to calculate how long we're going to be in Afghanistan and what capabilities and resources should follow to make such a plan. And avoid a situation where, if America pulled the plug, we would be caught unprepared. Were we making an indefinite commitment for a further ten years, a further twenty years? Were the Americans committed to that? Do we have any exit strategy for what we do in a hurry? There was, from the Defence Secretary and the Chief of Defence Staff down, a refusal to engage on that. I understand it's very difficult terrain for those that have lost comrades in Afghanistan. I think as leaders, we always had to press ourselves on the coherence and focus of the mission.

On 18 August, three days after Kabul had fallen, Prime Minister Boris Johnson gave a speech to Parliament:

I think it would be fair to say that the events in Afghanistan have unfolded and the collapse has been faster than I think even the Taliban themselves predicted. What is not true is to say that the UK Government was unprepared or did not foresee this, because it was certainly part of our planning. Op Pitting, the very difficult logistical operation for the withdrawal of UK nationals, has been under preparation for many months, Mr Speaker, and I can tell the house that the decision to commission the emergency handling centre at the airport took place two weeks ago, Mr Speaker.[14]

This raises the question as to why it would be almost two weeks later before 2 Para were on the ground. Johnson echoed Joe

Biden in the belief that the Afghan forces would hold, while at the same time stating the importance of America in the twenty-year war:

> I think that when he asked for a commentary on the respective military potential power of the Taliban and the Afghan forces, it's pretty clear from what has happened that the collapse of the Afghan forces has been much faster than expected. And as for our NATO allies and our allies around the world, when it came for us to look at the options that this country might have in view of the American decision to withdraw, we came up against this hard reality that since 2009, America has deployed 98 per cent of all weapons released from NATO aircraft in Afghanistan, and at the peak of the operation, when there were 132,000 troops on the ground, 90,000 of them were American.[15]

These two statements cannot rationally co-exist: if 98 per cent of weapons released against the Taliban were from American aircraft, and America was now leaving Afghanistan, then what hope was there for the Afghan security forces?

There would be further challenges for those left to fight on alone. A prisoner swap was part of the Doha Agreement, trading 5000 Taliban prisoners for 1000 Afghan security forces.[16] Raising sanctions was also agreed, making it quite clear that the Taliban were understood to be an emplaced force. After Doha, Afghanistan was going to be a fractured country at best.

Donald Trump ran on a ticket of ending America's wars, but in reality he inherited a mission that had been continually downgrading its commitment. The Afghan army was carrying the full burden of the fighting, as its casualties reflected. For almost a decade there had been on and off attempts at negotiations. Sometimes these stalled over the killing of US servicemen, but they continued behind closed doors.

There was nothing in the Doha Agreement about the Taliban laying down their arms. In fact, 2019 and 2020 were bloody years: battles and air strikes continued. If this was the road to peace, then it was a road paved with bodies. And yet, there was almost no deviation from the plan, except to extend the last day of withdrawal from May 2021, to the politically significant 11th of September, as agreed with the Taliban. President Biden, who replaced Trump that year, gave a speech on 8 July that deserves close attention, as it is illustrative of the attitudes and actions of the Western leaders during this period when 'the plan' was derailing, and NATO was entering the endgame.

Biden said, 'The United States did what we went to do in Afghanistan: to get the terrorists who attacked us on 9/11 and to deliver justice to Osama Bin Laden, and to degrade the terrorist threat to keep Afghanistan from becoming a base from which attacks could be continued against the United States. We achieved those objectives.'

Joe Biden's own chairman of the Joint Chiefs of Staff would seem to disagree: 'It's a real possibility in the not too distant future – 6, 12, 18, 24, 36 months, that kind of timeframe – for reconstitution of al-Qaeda or ISIS,' General Mark Milley told a Capitol Hill hearing, 'and it's our job now, under different conditions, to protect the American citizens against attacks from Afghanistan.'[17]

It is worth remembering that Bin Laden would eventually receive American justice in Pakistan, and terrorist groups such as al-Qaeda are still in the country, as are IS-K and the Haqqani network, despite the Taliban assurances to the contrary.

'It is our commitment that we will not allow anyone to use the soil of Afghanistan against any other country, including the United States,' said Suhail Shaheen. 'And we consider this as a part of our national interest, because we are going to have a country with peace that we want to pave the way for reconstruction of Afghanistan. That could not be achieved without a commitment not to allow anyone to use the soil of our country against other countries.'[18]

President Biden was of the belief – at least publicly – that the Taliban would not be in a position to make such statements. 'We provided our Afghan partners with all the tools,' he said in July 2021. 'Let me emphasise: all the tools, training, and equipment of any modern military.'

Billions of dollars' worth of this equipment would shortly be in the hands of the Taliban.

'We're going to engage in a determined diplomacy to pursue peace and a peace agreement that will end this senseless violence,' the president continued. One wonders which senseless violence he was referring to. Was this an admission that the policy following 9/11 was flawed, and that there was no sense in fighting for the idea of a democratic Afghanistan? The Taliban would certainly not categorise their use of force as senseless. It was about to get them exactly what they wanted.

Later in the speech, the president asserted that, 'It's up to Afghans to make the decision about the future of their country.' Why this was not the case in 2001 was not made clear, and how they were to do so as the Taliban swept across the country was equally vague. Biden gave out numbers of the Afghan security forces in the cool confident way that Vietnam generals once boasted about fire power, but considering the daily collapses to the Taliban, these statistics were as meaningless against the

Taliban as they were against the Viet Cong and North Vietnamese Army (a war which ended with a US air evacuation of 50,000 Vietnamese,[19] with estimates that a further 620,000 eventually fled as refugees).[20] There was nothing in the president's words that resembled a plan of how the Afghan government would prevail.

Perhaps one of President Biden's most illuminating statements was this: 'The Taliban [...] is at its strongest militarily since 2001.' Twenty years of war, and the ousted enemy was stronger than ever, with NATO heading out of the door. What chance then for the Afghan government?

'After twenty years,' said the president, 'a trillion dollars spent training and equipping hundreds of thousands of ANSDF [Afghan National Security and Defence Forces], 2,448 Americans killed, 20,722 more wounded, and untold thousands coming home with unseen trauma to their mental health – I will not send another generation of Americans to war in Afghanistan with no reasonable expectation of achieving a different outcome.'

Considering his previous statement about the Taliban being stronger than ever, this begs the question: what did more than 20,000 US casualties achieve?

He concluded, 'The United States cannot afford to remain tethered to policies creating a response to a world as it was twenty years ago. We need to meet the threats where they are today. Today, the terrorist threat has metastasised beyond Afghanistan.'

Was it not before 2001? Victims of the IRA, Boko Haram, al-Shabaab, and hundreds of terrorist attacks would insist that terrorism was not – and never has been – confined to Afghanistan.

Following his unconvincing speech, the president took some questions:

Question: Is a Taliban takeover of Afghanistan now inevitable?

Biden: No, it is not.

Question: Why?

Biden: Because the Afghan troops have 300,000 well-equipped
– as well-equipped as any army in the world – and an air
force against something like 75,000 Taliban. It is not
inevitable.

If numbers alone were enough to beat the Taliban, would it not
have been defeated when highly trained NATO soldiers were
on the ground? A well-motivated force with momentum behind
it can defeat numbers far larger, particularly when they choose
when and where to fight.

Question: Do you trust the Taliban, Mr President? Do you
trust the Taliban, sir?

Biden: You – is that a serious question?

Question: It is absolutely a serious question. Do you trust the
Taliban?

Biden: No, I do not.

Question: Do you trust handing over the country to the
Taliban?

Biden: No, I do not trust the Taliban.

Question: So why are you handing the country over?

[No answer]

Question: Mr President, will you amplify your answer, please
– why you don't trust the Taliban?

Biden: It's a silly question. Do I trust the Taliban? No. But I
trust the capacity of the Afghan military, who is better
trained, better equipped, and more competent in terms of
conducting war.

To President Biden's credit, he then states:

Biden: I opposed permanently having American forces in
Afghanistan. I argued, from the beginning, as you may recall
– it came to light after [our] administration was over [...]
– no nation has ever unified Afghanistan. No nation.
Empires have gone there and not done it. The focus we
had – and I strongly support it – and you may remember I
physically went to Afghanistan. I was up in that pass where
Osama bin Laden was – allegedly escaped or out of harm's
way.

We went for two reasons: one, to bring Osama bin Laden to
the gates of hell, as I said at the time. The second reason was
to eliminate al-Qaeda's capacity to deal with more attacks
on the United States from that territory. We accomplished
both of those objectives – period. That's what I believed,
from the beginning, why we should be and why we should
have gone to Afghanistan. That job had been over for some
time. And that's why I believe that this is the right decision
and, quite frankly, overdue.

Question: Mr President, some Vietnamese veterans see
echoes of their experience in this withdrawal in
Afghanistan. Do you see any parallels between this
withdrawal and what happened in Vietnam, with some
people feeling—

Biden: None whatsoever. Zero. What you had is – you had
entire brigades breaking through the gates of our embassy
– six, if I'm not mistaken. The Taliban is not the south – the
North Vietnamese army. They're not remotely comparable in
terms of capability. There's going to be no circumstance
where you see people being lifted off the roof of an embassy

46

– the likelihood there's going to be the Taliban overrunning everything and owning the whole country is highly unlikely.[21]

A month later, as the Taliban overran Kabul, helicopters evacuated staff from the roof of the US embassy.

3

The Downfall of a Nation

Look back over the past, with its changing empires that rose and fell, and you can foresee the future too.

— Marcus Aurelius

How a government acts in a country's darkest days can tell you a lot about the state of the nation. In Britain, we are rightly proud that our Prime Minister remained in London during the Blitz. Winston Churchill became a rallying figure for the embattled citizens, an embodiment of the 'Blitz spirit'. With those days some eighty years behind us, the Allied victory has long been taken for granted, but that was not the case in 1940.

The French had been knocked out of the war, the American people were against entering it, and Britain stood alone against the juggernaut of Nazi Germany. The evacuation from Dunkirk, spectacular as it was, was still a retreat, and one that left much of the British Army's equipment behind. It wouldn't be until the end of the Battle of Britain, which overlapped with the devastating Blitz, that Britain could breathe a sigh of relief and know that the very real threat of German invasion had passed.

One might imagine that the situation could have played out very differently. What if, rather than attempting a dangerous rescue mission, the British Expeditionary Force had just been abandoned in France? What if, rather than continuing the fight against the enemy, the Royal Air Force had flown to a friendly country and not returned? What if Churchill himself had taken an aircraft – perhaps stuffed with cash – and flown away from the war?

This is what happened in Afghanistan.

The Afghan government

In the months following the takeover of Kabul, protests would be held in the streets. The Taliban were a cause of much of the anger, but the fallen government was also a cause of their ire: 'Death to Pakistan, death to the Taliban, death to the ones who cheated our country!'[1]

Who were the ones who had cheated the country, and what had they done?

The most obvious example to point at is President Ashraf Ghani. On 15 August, before the Taliban were in full control of the city, Ghani got into a helicopter and left Afghanistan. In a later statement,[2] Ghani said that he did so 'to keep the guns silent and save Kabul and her six million citizens.'

Perhaps there is some truth to this, but such a decision seems to be one that would have been discussed with other members of the government, and this does not appear to be the case. Afghanistan's former Minister of the Interior recalls that 'at noon, [the president] supposedly informed his chief of staff that he was going to take a nap. The chief of staff was in the dining room eating when he heard the helicopter.'[3]

It is for the reader to decide if this action was one of a man fleeing for the sake of the country, or himself. The former president also denied claims that he had taken millions of dollars with him out of the country. These allegations came from a former Afghan ambassador, who alleges that President Ghani left with $169 million.[4]

According to US officials, it seems that the Afghan president had suffered a massive change of heart. The US secretary of state, Antony Blinken, claims that Ghani said that he was willing to fight to the death. Blinken could be making this claim to cover for their choice of president in Afghanistan. After all, it was America who had supported Ghani, and they had backed a lame horse.

That there was corruption in Afghanistan's government is not denied. Afghanistan was ranked 165 out of 180 countries by transparency.org.[5] Everyone from the local police to the highest echelons of the administration were collecting bribes. One reason the strength of the Afghan security forces was over-estimated was that unit commanders still claimed pay for men long dead or deserted.

Khalid Payenda, a former finance minister, maintains that a large part of the 300,000 strong force existed only on paper. They were 'ghost soldiers'. In his opinion, the idea that the ANA (Afghan National Army) greatly outnumbered the Taliban was false. Accountability rested on the word of the local command-ers, whom he alleges kept the bank cards and accounts of departed soldiers, withdrawing the money for themselves.[6]

More than two trillion dollars was spent on the war in Afghanistan. 'For that, it should have been like Dubai,' says war correspondent Hollie McKay. She believes that corruption wasn't merely a factor in the collapse of the country, but a primary cause.

'In many ways, it was the fraud that opened the floodgates to the Taliban. Multiple military insiders stressed to me that the level of corruption swelled throughout 2021 when it became clear that the United States was on its way out, with the Taliban able to pay off troops of all echelons for information and insider attacks. But long before that, cash flooded the country and into the hands of corrupt officials and their friends and family, with the US taxpayer essentially funding projects that never got off the ground or eroded in a season or two. Most of this money flow seemingly drifted unchecked and with little accountability, providing the Taliban with the perfect recruiting tool for disaffected and frustrated Afghans to pounce upon.'[7]

Detractors will point to this collapse as inevitable, the result of Afghan culture being incompatible and too corruptible to receive the massive amounts of wealth that were thrown at the nation, but one must look at the West's role in this. When President Obama announced the beginning of the end in 2010, many veterans of the campaign knew a Taliban victory was assured in a matter of years. If British soldiers could understand this, then Afghan officials also could. They knew they could not live under the Taliban, and some accumulated as much wealth as they could, so that when the end came, they could flee with their families and start a new, comfortable life in other parts of the world.

Many of us in the West are deaf to our own history of interventionism, but the developing world has watched, and learned. What became of the Vietnamese officials who sided with America, or with the French? What happened to them when the Western empires withdrew? A quick death, if they were lucky. Humans do not look kindly on 'collaborators'. Whether in 1940s France, 1970s Ulster or any number of other conflicts, there is often no mercy for civilians who supported the losing side. Afghan officials would have known they had to secure their own way out, and for many that meant 'looting the Treasury', a common practice in the last days of a nation.

Another fatal misconception was that the West believed they were building a democracy, but Afghanistan remained an extremely centralised government run on ethnic and tribal lines. President Ghani had a narrow base of support, and consequently, a tight inner circle. His governance seemed often more authoritarian than democratic, and this feeling of voicelessness disenfranchised those who fell outside Ghani's tribe and ethnic set. Particularly in the Pashtos of the south. This was key, as it allowed a continuous stream of recruits, trained fighters, and arms to enter Afghanistan from Pakistan. Without the support of the south, the north would always be at war.[8]

The Afghan security forces

In the summer of 2021, many Western politicians and commentators were quick to malign the performance of the Afghan security forces. That judgement is unfair and perhaps a reflection that most people making these comments had never spent a day in combat. 'The Afghan military collapsed, sometimes without trying to fight,' President Biden said.[9]

Did they give up, or were they abandoned? Two special forces units, Task Force 333 and 444, were both fighting with all of their strength in Lashkar Gar and Kandahar as the Taliban encircled them. A former 1 Para soldier, who had served alongside the Afghan special forces, said, 'Every day I was getting messages from the Afghans I'd fought with saying, oh, he's dead. Now he's dead.'

It is worth remembering that in 2006, units of the Parachute Regiment – some of the best trained infantry in the world – would have been overrun if not for sustained close air support. It took everything from Apache helicopters to the massive B2 bombers to stop these elite soldiers from being defeated, yet Western politicians now expected the far more poorly trained Afghan army to stand and triumph with almost no such air support. At best, this was an incredibly short-sighted, negligent assessment of what would happen. Either the politicians and generals had no real idea of the situation on the ground, or they knew and allowed the situation to unfold, regardless. Either scenario is damning.

How was it that the use of 'ghost soldiers' was unknown, or if known, not policed? Why was it not foreseen that withdrawing air support – vital even for first-rate Western soldiers – would take away the Afghan Army's biggest advantage? And how was it that the ability of the Afghan security forces was greatly over-stated? For this final question, we can at least offer a possible answer.

Military careers are competitive, and attract competitive people. In such environments, saying what people want to hear is a form of self-preservation. Years before Pearl Harbor, General William Mitchell warned that in the event of war, the Japanese would launch a first strike against the US naval base in Hawaii. His advice was unwanted and unheeded, and he was hounded out of the service. The same was true of Colonel David Hackworth, one of the US Army's most promising counter-insurgency leaders. After speaking out against the way the war was being conducted in Vietnam, Hackworth was put out to pasture. Following his demands for accountability for the events of 2021, a Marine officer named Stuart Scheller was also relieved of his position, and discharged from service.

Such lessons are ingrained in the subconscious of all officers, many of whom want to make changes to 'the system', but feel they must 'play the game' to get to a position that counts. In

Fallujah, General James 'Mad Dog' Mattis chose to follow orders, against his own judgement, to launch a full scale assault on the city, rather than dealing with insurgents with targeted strikes. Even a 'Mad Dog' knew when to sit down when told.

Training team after training team was sent to Afghanistan, many of them from the Special Operations Command. By their definition, these units attract individuals who are a cut above, many of whom eye long careers and high posts. The military is a bureaucracy, fond of reports, and by these reports is a man judged. It would be career suicide for a young leader to say: 'This Afghan Army unit was far below the standard I was led to expect. They are not fit for combat. They need at least another six months of training.'

Even if a soldier's code of honour did not forbid him from throwing a predecessor 'under the bus', that predecessor, by dint of longer service, would now be higher in rank than the person following him into that position. Even if a young officer was willing to go on the record and call out optimistic reporting, he would be throwing himself under the proverbial bus, too. The previous officer's peer group would not take kindly to their friend and comrade being tarnished.

No doubt there were many officers whose integrity demanded that they speak up about the overzealous reporting on the state of the Afghan troops, but given that they would be in the minority – likely with a career cut short – these opinions would be easy to dismiss.

'What does he know? He washed out as a captain.'

To progress up the ladder, an officer would not only need to accept his predecessor's positive view of the Afghan troops, but add to it. Anything else would be shown as a failure in his ability to improve upon them. And so, with every deployment, the ability of the Afghan forces became greater and greater; at least, on the paper of the Pentagon's reports. The situation on the ground was far different.

Ask anyone who fought alongside the Afghan special forces and you will hear stories of highly motivated, brave, and intelligent individuals who believed wholeheartedly in the new Afghanistan, and who would gladly give their blood to water the tree of liberty. This could also be experienced with conventional ANP (Afghan National Police) and ANA units, such as Major Adam Jowett had in 2006: 'The Afghan Police were having rare fun in their sector, I quickly saw. They were smiling, fighting to be the ones in the firing positions . . . You couldn't help but smile at the attitude. These men were born warriors and nothing less.'[10]

This was not the experience of all British soldiers, including one of the authors of this book. Serving in the same area as Major Jowett had done, three years later, the Afghan Army soldiers were usually late to operations, then tried to leave early, and even refused to carry one of their wounded British mentors out of a firefight. They were also known to shoot at British patrols – even when they were conducted with armoured vehicles, which the Taliban did not have. This may be down to drug use, which seemed rife in that Afghan Army unit. MP Johnny Mercer recalled one Afghan unit he had worked with where one soldier stabbed his comrade to death while on parade.

'Green on blues' were also a factor that led many NATO soldiers to be wary of their allies. This is the name given to an attack where Afghan soldiers turned their weapons on their Western mentors. It is safe to say that there was a large amount of distrust between the nationalities. Even in Afghan patrol bases, which were nominally secure, Brits would set their own sentries within the perimeter.

In late 2009, a quarter of the Afghan police drug tested in Helmand tested positive.[11] That same year, the *Daily Telegraph* ran a headline claiming that 15 per cent of the Afghan Army were drug addicts.[12] The British Forces themselves are not drug free – almost a battalion's worth of personnel were discharged for failed drug tests in 2020[13] – but on tour it is difficult for most soldiers to get a beer, let alone drugs. In a country where marijuana grows wild, and where poppy fields are as common as grass lawns in the UK, there was certainly scope for misuse. In the documentary *Combat Obscura*, made by a US serviceman who served in Helmand, drug use among US Marines is documented. While not reflective of the whole, it would be unfair to point to the drug use in the ANSDF, while not pointing out that it also existed in NATO forces.

While some Western soldiers were indifferent to ANSDF drug use, few – if any – were not horrified and disgusted by the often seen practice of Bachi Bala: sex with young boys. These acts of paedophilia were known throughout NATO ground forces, but Western soldiers were forced by policy and orders to turn a blind eye. This caused 'moral injury' in many to the point where they became suicidal. Sometimes, a Western soldier's conscience would demand that he act despite his orders. There is a recorded incident of a US Green Beret badly beating an Afghan officer who had raped a boy that he kept chained to a bed as a sex slave.[14] For coming to the defence of the child, the soldier was punished.

'At night we can hear them screaming, but we're not allowed to do anything about it,' a US Marine told his father of the abuse of young boys. In the same *New York Times* article, the special forces captain removed from his position said, 'The reason we were here is because we heard the terrible things the Taliban were doing to people, how they were taking away human rights. But we were putting people into power who would do things that were worse than the Taliban did – that was something village elders voiced to me.'[15]

The partnership between NATO and the ANA was never an equal one. The Afghan security forces took the overwhelming number of casualties and they served longer on the frontline. Western units rotated in and out, and came to battle with better training and equipment. That being said, it was often the Western units that were used as 'the shock troops'. They carried the war to the Taliban through large scale operations, and rigorous patrolling when ground holding. Afghan units were sometimes late or absent from missions that they were supposed to join, even lead. In contrast, young 'squaddies' from Britain and other Western nations, were chomping at the bit to get at the enemy.

In the years when both the ANA and NATO were in the field, these differences could be overcome. The ANA provided the bulk of the ground holding force, while the NATO troops could be the shock troops. An anvil and a hammer, battering the Taliban between them; but when the hammer left, the anvil became too heavy and unwieldy to take on their insurgent foe and win.

Could the ANA really be expected to defeat the Taliban when the best trained and equipped soldiers in the world had failed to do it? The special forces of many nations took the war to the enemy, but no matter how many heads were cut from the snake, more grew back. At the patrol bases, and in the towns and villages and mountain passes, conventional forces killed the enemy on a daily basis, but no matter how many Taliban were killed, more came in their place. According to Joe Biden, as we have heard earlier, the Taliban was at its strongest militarily in 2021.

Most of Afghanistan had held out with skeletal NATO support for six years. The *New York Times* reported that in 2016 the Afghan National Army was losing twenty-two men per day, which led to a decision to classify the total numbers for that year.[16] In just one week in 2018, the Afghan Security Forces suffered 400 deaths – almost as many as British forces lost in the entire war. What is clear is that when NATO withdrew, the Afghan Security Forces' casualities mounted steeply. Brown University's cost of war study put the total deaths of Afghanistan Security Forces at 66,000, the majority coming in the final six years of the war – this from a force that was alleged to be 300,000-strong in 2021, of which 20,000 were the country's commandos.

'The Afghans are up to the job,' is the essence of what so many Western commanders were saying, but even if that is true, at what cost? How long could that number of deaths be sustained? How would they continue to recruit? How long would morale last? Napoleon once said that 'morale is to the physical as three is to one'. In other words, it doesn't matter how many weapons and how much kit you give to an army, or how much you train them. The only thing that matters is if they have the will to kill, and the will to die, and by 2021, this will had fled from large parts of the Afghan forces. They saw the writing on the wall. So too did many Western pundits.

One of the most disturbing parts of the last days of Afghanistan was that many commentators expected the Taliban to emerge victorious in the end, but they expected the ANA to hold on for a little longer. Despite their shortcomings, the ANA did fight a rearguard action that lasted for several years. To many in the West, it seemed that Afghanistan fell quickly, but that was because they had ignored the war for a decade, at least. For an Afghan soldier, the war was not the few weeks that it was on Western television sets in 2021, but year after year of bloody fight after bloody fight. For them, it was bombs, boobytraps, and the murder of comrades. The Afghan forces did not 'collapse in a few weeks'. They gave up after years of battle, when their allies had left the field.

Did the West want all of them to die fighting, just so that we could feel better about ourselves? Why would an ANA soldier throw his life away in a war that even their long-time ally was now saying was unwinnable? And why would Western politicians expect him to? If a nine month to two year collapse was predictable, then so was a one month collapse. An army will not fight without morale.

There is much finger pointing at the Doha Agreement. This deal, made with the Taliban in 2020, proved to many that the United States was willing to 'do business' with the Taliban. It would be akin to the Americans making a deal with the Viet Cong while US forces were still in Vietnam, and the South Vietnamese government was still at war.

Sir Laurie Bristow was the British ambassador to Afghanistan in the summer of 2021:

> I arrived in the middle of June. As part of the preparation for becoming an ambassador, I was reading the files for much of the previous four or five months, doing the calls around Whitehall, getting the size of the thing. But the context, of course, was the Doha Agreement. And then Biden's review when he came in . . . where basically the Trump Doha Agreement set a timetable for

leaving. It didn't set many conditions for leaving, which . . . [was] the underlying problem . . .

It did three things: it put time pressure on the military withdrawal; it gave the Taliban a bunch of quite significant concessions upfront, including releasing prisoners, without really any enforceable expectations that the Taliban would even negotiate in good faith, let alone that they would actually deliver an outcome; and it pulled the rug out from under the government.

With Biden coming in, I think it's important to bear in mind a couple of bits of context. He'd been on the record for years about wanting to bring the military operation to an end . . . My own take on it was that the circumstances of the transition in Washington, the assault on the Capitol and all the rest of it, meant that he needed to deliver some important bits of policy early on to stamp his authority. And I think that's what he thought he was doing. So once it was crystal clear that the military were leaving and on that timetable, and there's no doubt about that, it's a question of how quickly rather than whether.

What we had was a direction from the NSC [National Security Council] to keep the embassy open to do what it was there to do. So about three or four key tasks. One, of course, is the National Security Task, counterterrorism task, and one was to support the government, the Republic, [another] was to press ahead with ARAP [Afghan Relocations and Assistance Policy], [which] had only just been announced and crystallised after all the goings on over the years about military interpreters and the finals to do the contingency planning.

So that was what I was working on from about April through to going there in June, on [the] principle that the person having to live most closely with the outcome of this, gets to do the preparations. And that was almost entirely about transitioning a vast embassy completely dependent on the military to a slightly less vast embassy, no longer dependent on military, who weren't going to be there. So loads of detailed stuff about how we're going to guard it.

Who's going to run the airport? We can't do anything without an airport, without an airport, we're gone, very simple. Without a serious trauma hospital, we're gone, because we can't fulfil our duty of care. Nobody can. And modelling through the scenarios if the shit hits the fan ... through the various iterations of Op Pitting, we're basically looking at [what are] called GROs, 'Graduated Response Options', ranging from pretty benign, to pretty scary. And on the benign end, we're leaving on Emirates essentially, and at the scary end, we're doing something like what we actually did.

One piece of policy may have contributed more to the collapse of Afghan morale than another, but in the end, it was a succession of events that degraded the support given to Afghanistan: from Obama's troop withdrawals, to Trump's Doha Agreement, to Biden's adherence to it. Add to these 'abandonments' the corruption, the high casualty rates, and the prospect of continuing 'the Forever War', and there is little wonder that the security situation ended as it did. Most armies are asked to fight for a few years, at most. The Afghans fought for two decades.

When Western politicians disparage their efforts, they should perhaps spare a moment for the 92,000 Afghan security forces who gave their lives in a war initiated by the West.[17] For every person murdered in 9/11, more than thirty Afghan security personnel died in the war that followed it. Western determination to defeat the Taliban had melted in the face of far fewer casualties, and yet it seemed to be expected that the Afghans should continue to die in perpetuity.

'Someday this war's gonna end,' said Colonel Kilgore, in one of the most understated, but damning lines of the Vietnam war epic *Apocalypse Now*. A line that summarises the futility of the conflict, the wasted lives and the broken dreams. Sooner or later, all wars come to an end.

Even the Forever War.

The advance

'You have the watches, but we have the time,' a Taliban spokesman is credited with saying, stealing the line from a Viet Cong commander. For years they had been harassing NATO and ANSDF forces, bleeding both, sapping morale, conviction and the will to fight on. In 2021, reassured by the Doha Agreement, and correctly judging that the COVID-19 world did not have the stomach for war, the Taliban launched an offensive that would have impressed the German architects of Blitzkrieg.

Even those expecting a Taliban victory were shocked by how quickly the insurgent force swept through the country in the summer of 2021. Ben Wallace, the UK's defence secretary, gave an explanation as to the difficulties of predicting the advance.

'At the very end, when something like a rout develops, you never really know what tips something to a rout and a rapid collapse because your sources dry up. So you might on any day in a normal time have hundreds of sources to inform you of the situation. As a country falls, of course, they all disappear, you end up with lesser and lesser, you might end up with three people in the presidential palace. And suddenly your information flow rapidly constricts. So you just don't know. Intelligence is a guidance. It's a cumulative assessment. And I looked at it and said, from what I know here, and what I can see there, and what it was like in Washington when I was there the summer before, the game was up.'

The political stage had been set for a Taliban victory, but they still needed to win the battles on the ground.

Summer offensives are a tradition in Afghanistan. It is far easier to move on the dirt tracks when they are baked hard in summer, and not the soggy quagmire that they become in Afghan rains. The 'green zone', the name given to the lush belts of irrigated farmland, becomes a haven for insurgents in summer. The poppy harvest is taken in, freeing field hands to become 'ten dollar Taliban', the name given to those who fight for a few dollars a day, rather than because they are committed jihadists. Summer in Afghanistan is a time when both sides jockey for position.

Indeed, the purpose of many British operations between 2006–2014 was to counter the Taliban's summer offensives, but following the withdrawal of NATO troops, the Taliban had been gaining ground. They took control of the towns that British soldiers and American Marines had fought so hard to hold before being withdrawn in 2014. Musa Qala fell within a year. Sangin a year later. In this town, 106 British Servicemen had given their lives for the cause, and many more than that their limbs. US Marine casualty rates in the town were just as high.

In a news article, a mother of a British soldier killed in Sangin said that: 'Most of all [I feel] a desperate sense of waste and fear that we are still not learning the lessons and that it's British troops that are going to pay the price for that failure to learn . . . We never knew what we were trying to achieve. The mission seemed to change constantly according to circumstance.'

In the same article, General Lord Richard Dannatt came to the defence of the withdrawal. 'We always knew that the situation once we left Helmand would be difficult. We left Afghanistan in a situation where the Afghans were in control and the future was in their hands. It is not a great surprise that the Taliban have continued to push in southern Afghanistan, it's their heartland.'[18]

If it were no great surprise that the Taliban retook the towns of Helmand within a few years of British soldiers dying there in their hundreds, one wonders why holding these areas was a priority for the British Army, of which General Dannatt was the Chief of the General Staff between 2006 and 2009, when much of the heaviest fighting occurred. The hundreds of British dead, and the thousands of civilians killed and injured, should not have been sacrificed for a cause that was deemed unlikely to succeed.

'Not a great surprise,' the general says of the Taliban's recapture of the towns. If only the same could be said for the families of those who died there. First, the knock on the door, and the news that their child had been killed. And then, years later, a story in the news telling that the town was now back in Taliban hands. If this angers you as a Western reader, imagine the thoughts of an Afghan who had his home turned into a frontline for almost a decade. It is not difficult to see why support for the Taliban – grudging or not – held firm and even began to grow in parts of the country. Empty promises and words were paid for in blood in Helmand.

Dannatt claimed Afghanistan's future was in Afghan hands, and that was true, but it was the Taliban who were in control, and at the wheel.

Ambassador Sir Laurie Bristow contends:

My personal view on going out there was that this is probably going to come to an end on my watch. I mean, that was the basis on which I took the job. Knowing that that was more likely than not. The purpose of those telegrams, as always, is to tell it as you see it. So there's an element of sort of [Iraq Inquiry chairman Sir John] Chilcot testing here. Are we telling ourselves stuff that isn't actually true? The job of an ambassador, an embassy, in those circumstances is to tell London the bad news, if there is bad news. And then, if there are recalibrations to be done with policy or with operational decisions, see them through. And that was a big part of what was going on there.

So it's been briefed into the foreign affairs committee that it was pretty bad, it was going bad, fast. But on balance the Republic had a fair chance of making it through the summer and out of the fighting season. And then, if that happens, what you've got is the opportunity to try and slightly change the calculation for all concerned. So the sorts of things that I was trying to do with the government at the time, was first of all get them to understand what was happening to them. And the problem we're all wrestling with is just lack of visibility and reducing visibility of what's happening outside the green zone [the diplomatic zone, as opposed to the fertile 'green zone' in rural areas where the British Army did much of its fighting], because of the security situation, but also, at least some senior members of the government who I think were not willing to believe what they were seeing. So a big dose of drinking their own Kool Aid.

As the Taliban's 2021 push advanced, more and more ANSDF units began to lay down their arms rather than fight. It was clear that America was not coming back into the war, and that Afghan units would stand alone. Even if they put up a fight, surrounded as they often were, there was no chance of resupplying ammunition, or evacuating casualties. Footage of these surrenders circulated on social media. One showed an Afghan soldier breaking down in tears, and having to be held by his comrades. This was not a man who wanted to surrender, but his unit had made the decision. They had families, and a life under the Taliban was seen as preferable to dying in the last days of a lost war.

The Taliban were prudent in the way that they handled the regular units of the ANSDF, granting clemency and forgiveness if they surrendered. As word of this treatment spread, and Afghan Army soldiers knew that they would not be tortured and killed, more and more of them were willing to lay down their arms. Disarmed, many of them were allowed to start the long walk to their homes. A Taliban spokesman later claimed that an amnesty was being observed.

'There is not any kind of reprisal nor any revenge under those people who are working with the foreign troops,' said Suhail Shaheen, the Taliban spokesman in Qatar. 'And so we have announced a general amnesty, they can lead their normal life and they also contribute to the reconstruction of the country, to people's economic prosperity, to their own prosperity. And they can use their talents, capacities, in the service of the country and people.'[19]

These surrenders of the Afghan security forces hastened the Taliban's advance in several ways. Not only did they not have to fight their way through every town, and by every outpost, but they now inherited the vehicles that had belonged to the ANSDF. One of the most bewildering – and for many people, frustrating – elements of the advance was the sight of the Taliban bedecked in US-supplied fatigues, carrying weapons and driving vehicles that had come at the expense of the US taxpayer.

The Pentagon has admitted that more than seven billion dollars' worth of military equipment fell into Taliban hands. They went to great pains to insist that it was equipment belonging to the Afghan security forces, and not US military, but the technicality of ownership seems like a moot point. It was paid for with US taxes, and now belongs to the Taliban.

'It's not state-of-the-art stuff,' a US defence official said, in contradiction to President Biden's July claim that the ANSDF were kitted out as a first-rate military. 'Everything that we provided to the Afghan forces was not on the same level as ours or those of our allies.'[20]

Behind the wheels of American-made Humvees and MRAPS (Mine-Resistant Ambush Protected vehicles), the Taliban continued their pushes around the country. Seven years to the month since Musa Qala had been taken by the Taliban, the end of the Republic of Afghanistan was all but assured. In August 2021, provincial capitals began to fall in quick succession. On 13 August, the capitals of Badghis, Ghor, Helmand, Kandahar, Zabul and Uruzgan provinces were taken by the Taliban. Helmand and Kandahar had been the main battlegrounds for British soldiers, and both were now completely under Taliban control. Days before the events in Kabul, almost every piece of ground that the British had fought for was lost.

Ambassador Sir Laurie Bristow describes two other events that were key to the changing situation:

> One was the rocket attack on the government on the morning of Eid. If those rockets had landed in a different pattern, that would have taken out a big chunk of, or possibly the entire government, the political elite. That would have been a very different situation . . .

The second event was the attack on [the Afghan defence minister] Bismillah Khan's house. So he wasn't at home. It was an absolutely epic firefight, the house was destroyed. The attackers were all killed, but it went on late into the night. And that was very close to the green zone. So the point was that, apart from what would have happened if Bismillah Khan had been at home, the Taliban are now bringing the fight to the Defence Minister in the heart of Kabul. What I was trying to do, particularly with the reporting around there, was essentially to tee up London to an understanding that now things were accelerating and going bad very, very quickly, and that things followed from that . . .

As far as the embassy was concerned, we [had] planned and modelled through [the process of] closing it. We've got it down to essentially a five-day closure plan. As the thing deteriorated progressively that had to come down to nine hours, which is why the mistake was made over the papers that didn't get burned properly. So there's that. And what we also had in mind, and this has been on my mind going right back into April and the planning for all this, it's the Saigon thing. So what happens when an absolutely humongous US embassy that, as far as I could see, hadn't done any serious planning at all, what happens when they move north of perhaps 100,000 people with them? . . .

We need to have started moving by the time that happens. Because what you don't want to happen is to get stuck in the sort of enormous gridlock in Kabul as the Americans pull out under God knows what situation. So that was an issue. If the moment comes, what's the optimal time for us to leave? To close the embassy and pull back. And there's another factor in play here, which is very important, you don't want to be the ones who actually collapse the whole thing.

So bear in mind that we were the second biggest embassy in Kabul. And we were responsible for a big chunk of the security on that corner of the green zone on the gates and so the moment we pulled out, all the Europeans would follow, if they hadn't already gone. It would be a very visible vote of no confidence in the government, in the army and all the rest of it, and it will take down a chunk of the defence of the green zone . . .

Imagine the situation we would be in if we had lost anyone on the way, killed or captured. That was the risk that we were trying to manage there. My take on it is that we probably timed it pretty much right, actually, in terms of leaving it as late as we could, but no later. And, we didn't lose anyone, we got bloody lucky to be perfectly honest.

On 11 August, a US State Department spokesperson, Ned Price, was grilled at a press conference by a reporter. During the lengthy exchange, the journalist asked many of the questions that were on American and British minds:

Question: So in terms of your grand promotion of democracy, human rights, which are going to be at the centre of US foreign policy, as we will see no doubt in December when the President hosts his summit of— for democracy, how does that relate exactly to Afghanistan and your promotion of human rights and democracy, when you have a situation where the country is rapidly coming under control of a group that has shown no respect for democracy and human rights ever?

Mr Price: I'm sorry, the question was . . .

Question: How do you reconcile this? How do you – how does the administration expect to be taken seriously in

terms of promoting human rights and democracy as being
at the centre of US foreign policy if it is prepared to allow
Afghanistan to deteriorate into a situation where a group
that has shown – that you yourself just days ago have
accused of committing atrocities – if you're prepared to
allow that to happen.

Mr Price: I would reject every single premise of that question.
The United States—

Question: Really? Because most of what I just said is actual – is
factual.

Mr Price: The United States – I think it is undeniable – has
over the course of twenty years done more to support the
cause of the Afghan people to provide humanitarian support.
Just numerically speaking, of course, we are the largest
donor, and that includes humanitarian assistance, it includes
assistance for the women and girls of Afghanistan, for
Afghanistan's minorities. That won't change.

I would also reject the premise that we are just prepared
to watch and do nothing as the violence escalates. That
could not be farther from the truth. The truth, Matt, is that
on every count, on every score, the United States over the
course of the past twenty years and now going forward is, I
would dare say, doing more than any country to try to bring
stability, security, and ultimately prosperity to the people of
Afghanistan.

Now, it is true that our tactics are changing, that the
President has made the decision to withdraw our military
forces. That says nothing about our support for the rights of
the people of Afghanistan and what we will continue – what
we have done and will continue to strive to do to bring
stability and security to the people of Afghanistan right now

as we speak through a diplomatic process. And I know you tend to discount diplomacy, at least in this case.

Question: Tend to? No, no, not tend to. [Laughter.] I just don't think and I don't see how you can realistically think that it's going to accomplish anything, because it hasn't in the past. And you say you reject the premise that you're prepared to sit by and watch and do nothing. Well, what have you done over the course of the last couple weeks as these atrocities that you've talked about have mounted, as the Taliban has taken over more and more territory? What exactly has it been that you have done?[21]

The reporter then brings up the Doha Agreement, which was the agreement made with the Taliban for the US-led forces to leave Afghanistan.

Question: ... they didn't agree in February 2020 not to seek a battlefield victory against the Afghan government.

Mr Price: What they agreed to do—

Question: Did they or did they not?

Mr Price: What they agreed to do was to seek a permanent and comprehensive ceasefire agreement.

Question: Yeah, through these peace talks, which have gone nowhere.

Mr Price: Correct, correct. And—

Question: Did they agree in 2020, in February 2020 did they agree not to attack Afghan provincial ...

Mr Price: What we can say—

Question: ... major population centres of the Afghan government and the Afghan forces?

Mr Price: What we can say—

Question: Did they or did they not?

Mr Price: What we can say is that the levels of violence are
  unacceptably high and what we have seen is inconsistent
  with the letter and the spirit of the agreement.

Question: But they didn't actually agree not to attack cities,
  provincial capitals, big, major population centres, or the
  Afghan . . .

Mr Price: Matt, attacking—

Question: . . . or the Afghan military. Did they?

Mr Price: Attacking – attacking provincial capitals and targeting civilians is inconsistent with the spirit of the agreement.
  It's this last clause of the agreement, the key point that I
  mentioned: a permanent and comprehensive ceasefire agreement over the future political roadmap of Afghanistan—

Question: I'll just put that down as a no.

'The spirit of the agreement' was that America wanted out of
Afghanistan, and not even a Taliban march across the country,
and the imminent fall of its ally's capital, would stop the exit. By
11 August, there was no longer any pretence amongst much of
the political establishment that Afghanistan's government would
survive. On that date, a US defence official cited US Intelligence,
saying that the Taliban could control Kabul in ninety days.[22]

Four days later, the Taliban seized the city.

4

Ready for Anything

They have jumped from the air and by doing so have conquered fear.
— Field Marshal Montgomery

In May 2022, almost a year after the fall of the Afghan government, the House of Commons Committee released a special report titled *Missing in Action: UK leadership and the withdrawal from Afghanistan*:

> When the Taliban took Kabul, the Prime Minister, the then-Foreign Secretary, the minister responsible for Afghanistan, and the FCDO's top civil servant, Sir Philip Barton, were all on leave. All returned that day, except Sir Philip, who returned on 26 August — the day civilian evacuations ended. Both the Foreign Secretary and Sir Philip told us that they regretted not coming back sooner, and Sir Philip admitted that his absence had had an impact on officials working on the crisis. Rory Stewart said that these absences reflected a systemic problem in the UK Government: a 'lack of seriousness, responsibility and grip around the issue of Afghanistan'.[1]

As the Taliban seized Afghanistan, the British Parliament was on its summer recess. While it is fair to say that the speed of the Taliban's advance surprised many experts, it is somewhat perplexing that it would be three days *after* the fall of Kabul that Parliament would finally sit in session.

Five months before the fall of the Afghan government, Parliament had been recalled in the wake of the death of Prince Philip. It wasn't until Kabul had already fallen that the collapsing Afghan state was given the same immediacy as paying tribute to a deceased member of the Royal Family. Perhaps if the 457 British soldiers who had died in Afghanistan were of Royal blood, Parliament could have convened much sooner. But, optimistic towards the Afghan government, and, underestimating the Taliban menace, ministers believed that the advance would soon grind down.

'It was kind of an incremental advance,' Johnny Mercer MP explained, 'and at every stage, I think a lot of us thought that they may take the countryside and Helmand, but they won't take Lashkar Ghar. Then they moved over into Kandahar province, okay, but they won't take Kandahar. Then they took Kandahar, and so this kind of pressure increased incrementally.'

Incremental or not, the Taliban were bringing down the country built on the backs of thousands of deaths, including British, and yet, day after day, the parliament who had sent those men to fight and die was not recalled. Rather than err on the side of caution, holidays were placed above the collapse of an allied government. Kandahar – Afghanistan's second biggest city – was claimed by the Taliban to have fallen to them almost a full week before Parliament would finally sit in session.[2]

Johnny Mercer and several other MPs felt severely hamstrung by the lack of will to recall Parliament, and the line the British government was taking over the Afghan withdrawal as a whole:

When the Commons is sitting, what you can do is put in things like urgent questions, and as a backbench MP, you can haul a minister into the House of Commons. A question like, 'What the fuck is going on in Afghanistan?' But that mechanism wasn't available, because everyone was on recess. So everyone watched this situation evolve, unfold. And you saw that played out in the papers, because the papers were reporting this and reporting it accurately, and trying to get reactions out of ministers. But there wasn't the real sort of democratic process as a world event was taking place, and Parliament didn't react in an agile manner to that.

I think when the Doha Agreement was signed by Trump, it was clear that it wasn't going to end well. And I think what was frustrating was that it was pretty clear, I think, to most people what was going to happen, but there wasn't really any sense of urgency in terms of planning for that within the UK govern-ment at the time. It was very much 'this is what the Americans are doing, and we've just got to go along with it.' Whereas some of us were sort of on the other foot thinking, actually, we're the second biggest troop contributing nation, we should have [a] fucking say in this.

And, the guys who died, and the families who lost loved ones, they didn't die for an American flag and American mission, they thought they were acting in the interests of the UK. So, for me, that was always a very important point. And this idea that, just because the Americans were leaving, we just collapsed. Obviously, we couldn't stay forever, but the idea that we just collapsed, I think, made it even harder for families.

Ben Wallace gave an honest assessment of the UK's preparedness:

The military preparation was second to none. I mean, that fateful Saturday night when we pressed the button to send in 16 Air Assault and, well, given the risk involved, that went off incredibly smoothly. No one really knew what they were flying into. Yes, we'd had recce groups out there, yes, and other people who we can't really talk about who've been out on the ground, so there was some texture of what was going on. But fundamentally, the speed of the decline of the Afghan government was so rapid, who knows what would have been there when you landed?

When it came to the political preparation, I think, the whole of government were not in the right mindset for far too long. I sent a general out to embed in the Afghan government in July, and his report to me was pretty damning of the direction of travel. It was not a view shared, necessarily, by other invested two stars and three stars and four stars [generals] around the system and the country who had had different views. But to me, it was clear. All you had to do is marry the Trump statements. Okay, it was then succeeded by Biden, but there's a sense in the political system of America to bring troops back home. And no one, no one's going to change the deal.

And then you had to see what the reports were from the functioning capability of the Afghans. And I think, to me, you felt quite strongly, I mean, in defence of the Foreign Office, Dominic Raab much earlier in the year, there was the more strategic question of 'Why are our troops in Afghanistan?'

Whatever the reasons that British troops had been there, the end was nigh.

'It's done,' said Wallace, speaking of Doha. 'It's a rotten deal, but it's done, and no amount of wishing it away is going to change that. There's no miracle that's going to suddenly change the Afghan government. And we need to think like that.'

'There was no one who challenged that continuous assessment,' said Dominic Raab, the Foreign Secretary:

To the extent it was questioned, it was me asking whether we were reading too much in the intent of the Taliban, given their capabilities. I'd met a Pakistani general in Islamabad, who was dealing with the Taliban at the time. I spoke to the Americans. I spoke to Europeans. Between, let's say, the beginning of 2021 and early August, of course, the scale of the advance, and when you saw big cities taken, required a questioning of that assumption. But even then, there was a consensus argument, certainly in the MOD, backed by Ben Wallace and Nick Carter, that the Taliban might snap up a few major cities, but we're not going to go to Kabul.

The way it works is you get the JIC [Joint Intelligence Committee] assessments. And we get the view from the Foreign Office, we get the view from the MOD, and you work on your best information. There are always snippets of what I would call 'low confidence information' coming back to you. And if you react to each one of those, they may make newspaper stories, but they're not a credible basis for you to plan.

To the extent that there was a canary in the coal mine, it was me. I, at every stage questioned, why if they got the opportunity, the Taliban would forgo the opportunity to hound us out of Kabul, because the PR coup would be just irresistible.

This raises questions as to why Raab remained in Crete on holiday until after Kabul had fallen.

'The truth is, in the modern day, foreign secretaries never really go on holiday and take a full break,' said Raab. 'You take the technology with you. So the idea that there was any proper rest and relaxation during this period is ludicrous.'

Whilst that might be the case, the optics of a Foreign Secretary remaining away when a British ally collapses into ruin are decidedly poor. If the end of a twenty-year war is not worth a four-hour flight, it begs the question, what is?

It would be unfair and untrue to say that all MPs were idle as Afghanistan was falling, but the fact remains that Parliament stayed in recess, and many ministers continued with their holidays uninterrupted. While many MPs were enjoying their vacations, thousands of servicemen and women were preparing to dig the UK out of another politically created hole. Leave was cancelled, soldiers were recalled to barracks and immediately put on standby to fly into the place that had seen so many of their comrades killed and injured over the last twenty years.

The Latin motto of the British Parachute Regiment is *Utrinque Paratus*, which roughly translates as 'Ready for Anything'. It is their pragmatism, eagerness and physical robustness that sets the Paras apart from the rest of the British Infantry. It is why they form the backbone of the British Army's 16 Air Assault Brigade, the unit set up to fly into any crisis, anywhere in the world, at a moment's notice. And that is why the Paras were the first unit to be sent to Kabul in February 2002 in the aftermath of the special forces operations in Tora Bora, and that is why the Paras were the last unit in Kabul almost twenty years later in August 2021.

'I was just a baby when 9/11 happened,' said Tom, a young private soldier in 2 Para. 'The first thing I really knew about Afghanistan was the Ross Kemp documentaries. I was probably about eight years old, and already playing soldiers a lot of the time, but the Ross Kemp stuff really cemented it for me. I wanted to be in combat like the troops that he was with.'

Soldiering is one of the few professions where someone may go their entire career without doing the job they signed up to do. For most professional soldiers, war is the anomaly in their service. Most of their military years will be spent on exercise, and camp duties.

This is less so for the Parachute Regiment than for other units of the British Army. Since their conception in the Second World War, they have formed a part of Britain's response to everything from conventional war to humanitarian missions. Though the Parachute Regiment has not jumped into battle since the Suez crisis of 1956, its men, because of their exceptional selection process and training, are considered an elite. If a soldier wants to up his chances of seeing a deployment, 'the Paras' are the regiment to join.

That was why Tom joined 2 Para, and in the ranks he found a wealth of experience. 'A lot of the lads had done an Op Toral [the codename for the British presence within Afghanistan post-2014 as part of NATO's Resolute Support Mission]. Full screws [full corporals] and above had done Herrick, and the CSM [Company Sergeant Major] had been part of the original invasion of Kabul.'

The Taliban's rapid advance across the country had been news around the world and was the kind of headline that eager soldiers latch onto, hoping to be sent into the fray.

'At first we thought the talk of us going was just a bullshit rumour,' said Tom. 'We were on exercise in Jordan, then came back and went on summer leave. They wouldn't have let us do that if they thought it was going to happen. It was a big if, but two days later we were called back to camp. My family was worried, but it happened so fast that I didn't really have time to think about it. The impression was that it would be buckshee [easy], and mostly stagging on [guard duties]. During the rehearsal drills, the processing was all done by people with laptops. We'd done public order training and mass casualty event exercises, but I don't think anyone at any rank had an idea of what it would really be like. We totally underestimated the size of the problem.'

Kabul would be a chaotic situation that required communication under the toughest conditions. Given the danger and desperation, this would be hard to do under the best of circumstances, but the soldiers who had come to aid in the airlift did not speak the same language as the people they had come to save. Fortunately for the Parachute Regiment, they had an ace up their sleeve.

Private Fahim

In 2021, after twenty years of war, there were many seasoned soldiers in the Paras. Some had spent years of their lives in Afghanistan, but none had as much experience in the country as the new private who arrived in Colchester in the summer of that year.

Private Ahmed Fahim stood out to his commanders for several reasons. Not only was he almost twice the age of many of his fellow recruits at depot – earning him the nickname 'Grandad' – but Fahim had been born and raised in Afghanistan. For most soldiers, the Kabul airlift would be their first operation. For Fahim, it was a homecoming.

'When you're growing up under the Taliban, I had nothing else to compare it to because that was all I knew. You couldn't be picky in Afghanistan. Nothing was handed to you.'

Entertainment was banned by the rulers, but Fahim and his family would take risks to watch black-market cassettes on a black and white television. 'We'd lie in front of the TV with the volume on number one, so it was barely a whisper. One of us would have to stag on while the others watched, to let us know if anyone was coming. It was a very restricted life. A lot of the time there was no electricity. You'd stay up until the candle burnt out, and then you'd need to wait for daylight to start doing things again.'

Life in Kabul could be brutal.

'There was the sound of gunfire every day. At the time I didn't know what tracer was, but I knew the red lights going across the sky were bullets. One day, I was going to the shop on my own, and there was a body lying on the path with blood running out of it. I told my dad, and I wasn't allowed to the shop on my own after that.'

When the Taliban regime fell in 2001, a young Fahim embraced the opportunity to look beyond his neighbourhood. He first did this by way of internet cafes, where he would practise English by talking in chat rooms. Then, with a few words and phrases under his belt, Fahim went to an American camp and offered his services as an interpreter.

'How old are you?' they asked him.

'Sixteen.'

He was too young, they said, but Fahim was persistent, and soon the Americans had put him on the payroll.

It would not be easy money. Though Fahim lived in that camp for the next five years, his English improving from a few words to fluent, he would have to risk the same dangers as the Americans. As the camp belonged to Special Operations Forces, operations came thick and fast.

On one such mission, Fahim was with the US Navy SEALs when they started taking fire from high ground on both sides of them. One of Fahim's closest friends was hit in the head and died instantly. It was only later, when they were loading the dead into a Humvee, that Fahim realised that he'd also been hit.

'There was blood on me, but I didn't think it was mine. It was only when I lifted my shirt and saw the wound that it started burning. It felt like it was being pinched, and salt was being rubbed on it. I spent the next few weeks in hospital.'

It was not something that he told his parents about. Not only because Fahim wanted to protect them from worry, but because he needed to keep them from physical danger too. Because of the Taliban, 'I couldn't just go and visit my parents. I had to sneak in at night, and I rarely saw them.'

As an American interpreter, Fahim could expect nothing but torture and murder if he fell into the hands of the insurgents. In 2012, after many years in the war, Fahim left Afghanistan and came to the UK.

'I tried all kinds of jobs, a lot of warehouse stuff, but after that experience of spending all my time around soldiers, and being a part of operations, I just didn't feel like I fit in with civvie life. And so I went to the army careers office.'

Fahim was a fit and capable individual with experience of conflict, and was fluent in Afghanistan's language. Given that British combat operations were still ongoing in his home country, one would expect recruiters to have signed up the Afghan on the spot. Instead they had to tell him that they could not enlist him into the armed forces, because of residency rules.

And so, as British operations continued in Afghanistan, the fluent Pashto speaker who had worked with US special forces waited five years for the red tape to say that he could now join the armed forces. Fahim was now in his thirties. The recruiter warned him that his back and knees would suffer, and tried to talk him into the Royal Logistic Corps, but Fahim wasn't interested in that.

'I'd researched every regiment, and I knew I wanted to be a paratrooper. I'm competitive. When someone tells me I can't do something, I want to prove them wrong. And I loved the maroon beret and cap badge. I wanted to earn that.'

Earning his maroon beret was a high point in Fahim's life, but not everything was going so well. Fahim had accepted risk for himself when he worked for the Americans, but now his parents were in danger. Somehow the Taliban had discovered who he'd worked for, and planned to take revenge on his family.

'Someone threw a grenade over the wall, and it went off in the garden. That was it. I knew I had to get them out.'

Fahim used all of his money, and borrowed more, to pay to get his parents out of Afghanistan. Smuggled from place to place, car to car, they left their home and almost all of their possessions behind to escape to Europe.

Good commanders know what they have in their men, and Fahim's leadership identified him as someone with a unique skill within the battalion. Fahim had arrived too late for an Op Toral deployment, but looking ahead, some of the battalion felt as though an operation to Afghanistan could be on the cards.

Fahim wasn't so sure. 'I wasn't expecting the Taliban to come back so strongly. The ANA and ANP had been holding the frontline for years. They'd shown that they could fight, and would fight. The problem was budget and supplies. I'd speak to friends out there, and they'd tell me that they weren't getting paid or supplied. What are they supposed to do?'

Fahim has no doubt that the blame lies not with the soldiers, but on their political leaders. 'It was the main government's failure. A political failure. It wasn't the ANA's fault.'

Over the summer, ground fought over by Afghan forces and their Western allies started falling more rapidly to the Taliban. A deployment began to look more likely, but it was 2 Para that were slated for it, not 3 Para.

Fahim didn't expect to be going anywhere, until: '3 Para CO [Commanding Officer] told me he'd been thinking about me over the weekend. A few days later I was told to pack my kit. 2 Para had requested me. I was the only one going from 3 Para. My green DZ flash [3 Para's unit insignia; 2 Para's is blue] stuck out, and everyone was looking at me.'

After leaving in 2012, Fahim didn't think that he'd ever step foot back in Afghanistan. 'I thought I'd missed out after Op Toral, and I couldn't come back as a civilian because of the death threats.'

For Fahim, Op Pitting would be the last chance to see his home.

Hurry up and wait

Op Pitting was a homecoming of a different kind for Major Danny Riley, a place he had served many times before fighting the Taliban. Joining the British Army in 1998, Major Riley had a deep experience of warfare, having served in Northern Ireland, Iraq, Afghanistan and Somalia. In the summer of 2021, he was serving as the second in command of 23 Engineer Regiment. His role on Op Pitting would involve 'wearing several hats', but foremost of these he would be the liaison officer between 16 Air Assault Brigade and the American forces at HKIA (Hamid Karzai International Airport) in Kabul.

'I'd been on the fringes of the planning. I got a good week's notice,' recalled Riley. 'The CO phoned me: "Do you fancy going out to Afghanistan?" I was expecting a combination of Basra and Helmand. I thought we'd be in the city. My kit was packed. I went to the ranges and test fired my weapon. I got to see all the guys preparing. I turned up the next morning and went to Brize.'

As to the short turnaround, Major Riley said, 'That's what we're designed to do.'

Riley then experienced the military phenomenon known as 'hurry up and wait'. Having been told to reach the Air Mounting Centre as quickly as possible, Riley found himself with others, sitting around and waiting. It was there that he noticed that there were some issues with equipment: 'We didn't see any radios or anything [until we were out there].'

Passing the time through conversation, Riley and others worked out who had been on the first operation to take Kabul twenty years before.

'We worked out there were a couple of people who'd been on Op Fingal,' he said. 'It was good to see the reaction of the blokes on the ground. You could see who was getting a bit nervous. To others, it was old hat. You made peace with whatever was going to happen. Some of the guys were only eighteen years old.'

Op Pitting was not Captain Aaron Nunkoosing's first time in Afghanistan. 2 Para's adjutant had served in Kabul as part of Operation Toral in 2019–20.

'My generation of officers, we missed the Herrick days. We didn't get to serve on Herrick, and that's probably what we joined for. We did Torals, but we wouldn't pretend that they were the same. A lot of us probably didn't believe that it [Op

Pitting] was going to happen. It started to ramp up the closer we got to the deadline. We started to see movement by the Taliban through the country from intelligence briefs, and that started to get a few of us concerned, especially because we had been to Kabul before and seen the effort that was put into keeping them at bay in the surrounding provinces such as Logar and Wardak.'

In one intelligence brief, Captain Nunkoosing and others were told that 'the J2 essentially said that the Taliban do not have the means or the intent to take Kabul, and if they do, they won't do it until March 2022.'

They were not convinced. 'When we saw that the areas where the Talibs had been successfully hunted as recently as 2020 were now the areas that were falling to them rapidly, we thought, hold on, there's no one keeping them at bay anymore. Surely there's a momentum to these things? There was a prison in the east of the city that had lots of Taliban being held in it. If you let them out, that's going to cause havoc. A few of us thought this could be worse, and there could be a momentum to it, but the intelligence assessments that most of us received, as well as the media coverage, didn't seem to reflect this until the very last minute.'

Major Steve White, Officer Commanding C Coy, 2 Para, was returning to the country where he had once fought. Not many soldiers in his company had similar experience. Many of the private soldiers were young, and fresh out of training. A handful of the more senior enlisted soldiers had experienced Helmand.

White took over C Company in June, and Lt Colonel Dave Middleton, 2 Para's commanding officer, suggested that White familiarise himself with the secret plans for Op Pitting. This is to the credit of both men, as the opinion of the intelligence community was that Kabul would not fall for some time. It was believed that taking Kabul quickly was not in the interests of the

Taliban, but 'they didn't take the effect of momentum into account,' White said. Once the Taliban's advance was crashing across the country, it gathered a power of its own. A phenomenon that White would see evidence of in Kabul.

Most operations have a pre-deployment training cycle of six to twelve months, but nothing like this would be available for Op Pitting. Having read the plan, and with the CO's blessing, Major White and his Sergeant Major came up with a 'DIY training package'. These 'serials', conducted in the 'slack time' between assisting another unit's exercise, focused around what the army calls public order training: in civilian terms, 'public order' can be replaced with 'riot'.

As a quick reaction battle group, there was an 'institutionalised readiness' within 2 Para. Despite this, the annual cycle of training and leave means that there are certain times of the year when 'compliance' is lower than others. The army has a large number of Mandatory Annual Training Tests (MATTs), which must be completed before a soldier can deploy. These MATTs range from battlefield first aid to values and standards; moral principles which define who British soldiers are as individuals and what the British Army stands for as an organisation.[3]

In the army of 2022, with a digitised system, it is easy for senior officers outside of the unit to scrutinise compliance. While well-intentioned, this can lead to distraction in time-sensitive situations. For instance, completion of fitness tests needing to be placed ahead of public order rehearsals. In such cases, it is sometimes possible for a unit to accept the 'risk' of not completing a MATT to meet operational requirements.

But not all bureaucracy is possible to overcome. For C Company's flight into an airbase in the Middle East, no charged radio batteries were allowed to be transported, and weapons and ammunition were flown on separate flights. This would not have been an issue if C Company were at the base for several days, but due to the situation in Kabul, they were needed at HKIA within several *hours*. As things stood, and due to rigid bureaucracy, C Company would be flying into a hostile environment with no ammunition or working radios.

It was a situation eerily similar to the battle of Isandlwana in 1879, where Zulus surrounded and overran a battalion of British Infantry. Most of the soldiers died fighting with their bayonets and out of ammunition, as the quartermaster had refused to distribute it without the correct orders and paperwork.

For such situations, the canny sergeant major exists. When a member of the RAF arrived to tell the Company HQ that they would need to leave for Kabul before their ammunition arrived on the next flight, the sergeant major 'borrowed' the man's vehicle, 'acquired' a set of bolt cutters, and 'liberated' a shipping container full of ammunition already at the base. It is decisive action such as this that has prevented many difficult situations from becoming disasters.

'That was a frustration,' said Captain Nunkoosing of the situation. 'The ops officer and CO are on the ground [in Kabul]. When we got word from them, they said, "Can you get hold of the ammunition? Consider whether you need to bomb up before you land." For the brief time that I was (at the airbase), I reiterated to the RAF movers that our priorities were: (1) Ammunition. (2) The next lot of 164 x Paras from Force Package D. (3) Freight, including comms equipment. (4) Remaining Paras from Force Package D and more freight.'

The adjutant of 2 Para explained, 'We were trying to get ammunition and comms forward, but they seemed to be stuck on freight, and for whatever reason we couldn't get them in.

When you have limited aircraft and many competing priorities, you see that stuff just gets bumped and things change, and it's got to go down the priority list. For us on the ground, ammo and comms were pretty fucking important. I thought we eventually got it nipped, but it just didn't turn up straight away.'

By the time that the secure radios had arrived in Kabul, 'We were already fully established on unsecured means. We were using burner phones, locally sourced Wi-Fi, the wrong laptops. Which is not the way we had ever practised to do things, but there was an element of, well, this is what you've got to work with, so just make it happen.'

Improvise, adapt, and overcome. A long-standing practice of service personnel.

'The situation just continued to escalate in ways that you couldn't predict,' said Captain Nunkoosing. 'You couldn't understand the chaos until you saw it. I don't think anybody thought there would be that number of people who wanted to get out. The initial estimate for EPs was something like four or five thousand, but actually when we did it, we evacuated more than fifteen thousand. I don't think anybody got caught out, but we didn't necessarily have the initiative at the start of the evacuation.'

As well as troops entering the country, there were also civilians heading towards the action. One of them was Tony, a security advisor for the UN.

'I did three tours with the military, and I was twice there with the UN. The first time for two years, and this time is now pushing three years. So I've had about seven years cumulative in Afghanistan, and a lot of that has been out on the ground. I've been around a bit, but I don't by any means claim to understand Afghanistan. I think it's like when you study at university. It's like the more you learn, the more you realise that you don't know. There's so many layers to Afghanistan that I don't think anyone will ever really truly understand it.'

Tony's previous rotation had involved visiting the places where the Taliban had taken over on the ground in order to gain the ground truth, 'so we could inform leadership, so they can make their decisions. When I came back in, there was no indication of the Taliban taking over immediately. Obviously, they were closing in, but we didn't have any intelligence, I suppose is the best word.'

Sergeant Andy Livingstone was one member of the RAF crews who would be taking people and supplies in and out of Kabul. Livingstone was a loadmaster working on A400M aircraft as part of No. 70 Squadron RAF, and Op Pitting would not be his first time in Afghanistan. In 2013, Livingstone had taken part in Operation Herrick, which involved close cooperation with the United States Marine Corps.

'At that time a lot of the big action had gone, and most of the stuff was surveillance.' As the British forces drew down, many of the IEDs that had been placed for them were now hit by civilians. 'I saw a lot of civilian casualties at that point getting brought in by the coalition. A lot of kids.'

Andy then deployed twice as a loadmaster during the British drawdown, including to Kabul in the early summer of 2021. 'I was in Kabul a couple of months before Pitting and it was a completely different place. Kabul still felt like an international airport, but it had that smell of Afghanistan, petrol and burning wood.

'I probably got about three days' notice,' said Livingstone. He was in RAF Akrotiri, Cyprus, at the time, working on the broader resupply operations for the Middle East. 'It was a fastball for everyone. No one expected it to happen. We could all see it happening but no one really expected it to go down as quickly as it did. I remember sitting in an intelligence briefing maybe four days before, and the feeling was that the Afghan government had at least another 90 to 120 days before the Taliban would be in a position to take over. Four days later, it fell.'

But despite the short window, the loadmaster felt absolutely prepared. 'That's where us crews make our money. All we do is train when we're not on ops. We pride ourselves on flexibility. You want to go on ops, that's why you do this job. All of us were fairly eager to go and help. We all knew that we could go there with the aircraft we had, with the crews we had, and with the experience that we had and make a massive difference, and prove what we could do. We were keen to go and help as many people as we could, because we knew we could.'

The same was true for 2 Para. On his own flight into Kabul, possible scenarios played through Major Steve White's head: 'Will we get shot down?' he wondered. 'Will we go straight into a scrap?'

There was no way of knowing. The aircraft carrying White and his men dived into a landing, losing height quickly rather than coming in gradually and making an easy target. It was a tactic developed during the siege of the American base at Khe Sanh, Vietnam, and has served as a timely reminder for thousands of soldiers that they are entering a place far more dangerous than the one they left.

Operation Pitting would be no different.

Exceptional and unremitting

Captain Sam McGrury, USMC, was born into a military family, and spent much of his life moving from base to base. His father served twenty-six years as a Marine, rising from Scout Sniper to the rank of Master Gunnery Sergeant (akin to a British Regimental Sergeant Major). Sam intended to follow in his hero's footsteps and enlist in the ranks, but his father had different ideas: 'If you do that, I'll bury you in the woods.'

And so, after taking a scholarship to Louisiana State University, Sam became the first military officer on either side of his family. Graduating in 2011, Sam attended The Basic School (TBS) and the Infantry Officers Course (IOC), the two arduous courses where Marine officers are trained, scrutinised, and shaped into leaders.

In his first ten years of service, Sam served in a variety of positions, and deployed twice to Iraq to take part in operations against ISIS. The size of the Marine Corps, and its commitments around the world, mean that deployments to a combat zone are never a guarantee, and Sam felt incredibly grateful to have not one, but two under his belt. Still, he couldn't help but feel as if he'd missed out on Afghanistan.

'We were supposed to be the last company to go there on a regular deployment, but then they extended the unit who were already out there, and we went to Iraq.'

It seemed as though Sam would see one of the main fronts in the Global War On Terror, but Afghanistan would elude him.

In May 2020, Sam was given command of A Company (referred to as Alpha Company), 1/8 Marines. It was a position of great responsibility, and on top of the 211 Marines under his watch, Sam had a young family with three – going on four

– children. If anything, there was some relief between him and his wife when 1/8 received their orders to take part in a Marine Expeditionary Unit (MEU) in European waters.

MEU's are air-ground task forces in the United States Fleet Marine Force, acting as quick reaction forces ready to respond to any crisis, be it a natural disaster or combat mission. 'We were expecting a peacetime deployment,' said Sam. 'We weren't expecting Afghanistan, or to be in harm's way.'

At least, not at first.

'In May, we started watching Afghanistan with an eagle eye. It felt like it was expected in CENTCOM [the US military command responsible for the region that included Afghanistan], but there was no plan that we knew of. Amongst the company commanders, we would dig through open source news and plot a map with different colours. One for Taliban control, one for contested, and one for government control. It looked like the board game *Risk*, and it was very clear that more areas were becoming contested, then falling to the Taliban. Still, the HQ's line on it was: don't worry about Afghanistan.'

While Sam and the other leaders in 1/8 did not worry, they did prepare.

The USS *Iwo Jima* is a massive amphibious assault ship, packed with close to 3000 people. Far from the open training areas of 29 Palms and Camp Lejeune, the Marines made best use of the space they had, using the ship's deck to carry out short, high intensity exercise and drills. While on ship, it was a challenge for commanders to keep the young Marines engaged with the idea that 'out there is a man who's been training his whole life to kill you.'

As well as fitness drills, Sam and the other commanders had their men conduct martial arts training. In a world where

Western militaries are leaning further into cyber warfare, and lowered fitness standards, Sam and his comrades knew the value of taking a punch in the face. In the coming weeks, it was this adherence to age-old physical standards – not any form of modern technology – that would save the Kabul airlift from total disaster.

The first clue that something was changing came when the MEU were 'chopped' into the 5th Fleet, and CENTCOM. The *Iwo Jima* and two other vessels went through the Suez Canal, and into the Red Sea. The Marines went ashore in a partner force country, and in the desert they conducted live fire exercises. Sam's company were the helo company, meaning that they had more than a dozen helicopters at their disposal, and as such, they were usually marked as the Quick Reaction Force (QRF) for most missions. Accordingly, the training of Sam's men put a lot of focus on the ability to read and react to situations on the ground, rather than the longer planning for a deliberate op. Both Sam and his men needed to be flexible, innovative, and willing to act decisively on their own gut instincts.

Every day made it more likely that these skills would be put into action.

'Any idiot could see that the dominoes were falling.'

Still no official word came, but the battalion's operations officer and other officers built training for Afghanistan into the programme wherever they could. 'When the MEU's deployment to CENTCOM was extended by a further month, things started to look real.'

All of a sudden, orders were coming down from above. Plans needed to be drawn up, including for operations to Herat, Kandahar, and Mazar-i-Sharif. As yet, none had fallen to the

Taliban. 'The idea was for us to take our people out, rather than fight.'

While some companies were performing these peripheral missions, other parts of 1/8 would help secure HKIA and Bagram.

'That plan went out the window quickly. From the changing map it was clear that we couldn't go into the peripheral sites with just a company. The Taliban were overrunning the country. And then we closed Bagram. I don't know the reason behind that.'

Although 1/8 had been deployed to Helmand, Marines change units every three to four years, and so there were no men left in 1/8 who had deployed with the unit on that tour. There were, however, several Helmand veterans in the battalion, including two of Sam's platoon sergeants: both veterans of the battle of Marjah.

'Seeing the country fall, there was a feeling of "what the fuck?" but it wasn't explicitly expressed.'

In late July, 1/8 planned for light, medium and heavy course of action in case of a NEO (Noncombatant Evacuation Operation) being called: something that now seemed an inevitability. Whichever plan was enacted, Sam's command, A Company, would form a QRF for the Joint Task Force. They would be the first company to go in. 'By the end of July, we had a solid plan.'

Not everyone thought that the die was cast. As two of the other troop-carrying ships steamed on to Kuwait, the captain of the *Iwo Jima* held back in the Gulf of Oman. For Marines chomping at the bit to get into action, this did not go down well.

Fortunately for A Company, they had their helos, and after President Biden's speech about evacuating SIVs (Special

Immigrant Visas), Sam's men were flown into Kuwait on 12 August. At 06:00 on the 13th, they began loading magazines with ammunition. The NEO had been called, and all of A Company's training and planning would be put to the test.

Sam was heading into Afghanistan with 139 Marines under his command. These were split into seven platoons, almost all of them with a junior officer and staff NCO to command them. It was rare to have such an abundance of these ranks, and it would prove helpful in the coming chaos.

Three of Sam's platoons would perform HQ or logistical functions. The four rifle platoons, with attached arms from Weapons Company, would be Sam's four chess pieces on the massive board of Kabul's airport.

Setting foot in the warzone – let alone being some of the last servicemen in Afghanistan – was not something that most of the men of 1/8 Marines had expected.

'We'd done some basic riot training,' said one junior NCO, 'which is typical for MEUs because that's the kind of situation we might get called to go to, but nothing specific [for Kabul]. We started training for the evac in a way that didn't apply. For three days we practised processing civilians, but these were in orderly single file lines. The training was whipped up quickly by the battalion's staff.'

If anyone had foreseen the chaos that would ensue, such disorder was not included in the training, which took place in the desert.

'We didn't think we'd use it,' said the Marine. 'We were given ROE [Rules Of Engagement] briefs, but we weren't expecting to see the Taliban.'

Like the men of 2 Para, the Marine belonged to a unit that had seen a lot of action in the last two decades. The First

Battalion of the Eighth Regiment of Marines was no stranger to tough deployments. Commissioned in 1940, 1/8's first years were spent in the bloody struggle of the Pacific Campaign, taking part in battles such as Guadalcanal and Okinawa. In the Global War on Terror, 1/8 found themselves involved in the fierce fighting of Fallujah and in southern Afghanistan. In August 2010, 1/8 was deployed to Now Zad and Musa Qala, which had been the scene of many British Army actions, tragedies, and dramas.

By the end of 2012, 1/8 had been on a cycle of constant combat deployments for almost a decade, and had experienced Marines at all levels of the unit. They had learned the lessons of war the hard way, but, like any fighting force, its members began to move on; some into other units, some into other positions, and many into civilian life.

A decade is a long time in the military. The Marine Corps rotates its Marines through different units, and many service personnel serve less than five years. By the time that 1/8 was deployed to Kabul, very few of its members had fired their weapons in anger, or been on the end of enemy fire. Iraq and Helmand had not been forgotten, but they were stories for the young Marines in the same way that the First Gulf War was to the soldiers of the 2003 invasion. A tale to be proud of, but which bore no particular personal relevance.

The same wasn't true for Warrant Officer Lee Bowden, leader of a USMC EOD (United States Marine Corps Explosive Ordnance Disposal) team:

My first deployment as an EOD tech was to Helmand Province in 2011. We worked Garmsir to the upper Gereshk valley. I went back to Helmand in 2013, this time to the south of Musa Qala.

On both deployments we were dealing with IEDs. Anything from 'toe poppers' in mason jars to hundred pound bombs designed to take out armoured vehicles. It was a very dynamic environment, and my second tour was more kinetic.

I took a lot away from the experience, like how to run a team, manoeuvre, and exploitation. Our team took risks to recover devices by rendering them safe whenever we could. This allowed for the collection of DNA and fingerprints. This evidence could then be used in building target packages, and Special Operations Forces could launch raids based on that and take out the bomb builders.

When we got news about something like that, it was really fulfilling, and some of the work we did wasn't realised until years later. In 2017, based on evidence our team had collected, a Taliban bomb maker was arrested as he tried to enter Heathrow airport. A lot of risks were taken to get these results, but we felt like it was worth it.

As a community, EOD [Explosive Ordnance Disposal] believe that every piece of ordnance we dispose of is one life saved. It's hard work, but we know that we'll never be doing it alone – we work in pairs – and that the risk is taken to save another life. Our Pararescue Jumpers have the motto, 'These Things We Do, That Others May Live', and we abide by that same ethos. When we go up against a device, we do so knowing that we need to be better than the person who built it.

I wanted to go back to Afghanistan, especially for something so monumental. I felt like it was critical for EOD to be a part of it, and we were the best-trained, best-prepared team.

As the EOD's warrant officer, Lee Bowden oversaw six smaller teams of two men apiece.

'The teams are detached to work alone, and this is why selection is so crucial. My youngest NCO was twenty-three, and the oldest was forty-six.'

By contrast, many of 2 Para were under twenty-three years old, with some as young as eighteen. 'I'd been in school when the older hands had been fighting the Taliban,' said Josh, a junior rank in the regiment. 'We were put on standby, and told to be ready to move, but some companies didn't think their turn would come. At the staging airbase we watched Sky News and saw a lot of [Sky's chief correspondent] Stuart Ramsay. A few days later I'd see him all the time in the flesh. That was really bizarre.'

While the Paras were gearing up for the now probable deployment, other soldiers were already in the country. Sergeant Stumpf was serving in the American Army's 10th Mountain Division as part of Task Force Polar Bear. They had come to Afghanistan during the summer of 2021, retrograding bases, assisting with COVID operations, and providing security for bases like Bagram. In June, soldiers from 10th Mountain had replaced the 250 members of 3 Scots in Kabul.

Shortly after leaving the country, the commanding officer of 3 Scots, Lieutenant Colonel Graham Sefton, gave an interview to official British Army channels. 'Afghan security forces are ready,' he said in July 2021. 'They've definitely got a challenge ahead, but we have spent a lot of time training, advising and working alongside them to ensure that they have the capabilities they need.'

A veteran of an earlier tour to Afghanistan himself, the 3 Scots CO went on to say in the article: 'A lot of our soldiers have never been to Afghanistan. For those young soldiers who've never deployed on an operational tour before, it's a very enriching experience, working with international troops and in a new and fascinating environment. Kabul is still a dangerous place for our soldiers and we need to recognise the risk those soldiers are taking; while the nature of the risk is different to that experienced by those who have served in Helmand, it remains significant. Now, it may be very different to what they might have seen on YouTube from Herrick, but it is still very challenging and the Jocks have remained sharp. For the more seasoned soldiers, it's totally different from Herrick tours.'[4]

Indeed, in 2009, 'The Black Watch' had seen some of the heaviest fighting in Helmand. They had also been put to the test in Iraq on several occasions, including at the infamous Camp Dogwood, which had been hammered by suicide bombers, resulting in the deaths of several Black Watch soldiers. It seemed fitting that they should be one of the last units to fly the flag in the War on Terror.

As the situation in the country further deteriorated, the 10th Mountain soldiers who had replaced 3 Scots were ordered to HKIA.

'We had about twelve hours of downtime,' Sergeant Stumpf recalled, 'and then everything started going downhill.'

5

Serve to Lead

Leadership is that mixture of example, persuasion and compulsion which makes men do what you want them to do. If I were asked to define leadership, I should say it is the 'Projection of Personality'. It is the most intensely personal thing in the world, because it is just plain you.

— Field Marshal Sir Bill Slim

The Royal Military Academy Sandhurst is where the British Army trains its officers, and it is justly regarded as one of the most exemplary academies for the creation of leaders. Its motto, 'Serve to Lead', encapsulates the idea that in order to lead their men, an officer must serve them. He, or she, must lead by example, from the front, and never ask a subordinate to do what they are unwilling to do themselves. A good leader is ultimately in the service of those under their command. Lieutenant Colonel David Middleton, Commanding Officer of 2 Para served his men in the highest tradition of military leadership during Op Pitting.

'He was the last man out,' a 2 Para soldier said of him. 'He was compassionate at every level. He didn't change at all during the op. I remember him greeting the 3 Para lads when they arrived. Saying things like, "Good to have you here. Great to be working alongside you again," that kind of thing. It didn't matter how low someone's rank was, he had the time for them.'

Private Fahim of 3 Para echoed this sentiment: 'Colonel Middleton was just awesome. I wish I could have worked with him for longer. He was brilliant. He trusted you, and that meant a lot. I was directly reporting to him and the brigadier. I understood the culture, and the enemy. The CO would say, "You know what you're doing, just do it."'

It is no surprise that a man who elicited such respect from his soldiers should downplay his own pivotal role in the airlift. When interviewed for this book, Colonel Middleton was humble and genial, lauding praise on his men while asking none for himself.

Like many of 2 Para's long-standing members, 'Colonel Dave' had fought in Helmand's poppy fields. He had waded through Afghanistan's irrigation ditches, lived in her pockmarked compounds, and now he would be commanding Britain's final battle group of a twenty-year deployment.

In 2 Para's role as lead readiness battlegroup within 16 Air Assault brigade, Middleton's HQ element spent a lot of time looking ahead at what would be the next flashpoint in the world, in order to foresee where they would need to respond. In the spring of 2021, it was clear that things were not going well for the Afghan government in Kabul, and Middleton expected that his men would be called upon sooner than later.

Having familiarised himself with the plans for Op Pitting, Middleton and his staff began to 'war game': playing out different scenarios that could take place during the evacuation of British citizens and their dependants from Kabul, and how they would respond to them. A crucial part of the war games were logistics – getting soldiers in, civilians out, and then the soldiers out at the end of the mission – and it was decided that 2 Para would deploy in several 'force packets'. Each force packet would land separately, and complete its own task, and this in turn would allow the next force packet to come in and build upon the success of the previous package. The CO and a small party would deploy first.

For Lieutenant Colonel Middleton, it was a matter of 'when, not if' the Afghan government collapsed. Still, 2 Para could not direct all of their time and training into specific training for Op Pitting. That would have left them under-equipped to other situations that may have arisen on the global stage. Instead, Middleton placed emphasis on competitions like the Bruneval Cup; a small-team level exercise that emphasises low level command ethos and team drills under challenging conditions, where Paras carry out section battle drills, stretcher races, command tasks, battlefield casualty drills, and other exhausting activities.

'Overwhelmingly there was a desire to get out on operations,' Middleton said of his men. 'We had maybe five or six soldiers who were on Op Fingal in 2001, and more who had been on Op Herrick 4 and 8.' Fingal was the initial operation to take Kabul. Now, twenty years later, those men would be returning to Afghanistan for the last time.

'Kabul hadn't fallen, and so there was still some hope. We had no expectation of fighting.' Familiar with the Op Pitting plan, Middleton was confident in his unit's ability to carry it out. 'The plan didn't change, but the scale did.'

Non-combatant Evacuation Operations (NEOs) are largely conducted by the military, but they are not military led. Rather, the FCDO has to make the decision of when to use the military, and when to hand over the reins if things get out of hand. Wherever possible, NEOs should be conducted pre-crisis, and not during one, as it was in Kabul, but the speed of the Taliban advance took the British government by surprise. When it became clear that the end was nigh, the CO booked himself a seat on a civilian airline and flew into Kabul ahead of his men. This was on 10 August. The first of 2 Para's force packets – A Company – would not arrive for another five days.

Large parts of the airbase were closing down as civilian companies began to pull out of Kabul. Support staff from the military – technicians, and the like – were flown out as infantry soldiers and Marines were flown in. As accommodation was left empty, the arriving units raced to claim the better spots.

The Baron Hotel had been an integral part of the Op Pitting plans for some time. According to a publication by the UK Parliament: 'In January 2021, the British embassy started scoping locations in Kabul for an Evacuation Handling Centre. The Baron Hotel, just outside the airport perimeter, was chosen in April, and detailed talks began with the hotel management, resulting in the signature of a contract for the provision of the handling centre. This made the UK the only country to have made this critical preparation. Because the UK had done so, the Baron Hotel would become a centre for international coordination when it came to the evacuation in mid-August.'[1]

This forward planning almost came to naught, for the hotel could not be occupied until C Coy arrived with the number of men needed to secure it: if the Taliban had chosen to enter first, then they had days to do so. Until the Baron was occupied by 2 Para, the CO and his team had rooms in the same buildings as American 'grunts': an endearing term for American infantry soldiers.

For 2 Para, there were five phases to Operation Pitting: recce, deployment, securing the airfield, evacuation and collapse.

The World Trade Center's Twin Towers after being hit by two planes in the infamous terrorist attack on 11 September 2001 in New York City.

The last stand of the 44th Regiment before the retreat from Kabul during the First Anglo-Afghan War, 1842, as depicted by William Barnes Wollen.

Operation Fingal in early 2002. 16 Air Assault Brigade took a lead role in the International Assistance Security Force (ISFA) and were deployed to assist the new Afghan Interim Authority.

US representative Zalmay Khalilzad (left) and Taliban representative Abdul Ghani Baradar (right) sign the Doha Agreement on 29 February 2020.

The Taliban's Badri 313 Battalion using US military gear left behind in Kabul.

Ashraf Ghani addresses the press at the presidential palace in 2017.

Ashraf Ghani was Afghanistan's president from 2014 until he fled the country in a helicopter on 15 August 2021 when the Taliban took over. Only a few hours later, the Taliban were posing for photos in the Afghan presidential palace in Kabul.

2 Para HQ: (L–R) Captain Jamie Robson (Ops Offr), WO1 (RSM) Steve Marsden (Regimental Sergeant Major), Lt Colonel David Middleton OBE (CO), Captain. Aaron Nunkoosing (Adjt) at Hamid Karzai International Airport, photographed as they were leaving Kabul at the end of the mission.

Vehicles were spray-painted as a way of identifying them.

Operation Pitting involved more than 1000 troops, diplomats and officials. 261,000 miles were flown by the Royal Air Force in 165 round trips between the UK and Afghanistan.

Ambassador Laurie Bristow (left) and Brigadier Dan Blanchford (right).
Bristow called Blanchford the 'mastermind of Operation Pitting'.

Scenes of desperation: three Afghan citizens – two men and a woman – fell to their deaths
on 16 August 2021 after clinging onto a US transport plane as it took off from Kabul.

Thousands of Afghan citizens crowded the tarmac of the airport after security lines were breached in a desperate bid to escape.

Afghan citizens were crushed to death in the crowds trying to get into the airport during the chaotic exodus. Many waited for days without food or water in temperatures above 30 degrees Celsius.

The Baron Hotel, just outside the airport perimeter, was chosen as an Evacuation Handling Centre and was the hub for processing some 20,000 civilians. Its protection from attack was crucial; 2 Para soldiers were posted outside.

Afghans had to have their passports and documents checked before they were allowed through various Taliban checkpoints and the airport gates. Even those with British passports struggled to get into the airport.

On 15 August, as part of the deployment phase, A Coy landed at HKIA. Within a short time they were sent straight into the next phase: reinforcing the US Marines on what became known as 'The Thin Red Line'. This was the human wall of NATO soldiers trying to hold back a crowd of thousands of Afghans desperate to leave the country. As A Company and other units tried to hold them back, the Taliban in the crowd cajoled them onwards. If the Thin Red Line broke, it would have meant a delay to operations at best, and disaster at worse. Securing the airfield was critical before the next phases of the operation could be entered into.

'It was a classic airborne operation in that sense. We had to secure lodgement.'

In the dark hours of the 16th, a deliberate operation by the Marines and remaining partner forces dispersed the crowds. With crowds building at Abbey Gate, the Baron Hotel needed to be secured so that processing could begin. The plan had called for C Coy and B Coy to move through A, but B Coy couldn't be spared because of the continuous threat of the airfield being overrun. C Company would have to do it alone, at least for the time being.

A deliberate operation was launched to clear the crowds from Abbey Gate to the Baron, allowing controlled access points to be put in. This involved having to push back a sea of people, and methodical, public-order street clearance was used to get everyone back, and connect the two gates. 'Baron became the centre of gravity.' It would be the hub for processing some 20,000 civilians.

As more American units arrived to secure the airfield, Colonel Dave Middleton was able to send his other companies to reinforce C, but even with all three rifle companies at the Baron, it was not enough. A further three would be needed, and these would arrive in the form of A and C Coys, 3 Para, as well as a company from 2 Yorks, who would operate the 'White Rose Taxis' that ferried evacuees from the Baron to their departing aircraft.

The deployment of 16 Air Assault Brigade HQ gave Middleton a layer of overhead cover, and meant that he could put his attention into the tactical situation on the crowd, without also needing to deal with the strategic issues that had come from being the most senior British soldier in Kabul. Brigadier James Martin and his team were a welcome sight to the 2 Para HQ staff, most of whom had not slept in days.

'The plan wasn't that complicated,' said Middleton, and now that he had six companies at his disposal, he could enact it without the real possibility of one of the elements becoming overrun.

While the plan was not complicated, the same could not be said of the ARAP process, or the difficulty in filtering those who qualified for evacuation from those who didn't. As family entitlement was 'one plus five', large Afghan families had to be broken apart, with several members left behind. Middleton recalled seeing such unfortunates sometimes having to be carried back out by his men.

'The more people the better,' was the colonel's attitude, as was, 'don't get fixed on emotion and certain cases.' His main effort was to get out as many people as possible, and that was best served by ensuring that the processing machine was running as effectively as it could.

In long days of no sleep, much becomes a blur, but several incidents stood out to the CO: 'A Coy landing into the airfield and going straight to the Thin Red Line; C Company holding out, and 3 Para reinforcing the chevron; B Company, on the twenty-first of August, clearing down to create an outlet and relieve the pressure on it; and the IED on the twenty-sixth.'

This was the bomb that killed thirteen US service personnel and more than 150 Afghan civilians.

'There was a degree of inevitability to it,' said the CO about the attack, but neither he nor his men shirked the risk. 'Staying was the right thing to do. Things were working well.'

By the time of the suicide attack, 2 Para were already handing over their parts of the operation to American units. Middleton said that the attack had no impact on their timeline for the British withdrawal. For the Americans, and the Afghans still waiting to leave, 'the size of the IED meant that time's up.'

Having fought against the Taliban in Helmand Province, Colonel Middleton found himself in the bizarre position of not only having to hold a truce with his erstwhile enemy, but working alongside them to facilitate the evacuation of civilians.

'Meeting the Taliban was life-defining. We had to interact with them through the whole thing, and it worked because there was a shared end.'

That did not mean it was easy. Professionalism demanded that enmity be set aside, but what the colonel could not control was who the Taliban sent to deal with him. The liaison regularly changed, making it harder to build a working relationship. With one of these former enemies, Colonel Middleton found himself experiencing one of the most unexpected moments of his military career.

'One day, I sat down with this Taliban commander. We were both knackered and dehydrated. We shared a look like, this is hard work. You expect to share that moment with another soldier, but not with a Talib.'

Asked about what he would have liked to have done differently, Middleton reflected for a moment before answering that 'the chevron was about a hundred metres short. I should have stayed up all night to not be shocked by that.'

On what could have been done differently at a higher level, he felt that 'starting the process of getting people out sooner would have been massive. International coordination was complicated and lacking, and that was the hardest thing from a leadership perspective.'

Another challenge was to remain functioning in the face of enormous human suffering. 'At the time, everything was compartmentalised because of work rate,' Colonel Middleton said. 'You tried to focus on specific acts of the recovery.'

And while the operation was about saving lives, rather than fighting a battle, it was achieved through the training, tactics and ethos of the Parachute Regiment. 'It felt like a classic Para Reg operation, and reaffirmed all the basic things that we know about soldiers, and soldiering.'

Both Colonel Middleton and Private Fahim, who worked often beside him, summarised the operation in exactly the same words: 'It felt like a six-month tour squeezed into two weeks.'

Such a challenge could never have been met without the highest standards of leadership, and a 2 Para soldier summarised his CO in British Army slang:

'The CO was ally,' he said, giving the highest praise known to a Para. Colonel Dave Middleton had indeed led from the front through service and compassion.

The Ambassador

As well as military leadership on the ground, the British ambassador Sir Laurie Bristow had volunteered to stay in Kabul so that he could better aid the efforts:

I'm not an optimist. I went through this absolutely eyes wide open, I think, about what was likely to happen, and what our options were. The political direction was to give it our best shot. Try to keep the embassy open, boil it down to the absolutely key things that you have to do, of which, the National Security Task was right up at the top, and I don't need to spell it out, do it. That's why we were there.

So what we're seeing is the prisons being sprung, very large numbers of Taliban fighters coming onto the battlefield, large, smaller than but still large numbers of Islamic State players coming out of prisons, particularly from Pul-e-Charkhi and the numbers are in my notes on that. And so what we're looking at is, well, what happens next? What are their intentions? What are the Taliban's intentions? What are the Islamic State [ISIS] intentions? And what conclusions do we draw from that? And, what I've got is the military saying to me, we don't have enough combat power. So at that point, essentially, the decision taken in London was we've got to get the civilians out.

There was then a to and fro about whether I should leave and the story has come out with slants, according to who's telling it. But basically, I agreed to stay. And that was what happened. You may have come across stories about, I think, at one stage I was ordered off a plane at gunpoint. I don't remember that. I don't remember even getting on a plane until the twenty-eighth, or whenever it was, but, for these purposes, there was a debate in

London about whether I should stay or leave. And I agreed to stay.

It's a situation where they're volunteer jobs, you can't be ordered to stay, and I would not have accepted an order to stay if I thought it was actually the wrong decision. Partly because it's my skin in the game. But also, because, you have to step back a bit and think, well, Chris Stevens in Libya, what was the impact on the Americans and on Hillary Clinton's personal career of losing an ambassador? That's the size of the risk that you're carrying here. And unless you are okay with that, I mean, think about it.

So I spoke to some of our military in Kabul, and essentially their advice boiled down to it's going to be very, very hairy, but we can do this. And, I'm rather more interested in that advice than I am of armchair generals, and we've never done anything of this sort back in London.

On 27 August, several news outlets ran the story that the British embassy had left behind papers that had endangered Afghans who had worked for the British:[2]

So the papers that were left behind me, first of all, it's important to be clear what they were. So they were piecing it together, it was a stash of papers that somebody had helped that, you know, they should have, people keep papers, I mean God only knows why. But what they were not, was a sort of full orbat ['order of battle' or command structure] of the embassy staff. It was some papers with names in them that shouldn't have been there and should have been destroyed. They weren't and there's nothing I can do about that. But, we're all going to have to live with that.

I spoke to the journalists concerned, it was Anthony Loyd [war correspondent of *The Times*] basically, to grill him on, so, what exactly did you see? What exactly was in those papers? Where were they, so we can try and work out what you had. He was fairly cooperative about it. And the long and the short of it is that he had tried some of the names and numbers on the papers. And of course, we tried them as well. What turned out was that several of them were already in the UK. They're already shipped out. At least one of those people passed on some more names, who were not actually on the papers, of people who they thought were at risk in Kabul. So I basically got clearance over the space of a couple of minutes or hours to say, okay, the only thing we can realistically do is just get those people out, no questions asked. And that's what we did.

So overnight, there was this, essentially an operation to sort of grab them, pull them in, put them on a plane. So what could have happened differently? Going back to the nature of the embassy, this is a twenty-year expeditionary embassy, at one stage our biggest in the world. So very, very complex. So three big sites, 130 buildings and a clearance happening in nine hours rather than five days. There'd been a lot of aggressive housekeeping going on, actually going back to April, May, before my time there. But some papers got missed.

I hope one of the effects of my reporting back was to accelerate that process as well and say, look, here's your unfolding situation. Now, go away and test your assumptions. And, I came to respect Dan's [Brigadier Dan Blanchford RM, Chief Joint Force Operations] judgement on that, what I saw of his planning, and then Ben Key's [Admiral Sir Ben Key, Chief of Joint Operations for Operation Pitting] planning was that they were on it, and that they were interrogating their system and ours pretty hard.

But bear in mind that there's a more extreme scenario than what we did, which is what you have to fight. You have to fight your way in and fight your way out.

The thing I most want to underline is that, in my dealings with the military in Kabul, they gave me absolutely straight advice. This is the size of the problem, here are your options. This is what we can and can't do.

6

The Fight for the Flightline

Then it's Tommy this, an' Tommy that, an' Tommy, 'ow's yer soul?
But it's 'Thin red line of 'eroes' when the drums begin to roll
The drums begin to roll, my boys, the drums begin to roll,
O it's 'Thin red line of 'eroes' when the drums begin to roll.
> – Extract from 'Tommy' by Rudyard Kipling.

By 14 August, most of Afghanistan had fallen to the Taliban.

'We're watching history happening,' said Stuart Ramsay, a British journalist who was reporting from Kabul at the time. 'A superpower supported by NATO countries, and obviously the United Kingdom, just lost to a bunch of guys on the back of pickups with AK-47s. I mean, it is quite remarkable. And we knew then what we were watching was history unfold.'[1]

It was clear that an emergency evacuation would be needed and – having abandoned Bagram airbase – the only available option to the coalition was Hamid Karzai International Airport (HKIA) in Kabul.

'It's a strategic location where lots of supplies and troops were brought in and out of [the] country,' said Lt Colonel Christopher R. Richardella, commander of 1/8 Marines. 'It was a military and civilian airport all at the same time – CIA, the Afghans and certainly some of our coalition partners had large portions of that base. There was kind of an outer perimeter wall, everyone kind of had their piece of that large pie, if you will.'[2]

For the Marines of 1/8, only elements of which had already arrived in Kabul, their first hours at HKIA felt like arriving at any US military base. There was no sign of crowds, yet, and no signs of the enemy. The day was spent with briefings that covered such things as 'chow hall rules', and 'COVID mask policy'.

'Looking back on it, that seems kind of stupid,' said a Marine.

A two-storey building behind a blast wall became home for a company of the USMC, who were soon put to work, processing German contractors who were being evacuated. This mostly involved searching bags, and was not the kind of action that had made the men enlist in the Marine Corps.

'I hate flying,' said Captain Sam McGrury, USMC, but there was plenty to keep his mind occupied as A Company 1/8 Marines descended into Kabul.

'I expected to find a situation with a high sense of urgency. Something like, "The Huns are coming, build the barricades!" Instead it was like landing at a regular base. Everything was done slowly, as though the Taliban weren't overrunning the country. People hadn't accepted that the Taliban were at the door, and there wasn't enough respect given to the Taliban's ability, or the fact that they had a vote in matters of the battlefield. I think that they came to the airfield to show us that they could. It was a very loud and clear "fuck you".'

McGrury recounted, 'We were given COVID screening and shown the chow hall, but there was no plan for us. No handover of accommodation, or duties. It was really a case of doing all the planning and thinking ourselves.'

Nothing about the planning would be simple. 'HKIA is like a village of multiple tribes, with many chiefs, and none of them talk to each other. You had all kinds of nationalities already there, like the locals, Turks, and a private force of Gurkhas, and then you had all kinds of other nationalities arriving, including all branches of US forces. There wasn't really anyone in charge. At least, not in a way that you felt. People just made shit happen. Go figure it the fuck out.'

'There was definitely a lot of stealing going on between units,' McGrury added, a skill fondly referred to as 'rat fuckery' in the Marine Corps.

Captain McGrury chose a walled compound for A Company that was close to the airport's aprons. Sam and his team now injected the sense of urgency that he felt had been lacking at the base. Looking over his notes from that day, he recalled some of the tasks that were of immediate concern.

'We needed to link up with Task Force Polar Bear and get left seat, right seats going,' he said, meaning familiarisation patrols. 'Cursory patrols to establish pattern of life. We may need to push into Kabul to establish an outer cordon. We had a hard talk about casualties, and threats. Suicide vest bombings. Suicide vehicle bombings. Complex attacks. Indirect fire. Sniping. Where's fuel? Where are the gates? How do the gates open? Where are the gaps in the fences? Who holds what buildings? Do they have radios? Do we have the same ones?'

The list went on. HKIA had grown up over twenty years, 'and we were trying to navigate and understand that complex network in a matter of hours using markers and a whiteboard.'

Like the British forces, an American NEO is called by a civilian branch of government. The troops can't go in until that happens. If the call is not made until the crisis is already at its height, it means that the troops are not up against a ticking clock, but one where the alarm is already going off.

'At 23:30 on the fourteenth,' said McGrury, 'we were tasked to assist in breaking down the embassy, who were already enacting their destruction plan, but this was called off and we were put to work processing Americans. We could only do that as far as a holding area, as there were no incoming flights. This was put down to a "low-density of aircrews", a brilliant piece of military jargon meaning "not enough people to fly the planes".'

Considering that C-17s would form the workforce of the NEO, this seems like an incredible failure of planning. The situation at the airport was precarious at best.

'There was fear,' said the British defence secretary Ben Wallace, referring to the possibility that the airfield could be overrun.

That night mortars were fired from the south of the city, jeopardising the flights which would be essential for bringing troops in, and taking civilians out. That same night, Afghan civilians began to sneak onto the base, looking to stowaway on aircraft. There were too few soldiers and Marines to hold the entire perimeter, and drainage culverts provided cover for anyone looking to evade the sentries.

It was decided that the company would form up in line and make a sweep of the airbase, and the Marines soon found themselves dodging C-17s on the runway. 'Their grey paint and lights work great in the dark,' said one junior Marine. 'You hear them, but you don't see them until they're right on top of you.'

Suddenly there was a crack in the air, like someone was lashing a huge whip across the heads of the Marines: 'A bullet went inches over my head. It was my first time getting shot at, and my staff sergeant was laughing his ass off.'

A crowd had formed on the edge of the airbase, and gunmen were appearing at the edges of it, firing, then melting back into the crowd.

'We couldn't really fire back much because of the civilians, but we clipped one guy in the shoulder. He ran through the terminal to the city. The first [firefight] lasted less than five minutes. I think it was probably the Taliban [rather than Islamic State]. There was no treaty with them at the time.'

In the space of twelve hours, the Marines had gone from briefings on COVID mask policy to dodging bullets.

A US infantry unit from the 10th Mountain Division was among the first reinforcements to have arrived at HKIA, coming from their base in the city, where they had taken over duties from 3 Scots earlier in the summer.

'We probably got about four hours of sleep before our immediate area started receiving ineffective small arms fire,' said Sergeant Stumpf of Task Force Polar Bear. 'As I understood it at the time, the city was already falling, and the embassy was sheltering in place.'

President Biden had assured the American people that there would be no one getting rescued from the embassy roof, such as had happened in Vietnam, but the next day, that is exactly what would happen. On 15 August, the US embassy released this security alert:

> **Event:** The security situation in Kabul is changing quickly including at the airport. There are reports of the airport taking fire; therefore we are instructing U.S. citizens to shelter in place.
>
> U.S. citizens wanting assistance in departing the country should register for any option that might be identified to return to the United States, and must complete this **Repatriation Assistance Request** for each traveller in their group. Spouses and minor children of U.S. citizens in Afghanistan who are awaiting immigrant visas should also complete this form if they

wish to depart. Please do so as soon as possible. You must complete this form even if you've previously submitted your information to the U.S. Embassy in Kabul.[3]

Confusion was the order of the day. The 10th Mountain soldiers tried to get a better understanding of what was happening, and what they needed to do. 'There were a lot of moving pieces,' said Sergeant Stumpf. 'By that evening, it was known that small groups of civilians had entered the airport from the civilian side and were trying to make their way to our side and the aircraft on the aprons. Half of our platoon responded to evict the civilians, and the other half secured the CRAM site near the civilian side.'

CRAM – standing for Counter Rocket, Artillery, and Mortar – is a radar-guided Gatling gun used for shooting down incoming fire. Against a night sky, the 'red beams' of their tracer fire look like something out of a science fiction movie. A mortar hitting a transport plane on the runway would be catastrophic for NATO forces, making the CRAM a priority to protect.

'Our enclave started receiving rounds more consistently,' said Stumpf. 'Our snipers could also tell with reasonable certainty where the rounds were being fired from. People were identified as being at least spotters, if not riflemen. Our snipers were leery of firing into that area as it was a civilian spot.'

The occasional shots remained an occupational hazard, and had to be largely ignored in order to concentrate on a threat that could soon turn the airlift into a disaster.

'Our platoons at the gates, and at the civilian terminal, were trying to push everyone back. They were short on manpower and the crowds were growing. We headed to the front terminal area. Driving over, we saw that there was a sizable group that had passed through our lines outside the terminal, gone through, and had finally gotten corralled by some Marines with concertina wire on the apron underneath and around some aircraft. We drove ourselves through a vehicle gate and joined our guys in a traffic circle, right below a billboard that said: "I $\heartsuit$ Kabul".'

The small unit of infantry was massively outnumbered by the crowd, which was in the mid-hundreds, and growing through the night. Despite the dangers, and the near absurdity of the situation, the soldier was unmoved.

'I wasn't feeling too much, strangely,' said Sergeant Stumpf. 'It was an "in the moment" kind of situation that you only process later. It was pure chaos, of course, thousands of civilians and family units clutching each other, crying, and holding whatever paperwork and documents they thought would get them freedom. I was glad I was with my brothers, and that we were the only ones holding the line in a fucked-up situation. I remember afterwards being amazed we didn't get blown up [by a suicide bomber]. I think it was sheer luck, and that everything happened so fast that anyone who wanted to do anything bad just didn't have a chance to put anything together.'

That did not mean that there was no contact with the enemy.

'We were the ones that took out the few guys in the crowd with weapons and hostile intent. We saw that the news said 'two' or 'a few' gunmen were eliminated. It was more like six or eight, but there was no collateral damage. Fire discipline was exceptional.'

The soldier, who had deployed on several previous tours to Afghanistan, now found himself living through an entirely new experience.

'Until that night I had never smelled fear. That's literally what it was. Fear, desperation and panic. Afghans would FaceTime with old American friends, showing me their phone, as if I could let them in. We were helpless to do anything. Just hold the line. As the night wore on, and the crowds kept growing, that became less and less likely.'

'Because people were so scared, people flooded the airport like a big wave. No fences or barriers could stop them,' said Haji Assadullah Agha, a local civilian. 'Everyone was running, running. People saw the Mujahideen as monsters who eat people, who kill women, children and anyone without a beard.'

'That was a terrifying time and it was full chaos,' said Beheshta Taib, a student and businesswoman. 'Everyone was moving towards the airport to get out of Afghanistan. We fear that a war may start, we were all afraid. It was about our families, about loved ones, it was about the city that I was born in, I was raised in.'[4]

Sergeant Stumpf understood the need of holding such desperate people back from the airfield in order to keep the runway clear and operational, and yet the entire situation gnawed at his conscience.

'Here were people that had raised families for twenty years believing in a new Afghanistan, and had paid blind allegiance to America and her allies. Promises were broken. It was fucking shameful.'

That did not stop the 10th Mountain soldier and his comrades from giving the mission every effort that they could, but there was only so much that could be done against the ever increasing crowd:

We held the line throughout the night and into the early day. I'd say at about 07:00 is when our line started to break. There were just too many people running around. We were running through ammo for warning shots at an alarming rate.

The crowd did this thing we'd later call 'the Afghan shuffle'. A line of them would surge forwards [usually pushed from behind], and we'd fire a few warning shots. They would drop to the floor, but inch their way forwards. This would happen again and again. We were constantly losing ground, but we weren't usually hands on yet, and we used our interpreters as much as possible.

Anyway, the break finally came in the direction of the parking lot, and the order came to pull back behind the terminal. It was haphazard. Guys were trying to find their original trucks, but everyone had been turned around when dealing with the crowd. I had to go and pull two guys out from behind a fence. I finally ended up in a random truck and we got in a line to pull back. There were people everywhere. They started climbing on our trucks and that's when it got physical.

I was worried about a grenade coming through our [manned] top hatch, so every time I saw someone climbing on my side I'd kick the door open and they'd go flying off. It took forever to get to the aprons [where aircraft are 'parked'], because people – mostly kids – were getting shredded on the rings of [concertina] wire that we were trying to pass to get to the aircraft.

Colourfully clothed crowds, hundreds of people deep, were milling beneath the massive wings of C-17s. In the distance, Kabul's mountains stood silent and serene against a pale blue sky.

'For the next couple of hours we rotated to a point mid-airfield,' said Stumpf, 'where we refuelled the trucks one by one, and topped off on food and water. That was a fancy piece of logistics. As one truck was conducting the resupply, the rest of the troops and trucks kept "circling the wagons" to make a new line and push people back. It was fairly effective. By about noon, I think, the rest of the Marines and the 82nd had arrived and reinforced us. It wasn't a moment too soon, as the crowds were now a horde in the thousands. That's when it really started to get dicey.'

As one of the first Brits on the ground, Major Danny Riley had arrived before the bulk of 2 Para. In his position as liaison officer between national forces, Riley watched as events unfolded across the airfield.

'When the airfield was overrun,' said Riley, 'common sense told us that these were just desperate people. I think that was, other than when I was right in with the crowd and probably immediately after the IED, I thought that was the moment I thought, it's getting a bit sticky. At the time I only had ten rounds in my magazine because there wasn't enough ammo to go about. And me and one of my American colleagues we went out because the way we were thinking, you could see all the crowd coming across on the monitors, and we thought, well if it's going to happen, let's give ourselves a fighting chance. So we actually went outside to fight our way through whatever.

'We quickly realised it wasn't a being overrun and killed situation. People were desperate. The irony of it all is that they were closing the place down by being so desperate. And we didn't have the mass on the ground to deter or prevent that from happening. It wasn't like Helmand. Some of the public order I did in Northern Ireland was horrendous, but this was nothing like it. These were desperate people, not angry people trying to get a name for themselves.'

By 15 August, almost 18,000 refugees fleeing before the Taliban had arrived in Kabul, many of them making their way directly for the airport. As his people came flooding into the city, President Ghani decided that the time had come to leave. So did many others. At least forty-six ANSDF aircraft were flown out of the country, carrying officers, government officials and their families. The aircraft did not return to continue the evacuation, but stayed in Uzbekistan and Tajikistan.

Major General Zia, Afghanistan's former chief of Army staff, justified the decision to fly the aircraft out of the country.

'The President had fled, and the Defence Minister was escaping. The chain of command no longer existed among the forces. I made the decision based on two main reasons. To save the lives of the pilots who had fought the Taliban and who were left alone – this was the least I could do for my colleagues as a veteran Army officer. And to keep the Air Force fleet from falling into the hands of the Taliban. Imagine if the Taliban had gotten those aircraft – how they would have been used against the people resisting them today in Andarab, Panjshir, and other parts of the country.'[5]

As the leadership of Afghanistan were flying out, 2 Para were on their way in. Reminiscent of airborne assaults, where a paratrooper must be prepared to fight as soon as he hits the ground, the young soldiers of A Company were quickly put to work.

'Once we got off we went straight to a tent city, bombed up, and went on QRF,' said one private soldier. 'We'd get crashed out to different gates, like Abbey Gate, for instance. All the civvies would be pushed up against the gate. We'd open the gates and shove them back. We were literally throwing them and scrapping. The younger ones would try and fight. It was like something out of a Spartan movie. My adrenaline was buzzing.'

Elsewhere on the airfield, the US troops were doing everything in their power to hold back the tide of Afghan refugees.

'It was human wave after human wave trying to make it to American aircraft,' said Sergeant Stumpf of the 10th Mountain. 'The crowd was extremely desperate. Family units generally stayed together, but women and children were collapsing left and right. Virtually none of them had water.'

'In that crowd I saw with my own eyes a mother and two children who both died,' said Muslim Hotak, an Afghan looking to escape. 'She left them there. She took her husband and remaining children by the hand and said, "Leave them, they're dead, let's go."'[6]

Individual tragedies were unfolding by the thousands amongst the chaos. The airfield was a riot of noise, panic, and confusion.

'The Marines began throwing CS gas and forgot to factor in the wind,' said Sergeant Stumpf. 'The gas hit us and we didn't have respirators. Half of my squad got cut off, and the gas really did a number on my lungs. I got swallowed up by the crowd and saw our trucks had moved back about a hundred metres. I started throwing elbows, muzzle thumps and using buttstock strokes to make it back. Fortunately, I didn't seriously injure anyone. A random Navy corpsman found me and flushed the CS out of my eyes, then it was back to work. The Turkish showed up, but they weren't effective in the least. People started getting run over left and right. I would see mothers with little kids just hanging limp in their arms. It was sheer pandemonium.'

The experience of 1/8's Marines was no less chaotic. They found the airfield's North Gate jammed up with civilians desperate to leave. The sound of screaming children was an ever present wail.

Sam McGrury, the commander of A Company, 1/8 Marines, led his men into flashpoints around the airfield. At the civilian terminal, TF Polar Bear were dealing with the increasing numbers of civilians. As the QRF, Sam was tasked to detach one of his platoons to aid them. In what felt like moments, he was also ordered to proceed immediately to Task Force Talon, and replace the privately hired Gurkha guards who were now withdrawing. Sam was forced to leave another of his platoons here, this one without an interpreter. It's not a decision he felt happy about, but it was 'becoming very clear that nothing about the situation at HKIA was going to be optimal.'

'All hell was breaking loose,' said McGrury. 'There were even Afghans coming in and stealing aircraft.' Due to a lack of vehicles, it had taken him two hours to put his detached platoons into positions around HKIA, and now he was told to pull them back, and consolidate his company.

The reason was a hijacked aircraft. Defecting members of the Afghan National Police had taken a civilian flight hostage. US special forces were going to raid the aircraft, and Sam was tasked to provide the outer cordon.

'I had no point of contact for them except a random [Delta Force] guy I'd met and had his phone number. I told my guys to double down on water and chow, as we'd have no idea how long we'd be on this cordon. We'd go in as an L shape on the objective, and then figure it out.'

But Sam saw that there was a potentially bigger, more critical threat approaching.

'I was looking at the TV screens, and there was a mass of civilians that Task Force Polar Bear were corralling in their wagons. I asked if this was going to be a problem, and was told not to worry about them. Five minutes later I got a message on my radio: "We have a breach on the flightline. We are about to be overrun."'

The hijacked plane was no longer a worry for McGrury's company. They were ordered to immediately reinforce TF Polar Bear.

'We loaded up as many guys as we could get into the vehicles, and sent those off. The remaining sixty of us ran.'

A Company 1/8 Marines ran to the civilian terminal, through it, and then formed a skirmish line. As he was running, Sam's phone 'butt dialled' one of the other company commanders, who was still in Kuwait.

'All they could hear was the sound of me running, and machine-gun fire. TF Polar Bear were firing 240s [machine guns] over the top of the crowd to try and get them back. There was maybe fifteen hundred civilians, and there were two hundred of us to push them back.'

For Sam, it was the beginning of forty-eight hours on his feet. He would lose all feeling in his left leg from a trapped nerve.

'To create separation we pushed two gun trucks out, and they were engaged by a platoon-sized element of Taliban with machine guns. The gunfight went on from about 00:00 to 06:00. The Taliban fire wasn't aimed at me or my men, but it was missing the trucks and going right over or between us. During this time the crowd's swelling. We're holding on by a thread, and we know that there's no immediate flights coming in, so relief will be a while. When they come, we're expecting the rest of 2/1, but it's some elements of 2/1 and the 82nd that arrive. There seemed to be no coherent order of unit arrival. By this point we're running on thirty-six hours of no sleep. 2/1 said they'd reinforce us, but I told them they needed to relieve us, so we could get off our feet for a bit to drink and snatch a little sleep.'

Such hopes were optimistic. As a C-17 began to taxi for take-off, the crowd surged over the concertina wire barricade and swarmed onto the runway, surrounding the massive aircraft.

'I had to get my men straight back up. There was an Apache [helicopter] hovering ten feet off the deck, trying to push the crowd back. One Afghan tried climbing onto it. The helicopter yawed and almost hit the C-17. I couldn't believe what I was seeing. It was a disaster waiting to happen.'

Sam expected the C-17 to stop. Instead it continued to roll forwards, and Afghans began clinging onto the undercarriage. 'They fell about fifty feet away from me.'

'We saw people falling from the planes,' said a Marine. 'We took stretchers to recover the bodies, so that their families could identify them. We all felt really bad for the Air Force guys who had to get frozen bodies off the landing gear once they landed.'

A lot had happened, and it was only mid-morning. McGrury was approached by one of TF Polar Bear. 'Their vehicles were almost bingo and Winchester,' he said, meaning that they were about to run out of fuel and ammunition. 'There were thousands of people between us and them. As they drove back, there were soldiers standing on the vehicles, pushing Afghans off.'

As the gun trucks pulled back, the Taliban followed.

'One of my guys said, "Sir, I've got guys with guns,"' recalled Sam. 'I told him not to fire unless they pointed a weapon at us. Soon after there was a gunshot, and one of them went down, shot in the head. The guy next to him picked up the fallen weapon, and started firing into the crowd. Luckily for us, the firers were on a raised platform, some kind of loading bay.

'We engaged and wasted all four of them,' he said, meaning that the four gunmen were killed. 'The situation was pure chaos. Other gunfights happened. There was plunging fire everywhere. I remember a civilian shot by a DShK [heavy machine gun].'

A Company, 2 Para, were experiencing that same chaos. 'I've heard that it was ten thousand civvies who broke the wire and stormed the airfield,' said a Private soldier. 'One of our multiples was over there so we went running to them. It was all kicking off. Civvies were climbing onto aircraft. It was mad. As we were running across the airfield planes were landing, Yanks called at us to stop, but our sergeant told them to fuck off. We were getting to our mates.

'It was carnage at the baseline,' said the A Company private. 'Turkish soldiers were swinging their weapons and butt-stroking people. Loads of warning shots were going off. There were civvies everywhere, shouting, and soldiers shouting back at them and to each other. The noise was mental. We joined the baselines and tried to regain order. All day we'd push them back, then they'd push us back. The first few days was non-stop, but then the rest of the battalion arrived and some of 3 Para. We gave it big licks in A Company, because we'd come in first. Once we had more numbers, we could start getting some rest and more of a rotation.'

For many at HKIA, the day of the 16th was spent wrestling and corralling the crowd. That night, A Company 1/8 Marines collapsed back to protect Apron 8. Partner forces were placed under Sam's command, and he used them to plug gaps in the defences and reinforce the gates. The tactics used by the Afghan forces left many in shock.

'I get a call on the radio,' said Lt Col Christopher R. Richardella. 'They're calling to tell me that we're going to partner with an Afghan special forces unit who's gonna come help us. I'm thinking, this is great. Okay, this is a host nation force that knows this culture, speaks this language, they're going to help out. Really at this point I just need extra people, I don't care who it is. The Afghan unit that was there, the way they got the people off was just running everyone over and shooting them. I watched from afar, it was dark at this point, so I can only see who's getting run over and shot by a vehicle headlight, and it was a horrific scene.'[7]

A US company commander added: 'There were people getting executed on the airfield and it was horrible to see that happen, but it cleared out the airfield.'

It was a night of bizarre experiences.

'My first time seeing the Taliban was nuts,' said a soldier of A Company, 2 Para. 'There was a big crowd of civvies who were standing off from us, and all of a sudden they went dead quiet. Then, an Afghan with an AK-47 emerged out of the crowd, and started telling them to move back. As soon as we saw him, we all dropped onto our belt buckles. My finger was on the trigger. We were on Card Alpha [Rules of Engagement], so we couldn't just drop him because he was holding a weapon, he needed to pose an immediate threat to life, and right now, he wasn't.

'More of them started to emerge out of the crowd. Some had RPGs. They were only fifty metres away. I was thinking that they must be trying to clear the civvies to make way for some kind of attack on us, but then this Delta Force guy comes flying down on a motorbike shouting "Don't fire, don't fire! Friendly Taliban." No one had told us that a deal had been made. I don't know how it didn't go to shit.'

'We came to conquer Kabul,' said Mawlawi Samiullah Fateh, a Taliban commander. 'Everyone was terrified of us.'

Perhaps not everyone. 'Twelve hours ago we had been killing them,' Sam McGrury recalled, 'and now we were face to face at a casualty clearing point.'

It was an uncomfortable truce, but one that worked. By around 03:00 the flightline was secure, and the airlift could begin in earnest.

For many, it was only the beginning of the nightmare.

7

The Gates of Hell

If you wanted to see the best and worst of humanity, you could find it outside of the Baron Hotel.

– Lt Col David Middleton, Commanding Officer, 2 Para

On 16 August, Ben Wallace said, 'I acknowledge that the Taliban are in control of the country. I mean, you don't have to be a political scientist to spot that's where we're at.'

Afghanistan had fallen, but Kabul's airport had not. Through the massive efforts of the troops on the ground, and the deadly tactics of Afghan forces, flights out of HKIA could now begin in earnest. However, there were still great challenges ahead. At the gates of the airport, civilians and soldiers alike would be put through a hellish experience.

Reinforcements continued to arrive. Among them was C Company, 2 Para, who had 'liberated' their ammunition from a container at a Middle Eastern airbase.

Major White and his men were unsure of what exactly awaited them on the ground, and first found themselves in a 'semi-non tac scenario', meaning that they were in no immediate danger. Many of the men were surprised to find themselves going through 'COVID processing' conducted by the Turkish forces, who were still nominally the airport's security. On Major White's previous trip to Kabul, the military part of HKIA had been rigid on rules such as the wearing of high-vis belts, and there was still an element of 'bullshit' as C Coy were processed into tents, where they stripped their gear down to the bare essentials.

For Private Fahim, 3 Para's Afghan-born soldier, the flight to Kabul was a homecoming.

'I didn't have a clue what my role would be. I'm proactive and I like to prepare in advance, but no one really knew what the situation would be. What I hadn't taken into consideration was how the training would kick in. As soon as we landed, I felt like I'd been preparing for this for the last ten years. All of my experiences in Afghanistan, and the training at Catterick and in 3 Para, just clicked and kicked in.'

Captain Aaron Nunkoosing was returning to the city where he had served as part of Operation Toral a few years previously. 'Even on the plane from the UK to (the Middle East) I didn't think that we'd go. A lot of us still thought that we'd get turned around. But the situation had changed in the air dramatically.'

Nunkoosing landed on 16 August. 'We started getting the footage coming out of people falling from the planes, and the crowds rushing the airport. I think that happened as my party was in the air. When we got to (the airbase in the Middle East) I established comms with the ops officer, I could hear in his voice that the situation had changed dramatically and then the feeling was, right, this is on now. When we landed it was like an apocalyptic scene. All these people are trying to get out, and we're going in. The smell of Afghanistan hits you. There's a strong smell of human waste sometimes. It's a different kind of air and atmosphere. This time there was an air of panic that wasn't there last time we were in Kabul. We were able to land but there was still a lot of people trying to get out. It did look like chaos.'

Aaron had last been in HKIA in 2019. 'There were coffee shops and diners. People cutting about on bicycles. It was mostly secure and functional. And then to see it now looking like the complete opposite – that was a bit of a shock.'

Josh, a young soldier of 2 Para, recalled his first impressions of HKIA. 'When we went from the airport to the Baron Hotel there were shots in the air. I thought, so that's what it sounds like, but the guys who had been in Helmand said the fire wasn't anywhere near us.'

For Josh, it was his first time experiencing the environment of Afghanistan. 'It was hot and dusty. In the distance you could see the mountains. I saw some of my mates who were now civilian contractors being processed out. That was strange.'

Major White met with his CO, Lt Col Dave Middleton, who handed him $30,000 and an order to secure the Baron Hotel. This plan was quickly postponed, as parts of C Coy were split off to support A Coy and the US Marines, still battling to control the crowd that was threatening to overrun the airport. 'There were armed Taliban in the crowd. It could have spiralled. Lots of small arms fire was flying around.'

Without charged batteries for their encrypted communications equipment, C Coy were relying on 'push to talk' civilian radios. 'You could hear the tension in the men's voices,' Major White recalled. 'It wouldn't have taken much,' he added, meaning a firefight between the Paras and the Taliban in the crowd.

White's men were 'on Card Alpha', which is the British Army's most restrictive set of Rules of Engagement. The legality of the use of force would become a problem in the following days.

Once the airport had been cleared of civilians, and the runway was secure, C Coy took over the Baron Hotel and the adjacent airport gate. The move from the hotel to the airport was done at night, on a slow patrol. 'It was only four to five hundred metres, but it was before the crowd was there, and I could see the Taliban through my night vision. They were shadowing us about a hundred metres away. It was bizarre. We were told that there were two Taliban "technicals" [a civilian pick-up truck with a machine gun mounted on it] nearby,' said Major White. This meant mobile weapons platforms that would be deadly to the Paras at such close range. It was a tense moment, but discipline held on both sides, and C Coy began to occupy their new home, and the site that would become pivotal for evacuation efforts.

The Baron Hotel

The Baron's website describes it as 'one of the most prestigious secured lodging projects in Kabul, Afghanistan. It is located less than one mile from Kabul International Airport and is an immediate neighbour of the International Security Assistance Force [ISAF], which puts the Baron within the buffer zone of security for both of these landmarks.'

This may have been true in earlier days, but in August 2021, the Baron Hotel became 'the frontline' held by British Forces in Kabul. Over the coming weeks, it would be a place of hope, hardship and death.

'It was bizarre to be in a hotel, which was still running to a certain degree,' said Josh of 2 Para. 'For most of us it was a case of find a bit of space where you can get your head down, but most of us didn't want to sleep, because we didn't want to miss out on anything. Obviously at some point you just couldn't stay awake any longer, and so you could head-to-toe it in real beds, one in, one out. Sometimes we'd eat ration packs and sometimes we'd eat in the hotel. It was good scoff. The cakes were really good. The hotel was still operating and some of the Afghans would pay for a hotel room and dining cards. Sometimes our blokes would have to chase them down in their rooms when it was time to move them onwards.'

'It's all a bit of a blur, because we were awake for so long,' said Captain Nunkoosing, 2 Para's adjutant:

I think I moved to the Baron on the eighteenth or the nineteenth, when we moved 2 Para Main [the controlling element of the HQ – maps, computers, comms, staff officers, watchkeepers, etc.], which had initially established an Ops Room in HKIA North on the sixteenth.

There's not a large distance between the Baron Hotel and HKIA North. We were debating where we put Main. Where can we control things from? Where can we offer value to Tac [the CO and Ops Officer, the command element of the HQ] and the sub-units? Initially Main stayed in HKIA North, which was useful to maintain links with the Joint Force HQ sat above us, and with the Turks and US through our liaison officers. However, we were not offering value to the forward elements of 2 Para, who were at the Baron. Once staff officers from the 16X HQ arrived and started to take some of the heat of 2 Para Main, we were able to move forward to the Baron Hotel.

I don't think I could appreciate what the blokes were going through until I got there. On my part there was a sense of disbelief. I had a sense of what was going on by hearing it on the radios, but it's not until I got there and saw it with my own eyes that I realised it was human suffering on a great scale.

I saw one of my old soldiers who'd been with me previously in the intelligence cell, and he'd now moved back to a rifle company. I saw him and I saw the look on his face, and I could just tell he was exhausted. I could tell he was fucked. That made me quite emotional when I saw him. I went over to him, we had a chat, and I put an arm around him and I basically tried to say, 'Look, mate, you're doing a great job, keep going,' and he said, 'Thanks, boss.' And then he looked at me and said, 'Boss, I can't do this right now. I'm going to fucking cry if I do. We'll have a whisky and a cry afterwards if we need to, but we can't do it right now and I need to keep going.' I agreed with him, told him I was proud of him, and then he just got back to work.

I saw him within minutes of getting to the hotel, and I instantly felt the gravitas of it, and I knew that even a few hundred metres back at HKIA, people probably weren't getting a feel for what was happening at the Baron.

Steve White then took me up [to the roof], looking down onto where the crowd had come up against the shield wall and the thin line of exhausted paratroopers holding it together, and that drove it home to me as well. Seeing the Taliban that close was unnerving for me, but the guys who had been there for a couple of days had already been inoculated and were less bothered, and although they were wary, they had to focus on holding the shield wall. You could already see it was a tense situation. And again, the smell . . .

The sound ebbed and flowed. During the day it was pretty hideous. You could hear gunfire every now and again. You'd hear the Taliban letting off rounds. You'd see and hear people getting beaten with rifle butts and whips. Then you'd get to night time, and people would calm down a bit out of sheer exhaustion. In the heat of the day, people would just be going crazy. It was hot. It was shit.

And it was not going to get easier. In the operation to move to and hold the Baron, Major White and the men of C Company had been shadowed by the Taliban.

This bizarre experience was about to become the norm for all soldiers at HKIA.

The Taliban

The Marines of 1/8 had a hard welcome to HKIA, and things would get even harder. As some Marines held back the crowd and pulled security, others worked on improving the defences, putting out rolls of razor wire and building barricades with whatever was at hand. This was all done in the knowledge that a suicide bomber could be in the crowd, and under the watchful glare of the Taliban. A treaty had been made. A fragile 'peace' held over the city.

'We were never even told that the [Afghan] government had fallen,' said a Marine NCO. 'We found out through texts from home. We eventually got a brief, but by then we already knew. I'm not sure if Command had even known themselves.

'Seeing them felt like a waste of twenty years,' he said of the Taliban. 'You'd see them beat women and children, but we had to cooperate.'

That need to cooperate was built on simple pragmatism, both for the coalition, and the Taliban. In *The Art of War*, the military strategist Sun Tzu wrote: 'Build your enemy a golden bridge.' Meaning that it is better to offer your opponent a way off the battlefield rather than depleting your strength in a fight to the death.

That was the source of the Taliban's pragmatism. For the coalition, there simply weren't enough troops to hold the perimeter alone, and any battle with the Taliban could be disastrous for the rescue effort.

'The UK state spends forty billion pounds worth of taxpayers' money on defence every year,' said Johnny Mercer MP. 'The idea you have to negotiate with the Taliban to secure an airfield is a bit embarrassing. I mean, basically, by not having enough troops to secure ourselves, that meant that we had to have Taliban checkpoints, which meant that the people that worked with us had to come through this. It just became absolute chaos.'

The troops at HKIA threw themselves into that chaos, rising above emotion to deal with the people who had been their enemy for twenty years.

'Sometimes we'd push units out, a five-minute walk from the gate,' said a Marine. 'You could see a subdivision of the city pretty well from there. Kabul looked like any normal city. There was an active road running right behind the blast wall called Russian Road, and the Taliban were heavily using it. They were a mix of ages, and had a blend of kit. Some looked about fifteen or sixteen years old, and they had the oldest weapons and gear. The older guys had some newer equipment and M4s.' This was some of the US taxpayer-funded equipment lost by the collapsing Afghan National Army.

'The Taliban didn't speak much. They were cold. Very observant, and always trying to gain height by standing on trucks, or walls. They were collecting intel on people. What people were saying, who had what kind of paperwork. It was a real Mexican standoff vibe between us and them. They even had a rocket launcher mounted in a flatbed, and it was aimed just over our heads.'

'I fought Jihad for fifteen years,' said Mawlawi Samiullah Fateh, a Taliban commander. 'The Americans slaughtered two members of my family. That's what made me want to fight Jihad.'

'Our units were very close to them,' said Qari Mohammed Zahid, a Taliban special forces operative. 'I had been fighting them for almost thirteen years. Now I watched them in their last moments here, surrounded with just some barbed wire between us and them. God willing, we'd kick them out completely in the next few days. They were leaving our country and that was so exciting. Since I was a kid, I always wanted to bomb them to bits. I was only little, but I felt it so strongly. I hated them for their savagery.'[1]

Such feelings made for a precarious truce.

Major White of C Coy, 2 Para, came face-to-face with his old enemy. 'I'd never seen a live Taliban up close, only dead ones. It wasn't so weird for the younger guys. The Taliban had an arrogant stare, which I suppose was fair enough. They'd just taken Kabul. But these weren't the guys we were fighting in Helmand. Not the big Pashtos. I think they saw which way the wind was blowing,' he said, suggesting that these men had taken up arms as Kabul was falling.

The Taliban held one side of the barrier at the gate, and the Brits the other.

'A lot of the Taliban we saw in the first few days were teenagers, or early twenties,' said one 2 Para soldier. 'Then the older ones started to turn up, a lot of them with American-made kit. Sometimes we'd be nose-to-nose with the Taliban. They'd keep letting people through, even when we told them to hold them, and this led to people getting crushed.

'We'd be having shouting matches from container to container,' he said, meaning the shipping containers that were used to form barricades.

'I'd been in school when the older hands had been fighting the Taliban,' said Josh from 2 Para, 'so I think it was less weird for me to see them than it was for the more senior guys. Most of them had never seen a live Taliban up close. Every Para who was at the Baron would have communicated with the Taliban, be that through an interpreter, broken English, or with hand gestures and eye contact.'

'When we came to Kabul, I was put in charge of the airport,' said Abdul Hadi Hamdan, a Taliban commander. 'We surrounded it with a thousand suicide bombers. The Americans were in the terminal and on the runway. At times, it was tense due to the high risk of a shoot-out with the Americans.'[2]

That the truce held did not mean the Taliban wanted to facilitate the evacuation of civilians. 'No mujahid, no Afghan, no Talib wanted our Muslim brothers and sisters to leave with the help of the infidels and adopt the American way of life,' said another Taliban commander.[3]

Major Danny Riley had expected such animosity, and more. 'If I'm being totally honest, I thought we'd be fighting an attack. The Talibs were moving up and we were getting reasonably good intelligence as they were closing. You can see how quickly they closed down Bagram.'

It was clear that HKIA would be the only way out.

'I thought we'd be fighting an Alamo,' said Riley. 'As it happens, negotiation channels with the Taliban were probably a little bit better than we thought.'

Major Riley was one of those who spoke to the Taliban, but stopped short of referring to it as working with them. 'It wasn't quite hand-in-hand, but there was a tacit agreement.'

'Reconciliation in any situation has to involve talking,' he added. 'Look at Ireland, look at Congo, look at Rwanda. All of these places have reconciliation, because people engaged with their once enemies. From our point of view, and to be reductionist about it, we didn't give a fuck. We just needed to get people out. I think that's where the professionalism comes in. But it was, when I was talking to the Talibs, the interpreter was not being quite as honest as he could have, when he was reading what he [the Taliban commander] said. The gist was the gist. "We need to do this, you need to do that. If you want us to go quickly, you need to let us do these things."'

While recognising that it was an unusual situation, the experienced soldier was unfazed.

'You just have to do it.'

Dealing directly with the Taliban was harder for some soldiers than others. Not only had Private Fahim been shot by the Taliban, but they had also tried to kill his family in a grenade attack on their home:

After we landed, a lot of memories I had left behind came to the front. It was unreal to find myself in that position and place. Coming face-to-face with the Taliban was hard. It brought a lot back, including the day I had been shot, and lost a best friend. It pissed me off to see the Taliban.

One day, at the gate, I could see five women being trampled to death. I tried shouting down from my position on the container, but the lads on the shield wall couldn't hear me, so I jumped down myself and pushed into the crowd. It was a silly thing to do, because I was away from our line, and the Taliban could have grabbed me or shot me and no one would have known who did it.

I wasn't thinking straight. I could hear these women dying. They were shouting, 'Help me! Save me son!' Any one of them could have been my mother. One of the Taliban was shouting at me, telling me that it was our fault for coming to Afghanistan. He showed me a bullet and said that it had my name on it.

I lost it, and went to pull my Glock from my holster, but I couldn't move my hand: the RSM [Regimental Sergeant-Major] had hold of it. He had followed me into the crowd. Between us, we got one of the women back behind our lines. She was still breathing, but she couldn't overcome her injuries, and died.

I was so angry, but the RSM calmed me down. He said, 'Don't react, that's what they want.' He was a great guy. He risked himself to come and get me. Later that day, he gave me an RSM coin for allyness. It means a lot to me.

Some years before, Private Fahim had paid for his own family to flee Kabul. 'When we first went to Kabul I was thinking, if only I had waited, I could have got my parents out this way, and taken them to Britain, but I changed my mind. I would have rather if my parents were shot by the Taliban than died slowly in that crowd. It was terrible.'

Civilian casualties

'As we entered Kabul, we realised that the city would fall. It was like a dream, everywhere I went I felt like I was in a dream,'[4] said Haji Assadullah Agha, but a Taliban commander's dream was a living nightmare for many other Afghans, who continued to flock to the airport to escape the new regime.

'My dad worked at the British embassy,' said student Malalai Hussainy. 'We knew that if the Taliban found out he worked there, they might kill him and everyone in my family.'[5]

Hasina Safi was the acting minister for women's affairs. 'I was told that if you do not leave in the coming three days, you will be assassinated.'

Similar stories were reported by thousands, but fleeing to the airport would prove equally fatal to many people.

'At first, there was nothing to hold back the crowd except razor wire,' said Major Steve White, 'then it was vehicles, and then it was shipping containers. The Paras and engineers were constantly trying to improve upon controls for the crowd, which were growing to be in the tens of thousands.'

Such conditions became deadly.

'There were surges in the crowd. Women, kids, and old people were crushed to death. It wasn't deliberate. I suspect it was like the Hillsborough disaster.'

To prevent the people in the crowd being crushed against the immovable objects of the barriers, the Paras would hold a shield wall ahead of them so that there was some flex in the crowd. 'They thought we were trying to keep them out, but actually we were trying to save them from getting crushed,' said Major White.

'During the American evacuation, Afghans suffered terribly,' said Mawlawi Samiullah Fateh. 'They were hungry, they were thirsty and conditions were appalling. When we went to Abbey Gate the heat was unbearable, I saw seven people die of heat and hunger.'[6]

'When we went to the airport, we came to a big gate,' said Hasina Safi. 'Taliban were standing there. We were afraid of being targeted. We came down, there was no electricity so it was good, because it was dark. No one could see us. It was so crowded that you would say there is no oxygen in the air.'[7]

Little wonder that some parts of the crowd tried to force their way through by whatever means necessary.

'At one point the barriers were getting overrun,' recalled Major White. 'I said, "Get the hickory sticks out and get them back," but I was told that we "don't have the authority". Apparently, using the riot gear needed to be signed off by a lawyer at JFHQ [Standing Joint Force Headquarters]. That was ridiculous, so I said I would take the flak for it.'

These were the difficult decisions made to keep the gates and airfield operational. Such conditions existed at every gate at HKIA, as a desperate mass of humanity attempted to escape life under the Taliban.

A US Navy nurse described the number of casualties coming into her station as 'insane'. She saw fifty to sixty patients a day. Navy Corpsmen treated many more at the gates, and in holding areas. 'It was an absolute crisis of humanity. There was no shade, no pre-staged water or food in the early days of the op. There were a lot of dehydration and heat injuries. Sick babies. Pregnant women. Our medical team was very female-heavy, so we saw a lot of women. Some people were bruised and beaten.'

She felt a strong kinship towards the plight of the Afghan women, knowing what life would be like for them under the Taliban. She also saw that those fleeing the Taliban could act in just as repugnant a manner as the oppressive regime.

'Afghan men would take blankets away from mothers and babies. They would try to push through the crowds to get on the buses faster, trampling over women with children.'

Captain Sam McGrury recalled similar tragedies. 'I saw a lot of women with dead babies. Mothers would be passing out into the concertina wire as they tried passing them over to us. And then there were men stealing live babies to try and use them as a way to get in. At one point, I had fifteen babies in my care.

That photo of the moustached Marine holding a baby, he's one of my guys.'

McGrury and his US Marines took care of the children until they could be moved on. 'We handed them over to UNICEF, who either found the families, or re-homed them.'

'The military were quite relieved to see the UN there,' said Tony, who was working as a security advisor in Kabul. 'They had this problem of all these kids who'd been separated from their parents and they weren't equipped to deal with them. So we helped set up a child-friendly place that was very makeshift, but helped with the processing. Some of these kids ended up in Doha, others were reunited with their families.'

Soldiers from 2 Para were also confronted with lost or abandoned children, or worse. 'With dead women and kids, the Taliban would just wash their hands of the problem,' said Josh. 'We would try and reunite the deceased with their families. We'd use the terps, and get word passed in the crowd.'

Asked how he dealt with such tragedy, Josh answered that, 'It was a job to do, with a start date, end date, and an objective.'

'The medics dealt with a lot of children and injured women,' he added. 'The non-entitled were getting in the way. Thousands of men squashing women and children. I think a lot of the men had come to just have a look, and maybe chance their arm. Sometimes we'd have to send people back out. We had a section of guys acting as enforcers. Some people would come in using fake docs and passports. The Afghan Border Force would be able to spot them. There were even photoshopped marriage photos. Locals married to Western passport holders, etc. You can't blame them.'

'This wasn't public order, these were desperate people trying to get away,' said Major Danny Riley, who had experienced such events in Northern Ireland. 'When you look at it from a parental point of view, you see it differently. Kids had been taken by people to use as bargaining chips to get through, then abandoned. We had to try and reunite them. There were also a lot of crush injuries. One of our female medics went on her hands and knees and crawled between the lads on the shields to pull a kid to safety.'

A 2 Para soldier recalled the frustrations of processing the civilians; or rather, the system that determined who could pass, and who could not. 'There was one Afghan who spoke good English and he was showing me pictures of him in America. He didn't have any paperwork and he was crying. He lifted his top and showed me scars from the Taliban. He was on his knees, crying and begging, but I couldn't let him through. Afghan commandos and police would turn up [trying to get onto the airport]. They'd show their ID cards, but that wasn't enough. They were begging. They knew they were dead if they didn't get on a flight, but we couldn't process them on just an ID card.'

Eighteen-year-old soldiers were making life and death decisions on a minute-by-minute basis.

'I don't know how I feel about that now,' the young soldier said. 'There wasn't any more I could do.'

'There was screaming as people were crushed,' said Private Fahim. 'People were crying, or shouting for help. Anyone could understand they were desperate and scared, but I understood every word that they were shouting and begging. On top of this, the Taliban were firing warning shots, but they were not carefully placed like our own. I had a few come really close. You had to watch where they were swinging their muzzles.'

The human tragedy took its toll.

'I felt helpless,' said Fahim. 'Officers cried on my shoulder. There was blood, sweat and tears from all ranks. Everyone had a nervous breakdown at some point. Every day of it was non-stop tragedy. People were shouting "Help me!", but we couldn't help everyone, and some of the more deserving people got left behind. Requirements on what paperwork was needed would change. It was very frustrating. Our lads were doing their best, but they're not experts on documents.'

In its way, this turned out to be a blessing. 'Lads passed through deserving people who wouldn't have got through otherwise [for bureaucratic reasons]. It took about an hour for the Home Office personnel to process one family, and they'd only sent two people. Once they arrived, the number of people we were getting out actually slowed down. If it had been that way from the beginning, we'd have got no more than a thousand out.'

Instead, by using their judgement and initiative, the Paras facilitated the rescue of some 17,000 people.[8]

'It was about using common sense.'

Despite doing all that he could to help the situation, Fahim could not help feeling a sense of guilt. 'I started feeling guilty of the life I was living. I had been in their shoes.' He found that in such moments of desperate humanity, 'little things made the difference, like opening doors. Being kind. The people were so grateful.'

Fahim's shared language allowed him to experience the gratitude of Afghans who were successfully passing through, but it also exposed him to the stories and pleas of those who could not.

'I knew first-hand from my own family's experience that they were not exaggerating [about the threats]. People were crying that they would die that night if I didn't help them, but sometimes there was nothing I could do. I think about those people now. Is he dead? Is he alive? At night, the crowd of people looked like they were in the wild, waiting to be hunted, and they would look to us for salvation.'

Life at the gate

The crowd at the gate was a constant scrum of pushing and shoving. There were still some ANA working alongside the Marines, and occasional ANA special forces would arrive. The difference between Afghan soldiers was noticeable in their demeanour, equipment and English.

'The ANA had a deal to get them out,' said a Marine NCO. 'They were promised flights, but then there was a misunderstanding with the Germans. The ANA had been firing warning shots into the air, and one of them hit close to the Germans. They thought the ANA were going green on blue, and returned fire.'

Green on blue attacks, involving ANA/ANP turning on their allies, had claimed the lives of many coalition soldiers. In 2012, they accounted for 15 per cent of coalition deaths.[9]

The Marine recalled that two ANA soldiers were hit in the return fire, and that once a US commander had been able to end the shootout, the remaining ANA at the gate downed tools and left their positions, never to return.

At the Baron Hotel, the Paras remained vigilant for threats among the crowd. This could be anything from a suicide bomber to a desperate civilian who wanted to get out.

'The Afghan civilians were different,' said a 2 Para soldier. 'The ones who had worked with us were OK to deal with. A lot more calm. Others were harder. Sometimes it was like dealing with wild animals. Some didn't care about their kids. Parents would just leave them in the crowd.'

'One day, two kids came up with a random bloke,' said a 2 Para soldier. 'When my CSM asked what relation he was to them, one kid said he was an uncle, the other said he was their dad. Something felt off. We separated the kids from him, and they didn't kick up a fuss, so he definitely wasn't a relation. How he'd come to be with the kids I have no idea.'

Such ruses were commonplace, and it was down to the intuition of the soldiers to spot them.

'We were stagging on an alley when a group of about six teenagers walked over to the Taliban and slipped them something,' said a private soldier at the Baron. 'When the group got to us, we threw them against a wall and searched them. Each had multiple phones and cash. Their demeanour was different to the people trying to escape. I think they'd been sent in to dick us,' he added, meaning that the teenagers were being used to scout out British positions, potentially to help plan an attack.

It wasn't only the civilians who were in danger at the gates.

'A few days before the Abbey Gate bomb, we got a threat warning that there was a bomb in a bag and it would go off at 13:48,' said Tom, a private soldier in A Coy, 2 Para. 'I looked around me and there were bags everywhere. I looked at my watch and saw I might have six minutes left to live. It was a helpless feeling, but you just kind of accepted it and made a joke. There was a lot of threat warnings like that which came to nothing. On another one, we got told that there was a suicide bomber on his way towards us along the track where we were resting. I was the sharp shooter, and I thought I had a great chance of dropping him. I was gutted when he didn't show up.'

Bomb threats are often met head on by the infantry, but there were also specialists at the airport, including a USMC EOD team led by Warrant Officer Lee Bowden, a veteran of two tours in Afghanistan.

'Arriving in HKIA felt a little like Camp Leatherneck in Helmand, but there were more permanent buildings and walls. There wasn't much of a sense of urgency around the place. We were made to feel welcome by the Army EOD, but the consensus seemed to be that there wasn't much going on.'

As specialists, it was up to Bowden to suggest to his commanders where and how his men should be used. Occasionally they would receive calls for assistance in the shape of a NATO 9 liner (request for assistance).

'A lot of civilian contractors were leaving, and the amnesty boxes at the airports were filling up with ammunition and grenades. There was a lot of foreign stuff in there. Anything from flashbangs to high explosives. How to dispose of it was an issue. HKIA was a working airport, and so a large controlled explosion was out of the question. I asked for permission to dispose of these munitions with smaller controlled dets, but I never got it. In the end, the shipping container full of magazines and grenades were left behind for the Taliban. Every day we received several nine liners. This could be anything from grenades to possible IEDs. Humongous credit is due to the infantry, who were patrolling and searching and remaining vigilant. Despite the fact they were getting hardly any sleep, they were still picking out anomalies.'

Amid the chaos and confusion, there were moments of happiness. 'There was a ditch that we called the pit, and it would fill with civvies,' recalled Tom of A Coy, 2 Para. 'It was like a gladiator arena. I pulled one guy out of there who spoke English. It turned out his family lived two minutes down the road from me at home! He took my phone number and we stayed in touch. He's just finished uni.'

'A lot of people in the crowd spoke English,' Major White said, 'and so when I needed a message relaying I would ask "Who speaks English?" and a bunch of hands would go up. I'd tell them what I wanted, and they'd relay it.'

As well as English speakers, there were passport holders and applicants from many other nations at the gate.

'Name a country, and someone from there would be at the gate,' said White. 'Other nations were using our security bubble to get their people out. It was very frustrating. Our blokes would calm the crowd down, and then some SF guy from another country would jump up on a container and shout, "Who's from such and such?" and everyone's hands would go up, and they'd all start shouting. It pissed me off. It pissed the blokes off. Usually there's a bit of hero worship between Toms and SF, but our guys were just gripping them.'

'Different nations had different characters,' recalled Josh of 2 Para, 'and some were easier to work with than others. You'd get certain passport holders arriving at the gate, in that heat, and no one from the representative nation would be there to be met. The French had one bloke with a clipboard.'

Major White was proud of his men's efforts, but felt like other nations were riding on the back of their work. 'It was all done on the back of the Brits. There was friction with the Yanks. They weren't as robust or as professional. I saw one of them throw this massive flashbang that went right off next to one of the senior Taliban's head. Things like that could have kicked it all off, but they did get better as it went along.'

One of White's biggest frustrations with the Americans had nothing to do with the Marines, but with the State Department.

'They'd keep changing the criteria. One day it would be passport holders, the next it would be green cards and passports, the next it would be something else.'

To add to the issue, some members of the Paras reported that many of the US special operations forces weren't familiar with their nation's paperwork process. As a result, many Americans and other nationalities would turn to the Paras for help.

'The Baron was supposed to be for British evacuees, and we took out 16,000, but we also processed thousands more who had come to our gate by mistake. If they were passport holders from a Commonwealth or NATO country, we'd process them.'

'We worked constantly,' said Private Fahim. 'I fell asleep standing up. British forces were the front belt, and other nations' militaries would be coming to us for their people, giving us lists. One of the things I needed to do was calm the crowd. Because I knew the people, they would listen to me better than they would do a Para with a riot shield.'

'We got along well with the Paras,' said a US Marine, 'but they kept trying to hotwire our cars, and stole our car batteries. They had two buses that you could hear coming from miles off. The Shag Wagon, and the Banter Bus.'

The Marines' time on duty was split between pulling security, and searching and processing.

'I didn't want to do it at first,' admitted the US Marine, 'but that feeling went away. We'd be getting into fights with people. At the start the Afghans were mostly hostile, but once they got inside they'd be grateful. I couldn't understand the behaviour of the men. At the North Gate you'd see men use kids as a means to get in, or they'd disregard dead kids, and just leave them. Some single mothers made it inside with their kids. They'd walk over to the wall and break down in tears.

'There were kids dying of exhaustion. Some were crushed. Some men would even use kids as blankets to get across the razor wire. The kids would be hanging, bleeding in the wire, and we'd have to go and get them. The crowd started throwing the bodies in the nearby river. You'd see them floating by. I was in disbelief. It didn't seem real. One five-year-old girl was brought in. We think she'd had a heart attack in the heat. She passed away in my arms.'

Under the burden of command and the pressure of the situation, many untested Senior NCOs buckled. 'A lot broke down and couldn't do the job,' the Marine said. 'Lance Corporals were stepping up. The command recognised they'd lost us, and let us be. It was *Lord of the Flies*. A natural hierarchy.'

In what was to become known as the 'Digital Dunkirk' (covered in Chapter 8) it wasn't ammunition that often proved vital, but an internet connection.

'There were special cases,' Major White said, referring to the people being helped by sources back in the West. 'Without WiFi at the Baron it would have been impossible to get them. When it got quiet at the barrier I'd go inside, download messages, get numbers, and then go back to the barrier and start making calls from a burner phone. We pulled the more high risk people from the crowd, including news crews.'

'It was about finding a problem, and being the solution,' said Josh. 'That could be handing out water, getting milk for babies or directing people. Sometimes it was a lot harder. I was handed live babies and dead babies.'

'What took us by surprise was the emotional burden,' Major White recalled. 'There was no respite, and it took more out of us than we realised at the time. Seeing the desperation of people in the crowd, it affected older guys more. It was a reflection of their own families in the crowd. You'd see battle-hardened Paras crying their eyes out around a corner. It was de-stigmatised. Everyone had their moment like that.'

The chevron

The escape from Kabul was a truly multinational effort, and as liaison to the US command, Major Danny Riley of 23 Engineer Regiment saw the value of that cooperation first-hand:

The biggest challenge we had was that we were broke in terms of equipment … We didn't even have radios, we couldn't communicate properly, which is a bit of a red flag. But other than that, without working with the Americans, with the Turks' permission, we wouldn't have been able to do anything out there. A lot of what we did, and what I did, was greasing the wheel to set conditions to put it in a position where we could do something.

The British embassy was now located at the Baron Hotel. It is only by good fortune that 2 Para managed to seal the doors and get themselves in there. The whole recovery of that was done through American capital and troops and equipment. Everything that we did was checked and cleared by the Americans. They had the manpower and they had the aircraft, they controlled the airspace, and they had the money and links to the Talibs. That's what was keeping the mobile phone network open. Without that it would have collapsed, so every time we would do anything we would run it by the Americans.

At no stage were General Sullivan [USMC] or the 82nd with-holding anything from us. I sat in all of their briefings in the ops rooms. I communicated everything with them. There were two headquarters. Someone was ejected from one and that created a seat for me. I know when Brigadier Martin arrived he already knew Sullivan and the two star [general].

I managed to get around and talk to everyone, so even the Foreign Office were talking to me. We were able to extract a lot of their people from different gates, so there was quid pro quo in terms of information.

Major Riley also worked with the Turks, who were the nation nominally in charge of HKIA's operations:

They were great. They were going to stay after we left, so without a shadow of doubt they were working their own communication with the Talibs. I mean they have to, because the Taliban were going to become the next government. It was in their best interest to, because they need to operate in a permissive environment. And we were aware of that. They were our primary means for getting supplies in and out.

For example, for the chevron [an operation to relieve pressure on the Baron Hotel], when we did the plan, when we worked out what our timings were going to be, General Sullivan went and spoke to somebody and came back and said, 'These are the timings that we work to.' And so they did have a direct line.

The Taliban were on the end of the phone:

When we opened up the Baron, it was me and one other who walked through the crowd to the Baron Hotel. We rattled the door. I spoke to Colonel Dave, and said we need to move the crowd back, we need to speak to the Talibs, here are the timings. He gave me a phone with a guy's number on, because he'd also been talking to the Talibs, so I reached out and arranged a face-to-face. There was many levels of [communication].

[The Taliban] had been told to screw the nut for the Brits, otherwise they're going to be here for a long time. They'd been told to screw the nut, because if it came to scrap, it would have been really quite unpleasant. But on the other hand, they would have known. They think long term. They think in consequential orders of effect far beyond us. We're there for a tour, they're there for a lifetime. Getting us out of there quickly would suit their agenda. Talking to them wasn't as difficult as people think.

If there was one operation that summed up cooperation between multinational forces, it was the mission to install 'the chevron'.

'The crowd had overwhelmed the route from the Baron Hotel all the way down to Abbey Gate,' said Major Riley:

2 Para headquarters, a portion of headquarters, and part of 9 Squadron felt cut off. A siege mentality had set in and they weren't leaving that place at all. What that had meant is that we could no longer process civilians coming in and out. We had to get it open.

The principal reason for opening it was to start processing civilians. And I was thinking not from a British perspective but from a Kabul extraction perspective. And so not only was I the liaison officer for the Americans, but I was organising all the movements of people from other companies. Everyone was coming to me because I was the link man for everything. So we and a couple of the Americans were mulling the problem over, and we realised that we were going to have to clear the people out of it.

Previously, 9 Squadron had built a barrier out of old vehicles and stuff like that. The problem with that barrier, and it was a problem, is that it was flat to the crowd. Although these guys wouldn't have realised it, after doing years of public order, the crowd acts like water. It has to flow, and people were being crushed against these vehicles.

Brigadier Blanchford [RM, Chief Joint Force Operations] was very keen that this did not happen again. So he came up with this sketch to change that flat barrier into something where the crowd could flow. We were in discussion with the Americans about how we were going to open up the thing to recover 2 Para. Blanchford's liaison officer came down and said, 'Well, you're an engineer, can we make this?' And we were looking at it and actually, yeah, we can make that. We can make this chevron and control the people. That was an easy fix. So I spoke with this American colonel and said, 'Can you get us this kit?' He said yes.

Another colonel, who was chief of staff of the MEU [Marine Expeditionary Unit] said, 'What would you need to clear this?' I said we'd need four companies. 'I need a company to push guys up, I need a company to clear the left flank, we've got a flank on the right, and we'll need another company to do transit. And I'll need some company to move things and build it. In my head I was thinking we'd use 9 Squadron, and in his very American way, the colonel said, 'Danny, it's going to be American-resourced, British-led, and you're going to lead it.'

This was welcome news to Riley:

Fuck, yes. We are going to do this. So we came up with a scheme of manoeuvre, sent out messages to everybody. We'd arranged a loose plan and we were going to go at 11:00 the next morning. I'd been given two American companies and two Brit companies and a troop of engineers. In terms of the move of stuff, the US were going to give me a platoon of engineers to move all the stuff up. But it all revolved around getting this crowd back. And I want to say there's something between ten and fifteen thousand people.

We'd have to push everybody back from Abbey Gate to the Baron Hotel and that was a mammoth task. Getting the Brits organised was difficult. 2 Para were a little late getting going. There were no radios. We were centralised with runners. I borrowed a push to talk radio. The US Marines were epic. They did this great '1, 2, 3 push' for well over two or three hours. Paras were filling in the left flank, but then the whole thing stopped dead. The Yanks wanted to keep pushing. Company commanders were falling out. I stood beside Jeff [one of the US company commanders] and coordinated. The crowd had become sandwiched between our barrier and the Taliban.

Major Riley needed to coordinate with the Paras at the Baron Hotel to get things moving again. He walked through the crowd and knocked on the hotel's door:

The Taliban had given a deadline of 05:00, but I wanted to push it to 08:00. Colonel Dave gave me a phone to speak to the Taliban and I went out to meet them. Jeff came with me. I took a good terp [interpreter], took off my helmet, and slung my weapon. What we needed was to push the crowd back. We needed the Taliban's permission to do that. The Taliban commander was skinny and lean and had probably been fighting us for the last twelve years. He was being a prick and having none of it, but I had the feeling he was just playing games.

Riley's interpreter was moderating what both men were saying, a common issue. 'I told him [the Taliban Commander], if you want us to go, we need to move this crowd. We eventually agreed to that, and that they'd treat the crowd fairly, but they didn't. Strategically the Taliban were on-board, but face-to-face they knew they had the upper hand. They were whipping people with the rubber from car windscreens.'

The commander of 16 Air Assault Brigade arrived on scene. 'He'd approved the scheme of manoeuvre,' said Riley. 'He brought us into the Baron to give us a pep talk.'

Through the efforts of those pushing against the crowd, momentum was restored and the plan proceeded forwards. Engineers were integral to it. 9 Squadron were clearing the way using plant operated machinery, while USMC combat engineers, directed by a Para engineer, put in the shipping containers that would form the chevron.

'It was an excellent example of combined ops,' said Riley.

Among the US troops that Riley was liaising with was Major Jared Lefaivre, a US Marine, who used social media to describe his experience of the operation to clear between the gates:

Word had spread that the Baron Gate was min-manned [minimum manning] and the roughly 400-metre stretch of ground between the gates was shoulder-to-shoulder. In order to continue the evacuation, the bottleneck had to be cleared.

The devised plan was solid, spartan-esque in nature, but so were the Marines who were assigned to execute it. Nut-to-butt, Marines and British Paratroopers lined up to rush the area in front of the two massive steel doors of the Abbey Gate. As the gate opened, an initial squad was to form a 20-metre semi-circle to establish a foothold. The remainder of the unit would fall in behind them, shoulder-to-shoulder and begin pushing the crowd back, foot by foot. Corpsmen, medics, PJs, and command and control would make up the third element to treat the injured, and grab any civilians holding US passports they happened to spot.

As soon as we opened the doors [the plan] fell apart. From an elevated position . . . I watched the first squad meet fierce resistance. Not from deserving interpreters and their families trying to escape the Taliban, but from a large group of military-aged males who didn't speak English . . . These men pushed their way to the front of the crowd, beating women and children in the process. Some had kidnapped children, trying to pass them off as their own to curry favour from us . . .

The second and third elements, seeing their comrades in trouble, heavily poured out the gate. Not in a straight line reminiscent of an organised Roman legion, but rather as a smattering of fire-team sized units, three or four at a time. We couldn't mass combat power and I knew we were in trouble. Standing next to me, a Turkish soldier began firing his weapon, agitating the crowd and instantly making things worse . . . I had never seen such fear before. I screamed at the soldier but it was to no avail. I finally reached over and ejected the magazine from his weapon. He looked at me in anger. My first instinct was to strike him, but I quickly turned back to the crowd.

From our position I could see one of the PJs [Pararescue Jumpers] in our group surrounded by civilians. He raised his M-18 and began firing in the air just so he could create enough space and move backwards towards the gate. Ghost Company's commander, bullhorn in hand, was also about to be swarmed. I leapt off the truck and waded into the crowd, trying to consolidate our forces. I grabbed Marines and tried to force them shoulder-to-shoulder. Hands reached out from every direction ...

Just when I thought things couldn't get any worse, a large group of Marines and Paratroopers formed a wedge and drove themselves through the crowd, taking no civilians with them in the process ... as they passed, the mob simply refilled into the void. We were even more outnumbered than before, our forces now split in half. The remaining Marines left in the crowd realised that we needed to regroup and fell back towards the closed gate. They were instantly pinned between the surging crowd and the steel doors. Agonising screams escaped from their mouths as they were being crushed.

I wasn't faring any better. I had found myself in a very bad position, surrounded and completely alone ... my body was being crushed between the ceramic plates of my body armour. I could barely force air into my lungs. This is it: I am about to die here in this crowd. [I tell myself] don't fall down, if you lose your footing, you are going to die ... A flashbang soared over my head and detonated just above me ... in that moment I was pulled back to safety. The doors had been opened and we found ourselves on the other side of the wall, back on our side of the line.

I immediately climbed back up onto my observation position. I could see that the British troopers from the edge made their way back to their ilk at the Baron Hotel, leaving a group of Marines still in the rear of the crowd ... The contingency was about to be enacted. CS gas was the only feasible way to get the crowd to disperse. As much as I hated the idea of gassing women and children, I agreed with the assessment. We had no riot gear, no shields, and no dogs.

Canisters began to flood the field with the pungent gas. It wasn't since my time at TBS [USMC officer training] that I had been subjected to CS. I had forgotten how much I hated the smell and how bad it instantly burns your lungs. Virtually no one had masks on, so we had to be careful to throw the canister far away so that it wouldn't affect us, but keep it close enough that the crowd was subjected to its effects. There was no wind, just unspeakably hot stagnant air. It was agonising to be exposed to it. I could only imagine how the children in the crowd were reacting. I prayed that it didn't kill them . . .

The screams were worse now. They were so loud they drowned out the persistent high pitched ringing that was currently raging through the eardrums, a direct result of the gunfire, flashbangs and my absence of hearing protection. My eyes met a father holding his little girl, who was about the same age as my daughter. His wife was clinging to him using her chadar to cover her mouth and eyes. She desperately reached with her other hand to find her daughter's mouth to protect it. His eyes met mine and in sheer terror mouthed 'please don't' as he pointed to his daughter . . .

Once the gas billowed, some of the crowd fled towards the gate. It was chaotic but there was nothing we could do. A couple of NCOs cut a relief hole in the chain link fence on the side of a gate that aided in funnelling people out of the area. All told, I think seven people were killed in the events of the day.

'It took the rest of the day,' said Major Lefaivre, 'for the Marines of 2/1 to clear the area, but they were finally successful. They were tenacious in their resolve; you could tell that they were incredibly well-trained and led.'

Josh, the young private in 2 Para, recalled the efforts between Abbey Gate and the Baron. 'Once the containers were put in, it was realised that there would be no flex against them, and the OC [Officer Commanding] ordered a multiple to go out and form a baseline ahead of it, but a section commander had already anticipated the order and was leading us guys out into a shield wall. That action saved many lives, as it allowed some give, but it meant that our blokes had to hold it all day against thousands of people. Young, fit lads were just passing out from exhaustion. You'd pull them back and another lad would step in. It went on like this all day.'

'The Yanks helped out for a bit, but then they all sat down with their helmets off,' another 2 Para soldier recalled. 'I saw one of our officers lose his rag with them. He was trying to find someone in command, but everyone was just ignoring him. He jumped down off the container. "You call yourself elite troops?" That pissed one of them off and they got in a shouting match. The officer told them to either get up and help or fuck off.'

The soldier was quick to add that this was not reflective of the US Marines' effort. 'To be fair, that was just a snapshot of them. They'd reached their breaking point and we hadn't. I don't think that says anything bad about them, but speaks to the standards of the Parachute Regiment. No other regiment could have done what we did.'

That praise extended to C Coy, 3 Para.

'I was up on the container and you could see them formed up in three ranks, running from the airport at the double. They came straight to us and got stuck in.'

The shield wall held.

'We saved a lot of lives that day.'

Major Danny Riley saw things differently. 'The US were on

line for hours and hours, and the Brits weren't. The Marines had done all the pushing and the public order stuff. The Marines were doing one hour off, four on. Jeff [one of the US company commanders] came to me and said, "Why aren't these guys helping out more?" There were misunderstandings like that.

'The Marines were great at public order. We made the chevron sound like it was all us. It's really important for people to know that we couldn't have done it without the Marines. The guys did really good work. From the outset the US Marines were in the thick of it, front and centre. If the chevron hadn't gone in, the whole thing wouldn't have worked. The concept by Brigadier Blanchford, and the plan enacted by the units involved, it was just as important as the air bridge.'

8

Digital Dunkirk

Until they are home, no man left behind.
– A motto of the United States Marine Corps

For some of the Afghans now falling under Taliban rule there was a glimmer of hope: the Afghan Relocation and Assistance Policy (ARAP).

The ARAP scheme launched in April 2021, with the aim of offering 'relocation or other assistance to former Locally Employed Staff (LES) in Afghanistan to reflect the changing situation in Afghanistan.'[1] The UK Government's website defined the criteria:

Eligibility under the ARAP:
There are four categories for assistance, against which all ARAP applications are assessed.

All applications received can be amended by the team if more information is received, as well as be retrieved if additional information is presented which would change an eligibility decision.

Where an applicant who was directly employed by, or contracted to, an HMG Government Department or Unit was dismissed from their job they will be ineligible for relocation to the United Kingdom under ARAP (except in circumstances where HMG considers that the person was dismissed for a minor reason).

The aims of ARAP were laudable: those whose lives were at risk, and who had thrown in their lot with the British mission, should be saved from Taliban reprisals. Unfortunately, as the Taliban began to make their rapid advance across the country, many worried that the system had been set up too late, was not moving fast enough, and it was often too complex for people to meet the requirements.

'If I said to someone in the UK, you need to go online and fill in this form, and if you don't know how, just google it, they would probably understand,' said Private Fahim, the Afghan-born member of 3 Para, 'but that wasn't the case in Afghanistan. A lot of people didn't know about ARAP, and those that did, didn't know how to fill it out. The scheme was not matched to the reality of abilities in Afghanistan.'

In May 2022, a House of Commons Committee Special Report recorded the evidence of a whistleblower at the FCDO: 'I believe no member of the Afghan Special Cases team had studied Afghanistan, worked on Afghanistan previously, or had a detailed knowledge of Afghanistan. [. . .] Members of the Afghan Special Cases team usually heard of an Afghan organisation for the first time when they were asked to decide whether its staff should be evacuated. [. . .] There was no access to additional information about organisations or individuals beyond what could be found on Google. There was no ability to process applications in any language other than English.'[2]

The Special Report also stated that:

There was chaos within the Foreign Office as thousands of emails and phone calls flooded in from people seeking help. The existence of the three separate channels for evacuation

– administered by three departments – added to the confusion. Many applicants submitted their cases to each one, and the information was further duplicated by MPs and others trying to help them. The FCDO's Lessons Learned review flags up the lack of clarity about the different schemes, and which Government department should be contacted by those seeking help. There were at least six crisis email inboxes in use in the FCDO alone, and emails were repeatedly forwarded between them, facing long delays at each stage. One whistleblower told us that there was no standardised FCDO process for handling this correspondence, no system to track what had been done with any emails, and no process to identify duplicates, while the very existence of some inboxes was forgotten about entirely between shifts. There was poor cooperation with the MOD, which was responsible for the operational side of the evacuation. Many emails from desperate people simply went unanswered, or even unread.[3]

Perhaps much of the confusion lay in the fact that ARAP was not a FCDO programme, but an MOD one.

Ben Wallace, the British defence secretary, spoke to its origins. 'To be fair it was actually the *Daily Mail* who instigated [it]. It was Larisa Brown, who ran a campaign. So there was definitely a sense that we needed to do something about it. I could see the slight direction of travel in this, which was that it was getting more dangerous, certainly in places like Helmand.'

At the MOD, Wallace wanted to change the conditions for those who could apply for the scheme.

'To be fair, Priti Patel [the Home Secretary] was very supportive. We did it through the government, agreed it and rapidly changed it. You couldn't just get away with parking people in other parts of Afghanistan. We had to get it through. And to be fair, the Prime Minister was very supportive.'

During Britain's twenty years in Afghanistan, thousands of Afghans had worked in positions ranging from camp cooks to commandos. Many had not applied to leave Afghanistan until the Taliban's rapid advance: a testament that they did not want to leave their homes unless their lives depended on it. Estimating how many of these people the UK would need to evacuate was a challenge.

'I think we estimated at the time fourteen thousand,' said Wallace. 'In total, including dependants, I think it's double that really.'

One issue facing the UK government was when to open the programme to members of Afghanistan's military.

'Six months before all this evacuation, if not longer before, we wanted the Afghan Army to stay and fight. What we didn't want is for them to lose all their most capable commanders, because that really would be the end. So there was definitely a line drawn up between supporting cast, probably less well-trained people who were interpreters, people who lived in the communities. And then there was the Afghan Army, because that's what you've signed up for. So we wanted to change some of those rules and bring them forward. But it meant it was in a good position when something really kicked off. And then the other challenge was the size of the family.'

Wallace believes that one of ARAP's greatest strengths is that it relies on verification from those who worked within the British military or government.

'Our ARAP is finite. We have verification people to say, "I know him, I did ten years with him." The hardest bit is the security bit. Where I might know intelligence that I can't talk to people about, identifying them as having aided and abetted the Taliban, or having actually aided and abetted the targeting of British soldiers.'

But the programme was not without its detractors, including Lord Dannatt, the former Chief of the General Staff. On 28 July, a letter was published that criticised the speed and scope of the programme.[4]

'Lord Dannatt had a habit of not actually reading the details before he put his name to letters, in my honest opinion,' said Ben Wallace. 'I have quite an experience of former armchair generals ... former generals who seem to ... someone comes and says, "We've done a letter, would you sign it?" Right, and that's fine but, first of all, I didn't ever get any letters from Lord Dannatt when I was doing all this stuff previously. I didn't get any lobbying from ... I mean, some of the great champions of this scheme never mentioned it to me, right? ... I credit Larisa Brown, *Daily Mail*. It was her article that sparked me last September to go to the Home Office and do some work with Priti Patel.'

Patel and Wallace replied to Dannatt and the others who had signed the letter with one of their own.

'I thought it is important to push back and we put some facts there in the domain. And the other thing for generals is that they were the ones who decided on the rules of dismissals for offences,' said Wallace, referring to those who fell outside ARAP because they had been dismissed from service with the British. 'So forgive me if I'm a little bit cynical to the sort of, after the fact people, who themselves administered all these schemes, who saw lots of people dismissed, and they're writing to me about *their* schemes. It's a bit cheeky, really, but what I would say of the ARAP scheme, it has been pretty successful.'

In the months before Kabul fell, Ambassador Bristow tried to instil a sense of urgency into the programme.

'What I was trying to do from Kabul was up the pace. So get London to understand, get the lead departments in London to understand, you've got less time than you think. So front load this, do everything you can to speed the decision making up. Absorption capacity in the UK is, of course, a problem, but so is having people stuck in Kabul or in Afghanistan, if that's where it goes. And this picked up the big question of ARAP category four, so the people who could conceivably fall within ARAP, but they weren't really covered by it, they hadn't been military interpreters, they weren't embassy staff.

'There's all the difference in the world between somebody who's worked on a frontline patrol with the military, and somebody who's worked in an embassy in Kabul. The lives of both may be at risk for different reasons, but the outcome is the same in the end. So my point there was to boil these questions through to decisions fast. Bureaucracies can always work faster. But the underlying point was to get London to understand you've got less time than you think. That was the key message I was trying to get across.'

Johnny Mercer points to the Doha Agreement as the time when Britain's evacuation effort needed to go into a higher gear:

Look, I think, and I was in the MOD at the time, that the Doha Agreement came out, and to be fair to Ben Wallace, he was very clear, this is a terrible agreement. It's a terrible result. It was an agreement reached without the government of Afghanistan. And the writing was on the wall there. But that's where I split from others, and I think at that stage we should have really woken up to the threat of leaving behind so many people and really upped our programmes.

So people have campaigned for many years, and more than me, around, for example, the Afghan interpreters. Dan Jarvis has done a great job on this. Our programmes are so tight, we were letting through like four or five, six, every six months. Absolutely absurd. Whereas we've got thousands out there that we owe this debt to. And then it was kind of revamped in April, May 2020. But again, it was just far too restrictive and constrictive. For example, if they were employed by a contractor, they were initially excluded there, but then included, but that initial exclusion undoubtedly cost lives.

And the net result of that was that when Kabul did fall under the Taliban and they are like, right, you've fourteen days to get as many people as you can, inevitably, right, if the Taliban are on the roadblocks and stuff, you're going to bring out a lot of people, but the vast majority of them will not be the people that you owe to. Consequently, we've got a lot of people over here, still in hotels, some of whom have absolutely nothing to do with helping the UK mission in Afghanistan.

And it makes people like me, who are trying to help the security community, our jobs a lot harder, because we brought back loads of the wrong people and left loads of the right people in Afghanistan. For me, that's the bit that could have been avoided ... Biden's been rightly criticised for his performance during this time.

Mercer recalls how frustrated he was at the lack of progress to streamline the ARAP process:

I mean, every kind of inch was fought for, so when you say, like I said, it was so stingy with all and hardly anybody was getting through and people weren't getting the assistance they needed. To be fair to them, more or less, he then did revamp the programme. But again I said this to him at the time that it wasn't really up to standard, and it wasn't going to be permissive enough to fulfil our debt to all these people.

Mercer put his name to the letter cited by Ben Wallace:

I signed a letter with forty other defence figures, service chiefs, and so on in July, saying our programme is going to leave loads of people behind. And Priti Patel then wrote back to us, basically saying that all our concerns were unfounded. And then Kabul collapsed, and we left them all behind. So that I found that very, very difficult at times, I felt very bitter about it. And I had some huge rows about it with others, because I feel like they were very protective of their scheme. But it wasn't actually delivering what we needed it to.

Despite the best efforts of those on the ground, and many at home, not enough was done, in Mercer's opinion. 'We left all these people behind. First of all, I felt quite bitter, because I knew how government works. I knew how easy it was to pull a lever and change stuff. And, for whatever reason, Priti and Ben had not done that. And I find that very difficult to deal with. Because then you're in the 24-hour-day scramble in dealing with Pratty [a veteran who worked to extract Afghans], trying to get all these people out before the deadline, and it was fucking dreadful. I was on holiday at the time, you hardly sleep. And so during that period, I just felt very embittered towards ministers for the way the ARAP scheme had been handled.'

'Never in my career seen anything within the civil service so badly managed,' a whistleblower told the House of Commons Committee.[5]

The Special Report continued:

There was no induction for new staff on the team, no clear tasking, no system for recording decisions or actions, and no system for handovers between shifts. The team was severely understaffed, and the rostering system was ineffective. The department's Lessons Learned review conceded that 'the necessary resource was not consistently delivered at the volume or for the duration needed' resulting in 'staffing gaps in some teams'. This repeats some of the problems we identified in the department's response to the pandemic. According to the whistleblowers, the situation was so dire that team members resorted to asking for help from their personal contacts elsewhere in the department.

Attempts to bring in reinforcements were hampered by technical problems, such as an inability to share files with former Department for International Development (DFID) staff, or to give security clearance to soldiers. A junior official with two years' work experience was the only person monitoring the Special Cases inbox on the afternoon of 21 August, as hundreds of emails poured in. This was the height of the evacuation effort, which would end days later, and the last chance for many Afghan judges, journalists and human rights defenders seeking help from the British Government.[6]

The report went on to criticise the 'Special Cases Scheme':

The FCDO told us that the Special Cases scheme was designed to help those 'likely to be of particular vulnerability as a result of the Taliban takeover – those on whose behalf MPs had made representations.' According to one whistleblower, a week into the evacuation 'primarily or exclusively cases put forward by MPs appear to have been entered into this spreadsheet at the expense of other cases.' As a result, those who made it onto UK evacuation flights as Special Cases may not have been the most vulnerable or those who had made the greatest contribution to UK objectives, but those who had the best contacts in the UK.

According to the whistleblowers, in late August the Special Cases team was instructed to focus solely on opening emails from MPs: this was purely in order to enable the Foreign Secretary to say that all emails from MPs had been read, and to issue a generic response. I do not believe that anything was actually done with any of the information in these emails at that time. The only urgent requirement was to manage the political fallout and to appear to MPs as if something was being done.

This channelling of resources into opening MPs' emails was apparently little more than a public relations exercise. Despite the Foreign Secretary's promise to reply to these emails by 6 September, having 'read and assessed' them, MPs received only a generic letter setting out how to apply to ARAP, and promising that ACRS would open soon.[7]

Afghans were falling through the cracks. Those who had fought alongside British and NATO soldiers were in danger of being left behind. For many, this would be nothing short of a death sentence.

What happened next was known to some as a 'Digital Dunkirk'. For others, it was 'the WhatsApp War'. Unique titles, for a unique moment in history.

The WhatsApp War

Britain has a history of recalling veterans into service in times of need. This did not happen during the fall of Afghanistan. Instead, veterans who had fought in the country more than a decade ago now volunteered to come back to the conflict, but they did so in a way that was a first in military history. They joined the war via their phones, laptops, and social media accounts.

Mike Pratt was one of them. 'Soldiers don't pick their battles, but veterans chose this one.'

In August 2021, Pratt was in his home in Wandsworth. His 'WhatsApp War' would be conducted from his kitchen table.

A veteran of the Parachute Regiment who was now involved with security for CNN, 'Pratty' found himself in the unique position of knowing those at the Baron Hotel, and other enablers within the city. These were people such as 'Smudge', who ran a low profile guest house in Kabul. Smudge provided 'fixers' in Kabul, many of them former Afghan special forces. Another key to Kabul was 'Bill'.

'He's a big South African white guy with a beard,' said Pratt. 'He was driving people around, taking them to the airport. In the end the Taliban detained him for three weeks. He didn't even tell his wife what had happened.'

Pratt said that 'my role was to identify the personnel and establish comms. Often it was Bill who would then drive them to the airport.' From there it was the old boys network of the Parachute Regiment that took over.

As an example of how this might happen, both authors of this book were contacted by people who were trying to get their former Afghan allies out of the country. Having relayed their information to Pratt, he would then go about putting the Afghans into 'packets' that could be collected and taken to the airport. Or, if they were in the crowd, Pratt communicated with the Paras on the ground to find and extract them.

Open sourced maps such as Google were marked with known Taliban checkpoints that needed to be evaded. Particularly for those who had served in the Afghan special forces, being caught could be deadly. From kitchens and living rooms at home, British veterans had to ask for the total trust of Afghans fleeing the Taliban. For some, it was too much. Others knew that they had nothing to lose.

'You'd tell them this is your only chance. I had people in tears on the phone to me. They were too scared to go.'

It was an understandable fear. Perhaps this is what drove others, such as Gus, one of Pratt's CNN security members in Kabul, to forgo their flight out of Kabul. Instead, they stayed and helped at the gates until the last possible moment.

'It could never have happened without digital assets,' Pratt said. 'At first I was getting requests from people at CNN, asking to help their fixers, etc., but it got bigger quickly. It started out with people doing their jobs, but progressed to people doing their jobs plus evacuation moonlighting.'

The urgency was clear. The life expectancy of some Afghans was measured in days. 'The Taliban were going door-to-door looking for these people.'

Pratt recalled one case of an orphaned child. Both of her parents had been shot by the Taliban. 'She barely spoke English. A CIA contractor went out of the gate to go and get her, then two Toms let her into the back gate at the Baron.'

The child was later taken in by a US senator's family.

Pratt showed two photos of an Afghan teenage girl. The first is of her outside the airport, clad head to toe in black, holding all of her possessions in a small bag. In the next photo she is in the UK with a large smile.

Despite these successes, many other deserving Afghans were being left behind. 'Every plane the Afghans saw leaving was one less for them to get away.'

With Smudge, Pratt came up with a plan that could have taken out seventy Afghans a day via Pakistan, but no one in 'UK higher' would sign off on it.

'ARAP paperwork took ten minutes, but no one at the FCDO was reading it. Channels were too slow no matter who you were. Instead, informal channels started usurping traditional ones. There was no effective comms between HMG and private companies. There should have been a matrix of Brit assets in the city.'

CNN has a huge network of influential people, but they couldn't get their people out. It was Pratt who got them onto a transit.

Johnny Mercer also turned to 'Pratty' for help. As a veteran and an MP, Johnny had found himself involved with Afghans trying to escape Kabul well before August, particularly with his own former comrade 'Naveed'.

'We were on holiday [when the Taliban were advancing]. And basically I've been in contact with Naveed for like nine months. And I was trying to get through the ARAP process. So it was a fucking minister trying to get this guy through. He's a sergeant and 333 operator [Afghan special forces], right? So they didn't come more bona fide in this way, but I just couldn't get him out. So I was in contact with him the whole time. And I was getting these more and more frantic messages. And then I just remember, I woke up at about six one morning, I had like thirty missed calls, messages. This is just a race, right? It's just a race trying to get people out. And it's hard.

'I think everybody feels this, whether they're helping veterans or whoever else to get out, there is this constant pressure of time. Because you know that if you don't get them out, maybe they'll get a knock on the door that night, then how are you going to feel when they send you pictures of his family being killed that night? And you didn't make a call, or you didn't send an email. I know that has really affected quite a lot of people, particularly people who've not been in the military and had to deal with these things before, journalists who've tried to help, lawyers, and so on. They've done twenty-hour days, pinging off emails to the foreign office, or contacts, trying to get people out and it's exhausting. I hear them in interviews on radio, like breaking down. It's hard.'

Despite Mercer's best efforts, he found himself frustrated and unable to get things moving through the officially laid out channels. 'I was reaching out to the Defence Secretary, to the Prime Minister's Office, to Afghans, and then basically I found the best way of working was to go back down to the tactical level, and use people that I knew like Lev [Levison Wood, author] and Pratty, and guys on the ground.'

With the help of Mike Pratt and others, Naveed and his family were eventually rescued.

'I'd give the evacuees quick clear briefs over WhatsApp,' Pratt said, parlaying his military skills into the rescue effort. This was also needed when it came to prioritising who would make 'the list', and who wouldn't. It was a brutal but necessary form of triage.

'You had to think of people as units instead of as people.'

Such compartmentalisation was vital to function. For weeks, Mike barely slept. The support of his heavily pregnant wife kept him fed and functional.

'I'd tell him that it would be better if you get some sleep, and get some food,' said Jo Pratt, who was 'an extra pair of eyes and ears', and 'Mike's cheerleader'. 'I made sure that he didn't need to worry about anything else.'

Jo's due date was close by. At the baby's scan, Mike was coordinating rescues on his phone.

'This was the only operational tour that I did in my kitchen,' said Pratt. About the power of the veteran network, Pratt smiled and said, 'It's a big endorsement of getting on the piss.'

Tongue in cheek, but true. Many Afghan lives were saved because 'someone' had met 'someone' over beers, and was now in a position to 'call in a favour'. But it wasn't all success. Jo recalled 'coming down in the morning and getting the tally of who got out. It was gradually getting worse.'

One day Mike came to bed at 4 a.m. He was downcast. 'It didn't work,' he told his wife.

'Mike was living it with them,' said Jo.

'It was a rollercoaster,' recalled Pratt. 'Highs when we got them out, and lows when we couldn't.'

All told, Pratt was able to coordinate the rescue of more than seventy Afghans. He is the first to praise others, particularly Gus, Bill, Smudge, and the members of 2 Para on the ground.

On the ground

Captain Aaron Nunkoosing was one of these people, but it was not a role that he was expecting:

My job as the adjutant is also to be the primary battle captain on an operation. In a traditional operation, I should be controlling the Ops Room where we usually have the benefit of all the feeds, maps, comms and IT that those further forward don't have. I should be maintaining situational awareness, so that I can feed it up to higher or down to the blokes on the ground, and primarily to the CO and Ops Officer, so that they have the information they need to make decisions.

In reality this was not a traditional operation and the HQ just had to fight to try and solve problems as they arose. The HQ was incredibly lucky, because we had two or three really good staff officers who were very capable, and they were doing a lot to keep that Ops Room going. I'm not sure what we would have done without them. Despite how good a job they were doing, it was getting frustrating for all of us to be continuously bombarded by external requests to pick individuals out of the crowd. We were getting people coming to us non-stop, asking, 'Can you help out with this, can you help out with that? This man or woman is much more important than the thousands of others outside the gate.'

I was guilty of it myself initially. When I was back at HKIA, I would do things like forward an excel spreadsheet that had been sent to me from higher asking, 'By the way guys, do you mind just picking these people out of the crowd?' When you get there [to the Baron], you realise it's absolutely impossible. You cannot go into this crowd and start calling names, because no one will hear you, and you're going to highlight people who are potential targets to the Taliban, because they're right there in your face.

It was getting frustrating batting people off. Then, my regimental headquarters emailed me with a specific request, and this was for a guy who had been a translator for 3 Para back in 2006.

He was now safe in Europe, but his brother was in Kabul, and a guy called Adam Jowett emailed this to me and said, 'Look, mate, they've just killed his dad. They've gone into his home, they've killed his father, and now his family are on the run, and they're trying to get in. Can you help them?'

This was the same Adam Jowett who had commanded a composite company of Royal Irish Rangers and Parachute Regiment soldiers in Musa Qala in 2006, seeing some of the most intense combat of the war in Afghanistan.

'That story got me quite a bit,' said Aaron, knowing how instrumental Adam's interpreter had been in saving British lives. 'And I also knew that this would just end up becoming a nause [annoyance] for Colonel Dave and the ops officer who had enough on their plate, working flat out.'

Captain Nunkoosing went to look for the family himself:

I couldn't find them. The first problem was trying to pin down where they actually were. There's an issue with terminology and battlespace management. So someone might be saying they're at the Abbey Gate, but what they mean is they're at another gate. They might say they're at the Baron Hotel, but are they at the back gate? Are they at the canal? Are they at the chevron?

So that was the first thing, and we're trying to do it on unsecured comms through various people, with a language barrier, and we're also not sure who is friendly or not. There was always this thing in the back of my mind like, these are unsecure comms and I don't know the other person on the end of this chat, is this actually gen?

I ascertained that the family were close to the back gate through pictures they were sending by WhatsApp or email, but there was so much going on at the back gate that we couldn't get close, and we tried two or three times. I'd pass a message to them via an email to Adam in the UK, then I'd walk to the gate, talk to the guys who were maintaining security on the gate, and say, 'Can you try and ID these people?' I'd be holding up a photo to the guys in the sangar, who would try and lase them with an LLM [Laser Light Module], and then blokes would then punch out, grab them, and get them back in.

It took about thirty-six hours to find them through the crowd, but there was a great feeling of jubilation when we got them. I remember seeing the terp's brother as he came through holding one of his kids. They'd taken a battering to get through the crowd. To get them in was a great feeling.

Once that happened, I realised I was in a comparatively unique position. I had access to more IT and comms, and the men on the shields are being exhausted maintaining order and security – I was not being physically drained in the way that they were. But don't get me wrong, a few of them were still getting messages on their phones. A few of them were still doing things to get individuals through, once we knew they were particularly at-risk individuals, although we couldn't really show preferential treatment to anyone as this would just whip the crowd up even more.

The family of Adam Jowett's interpreter was the first of many whom Aaron helped to get through.

'The next one that we did was an ANA officer called Abdul. He went to Sandhurst with a mate of mine, who knew I'd been out there, so he passed my name to a colonel, Colonel Sarah, and Colonel Sarah set me up on a WhatsApp group. We managed to go and get him and his family out.'

Nunkoosing and others would use a phone's location services to guide people to the gates past the Taliban checkpoints.

'Sarah had linked in with this guy called Ed. Ed, back in London, had been working various networks to get people out. Our ad-hoc team managed to send three former Afghan special forces soldiers to meet with Abdul, they secured him, looked after his kids and risked their own lives to get them through the crowd and past the Talib checkpoints. I linked up with them once they got close to the canal, talked them on to an RV, and we got them in. This was all coordinated on WhatsApp and by people in both Kabul and the UK.'

But it was a short-lived victory, as the three Afghan special forces were then taken off their extraction flight by the US State Department, and sent back into the crowd:

I was gutted to hear that. I spoke to Ed on the phone and I went back out again and got them again twenty-four hours later. We coordinated with an ex-US Ranger turned journalist to help out once I got them in, and this time the US didn't throw them off the plane.

To backtrack a bit, when Ed was trying to convince me to conduct extractions for him, he said, 'I know who your CO is, this is really important, this is one call away from the Prime Minister.' He was basically bullshitting me, and I was standing right next to the CO, so I turned around and said, 'Well tell him, mate, he's right here.' A couple of times I think I put the phone down on him. I told him, 'This is an unimaginable situation here, you are not going to get individuals out,' but eventually Ed's persistence paid off, and I gave in, partly to keep it off my boss's desk.

The next time I spoke to Ed, I said, 'I know you're bullshitting me, mate,' but that felt good and we helped someone there. And we kept on, and between Ed and I, we just kept on doing it. There were some people in the Ops Room rightly saying we shouldn't be doing that for individuals, because there are ARAP out there that we can't get, but there was just this ethos of do good where you can, because there's nothing we can do for the people we cannot physically get to. He would link up with his contacts to talk people on [to where they could be extracted].

The thing was, as soon as you tried to put something like a friendly forces indicator out there, like telling them to turn an empty water bottle upside down in their right hand, as soon as you've done that a few times, everyone else would do that, so you had to keep on changing the identifier.

Other forms of ID included blue squares that represented 2 Para's DZ Flash, a unit identification worn on the right sleeve. Some were more inventive and designed to catch the attention of the Paras, such as a sign that read 'I HATE CRAPHATS', a derogatory term for any military member outside of the Parachute Regiment.

Aaron would mark himself with bright pieces of clothing discarded by the crowd, which he would tuck into his plate-carrier in a way that would only be obvious if you were looking for it.

'I'd say, "Look for me, but don't shout and wave. Just make eye contact with me. I've got a photo of you on my phone," and the reason we had to do that was because these people had been sitting in this canal for days, standing in the sewage for hours or days. They just want to get out, and the second they start seeing you pulling someone else out, it whips it up. We had to be very careful about it.

'And there were many we just couldn't get out. There were seventy women and their dependants [including MPs] that had been identified as vulnerable, and on the last day we managed to get thirty of them close to the gate, but the crowd was too violent and we just couldn't get to them. Separately, between Ed and myself we managed to get forty-three high-risk individuals out. I don't know if Ed was working with other networks as well, he probably helped far more people than I'll ever know.

'I wasn't the only person doing this,' said Nunkoosing, referring to his off the books work at the gates. 'There were people doing this all over the place. When you were sitting next to someone in the Ops Room, they were probably doing a similar thing, but neither of us wanted to tell each other, because we felt like we were going to get in trouble for it at some stage. Only because no one had told us to do it, so there was a bit of uncertainty.'

They helped them escape from hellish conditions in the crowd. Wikipedia's page for the Kabul airlift records that eleven Afghan civilians died in the crowds.[8] Aaron believes that the true number is far higher.

'Our doc, our padre, our regimental sergeant major, were dealing with the deceased where they could, and the Taliban would be conducting casevacs and moving bodies too. And our doc said [that] if we handled ten dead bodies, the Taliban probably handled ninety more, because of the crush injuries further back in the crowd that we couldn't see. I don't think we'll ever know the full number of how many Afghan civilians died.'

Ben Wallace saw the dangers of having British troops like Captain Nunkoosing pulled in different directions.

'Of course, a new part of modern warfare is there were guys from 2 Para, they're sitting there trying to do their day job. [They are getting] hundreds of emails into the inbox from mates, ex-serving, current serving … saying: "Yah, will you get Joe Bloggs out …" You need to try and separate the guys that do the day job from, unfortunately, the lobbying that will inevitably happen. My point is that it's a modern day challenge. It'll be interesting to see in the wash up. I think, fundamentally: leave the ops officer, leave the sergeant majors to get on and do their job. And somehow protect them from you and me … I think that's a challenge.'

It was a challenge that Jeff Phaneuf, a former USMC officer working on his own Digital Dunkirk, was well aware of.

'It was something I was cognisant of at the time. Obviously these guys were under incredible duress on a chaotic mission, and so the way that I approached it was that if one of my friends wasn't able to help, or didn't get back to me, I did not pester them. The friends that I talked to on the ground, though, when they said, "Hey, I've got some time, I've got some Marines, and I can get stuff done," then I would push: "Hey, can you get this group out." But I was cognisant of the fact at the time that they had a lot to deal with, and I never wanted to take them away from their main mission.

'At the same time, most of the feedback I got was really positive. Like, "Hey, getting people out, getting people to safety is what's keeping my Marines motivated." But there were plenty of times when they couldn't help, they were pretty blunt, and I think part of the reason that I was able to maintain the relationship with them, and continue asking them for help on this, was that I was mindful of the fact that if they said no, then they were doing it for a damn good reason. Plenty of people afterwards have tried to criticise those who were on the ground for not bringing in a certain bus, or not going out to get a certain group, but I think that's the wrong approach, because anyone who's served downrange knows that when the guy on the ground says I can't do X, Y, or Z, they're probably telling you that for a very good reason.'

The US effort

Digital Dunkirk was a multinational effort. Western soldiers from different countries shared contacts and stepped in to be the 'link' in the chain that could pull out a stranger and their family. They did so because of a sense of duty and honour.

Former USMC officer Jeff Phaneuf had served in Iraq as part of the counter ISIS campaign. At the time of the airlift, he was finishing graduate school on America's east coast, and preparing to move on to study at Stanford University, California.

'I got a call on August 19th from a friend who was on the ground, another Marine Corps officer. He basically laid out to me that the situation was far worse than we were seeing on the news. I could hear chaos and gunfire in the background.'

The friend asked Jeff for help in verifying people's documents.

'They gave me a list of six pieces of information.' If Jeff could get the information, and if the people could get to the gate, then his friends on the ground could try to get them into HKIA.

The US's equivalent programme to the ARAP was the Special Immigrant Visa (SIV).

'The SIV programme was created in 2009,' said Phaneuf, 'and the intent was for people who had worked as interpreters initially, and that expanded to other government contractors, to have a visa pathway to the United States. The programme has changed over the years. Initially there was an Iraq programme and two Afghan programmes. The legal expectation was that visas would be processed in no more than nine months. Right now, they're still being processed at more than twice that.

'I spent the last twelve days of August without really sleeping, and just constantly trying to run people into the gates. It started out with people that I had some relationship with, or that my friends knew, and quickly the word got out that I had direct access to the Marine Corps captain who was at the gate, who could make decisions on the ground. It proved that that relationship was even more valuable than knowing the commanding general, because that junior officer was able to make decisions on who got in on an immediate basis. Whereas you could have the president on the line, and the president couldn't have accomplished that in the same way that my friend did.

'My phone started ringing off the hook at that point,' Phaneuf said. 'I got calls from everything from state department officials to a colonel at the Pentagon to a group called Skatestan, which is a subsidiary of the Tony Hawk foundation, and they taught young girls to skateboard as a means of empowerment.'

Not all of the people that Jeff helped were SIV qualified. Some had refugee status, but were turned away and sent out of the gates they had just come through. The next day US troops were advised to take in such cases, which meant Jeff and others had to guide more than eighty people back through Kabul and through the gates on consecutive days. The effort paid off, and the group, which included the skateboarding girls, were evacuated, and just in time.

'It was only a few hours before the suicide bombing at Abbey Gate. They got brought through by the Marines who were manning the gate at the time.'

Jeff became wary of those who came to Kabul with camera crews.

'I look at it through mixed eyes. On the one hand, I think that people who were using their voice to genuinely draw attention to our mission, and to what we're still trying to accomplish now, still over a year later, can be very useful, but I think there were also a lot of people who did this to build their own personal profile, or to build out their own personal brand.

'I know certain military celebrities who were on the ground were very much in the way of the Marines and soldiers and sailors who were trying to get the job done. And I've heard from personal friends who had to tell some of these military influencers that they were in the way, that they were causing more problems than they were solving. And unfortunately I think some of those folks have continued to try and capitalise off of this, and they're even some of the same people willing to criticise the military leadership on the ground for decisions they had to make under incredible duress.'

For many, Digital Dunkirk ended with the last coalition flight, but Jeff continued the mission from home after the Marines had left.

The end of the airlift was signalled by the bombing at Abbey Gate. 'One of my friends lost nine Marines in the blast,' said Jeff Phaneuf:

Another friend was nearby and had a Marine who was severely wounded. As soon as that happened I knew that there wasn't going to be a whole lot more we could do in terms of the immediate evacuation, but I still had a lot of people on my list. I still had people calling me, begging for options, including, right after the blast, the family of an American citizen baby who wasn't able to get in the gate. And so we still kept working at the time. I contacted another Marine I knew who had a little bit more of a prominent position, and he made an effort right at the last minute to get through the gate right as they were about to engineer the gates shut. This was a separate gate, because Abbey Gate was closed at that point.

Once the US military fully withdrew, I was in the middle of a cross-country move. I had pushed back the move several days in order to keep working on this, then jumped in my jeep and drove from New Jersey to California, fielding phone calls all the way. For a few weeks there was a desperate attempt to figure out what the options were. At that point I started at Stanford, and I was spending more time on Afghanistan work than I was on school.

I was skipping class, or I was leaving in the middle of class because I got a phone call from somebody whose safe house had been raided by the Taliban. Because of that I realised I couldn't do both things well, and so I applied for this job I have with No One Left Behind. They were the non-profit who had been doing this the longest. It was a way I could do this full time and really focus on saving people's lives, and that's a whole lot more important than accounting class.

No One Left Behind is trying to evacuate people, help the people who get resettled in the US, and also advocate to the US government to fix this system and make sure this never happens again. My plan had been to go to business school and launch a business, but this was too important. Eventually I want to go back to school, but not until I do this work.

'No man left behind' is a sentiment drilled into soldiers, whether or not they knew the other soldier personally. For Major Tom

Schueman, however, things were incredibly personal. Tom had been trying since 2016 to bring his former interpreter into America.

'I paid the $1800 bribe to the clerk,' said Zainullah 'Zak' Zaki, who had been Schueman's interpreter in Sangin. 'We both acted like it was a normal part of applying for a passport.'[9] Despite the bribe, one of the family's passports did not arrive. 'I did not know if I was angriest at the usual corruption, the usual incompetence or the usual apathy. I knew it would not matter which got my family killed.'

When President Ghani left the country, Tom Schueman told Zak that it was time to go to the airport. 'By August 14th, I had failed Zak countless times. That I had not secured a visa for him felt like a personal failure I could not justify. Zak and I had been working on it for almost six years.'

Six years. Here was an interpreter who had stood shoulder-to-shoulder with Americans in some of the hardest fighting of the war, championed by a United States officer, and they were still not successful in their visa application in *six years*. It is a damning indictment of the American programme, SIV. Like ARAP, the idea was noble, but the execution was so poorly done that it left many at the mercy of the Taliban.

After contacting Marines he knew at HKIA, Tom told Zak to go to the airport. 'I thought about the implication of that. It was as if someone called me late at night and said, "Get Andrea, Amelia and Jack ready for someone none of you know to take you to [the airport]. Bring one bag each. Bring your passports and your social security cards. Forget your family pictures. Forget your kids' toys. Leave every item of your hard-won, middle-class existence behind. And, oh yeah, you can never go home again."'

Zak's driver decided it was too dangerous to take him to HKIA and so, in the middle of the night, and as the country fell apart, Zak and his young family walked the four miles to the airport. After discovering that they were at the wrong gate, Zak now had to walk his family another mile around one of the most dangerous flashpoints on earth.

The heat was baking hot, and the Marines that Tom was in contact with were no longer answering their phones, consumed by the chaos at the gates. After a hail of gunfire at Abbey Gate, Zak walked his family back to their apartment.

The power of social media now came into play. 'A former British Army contractor in Kabul saw Zak's story on my Instagram and reached out to me,' said Schueman. He was introduced to Milad, a local. 'This guy's got balls of steel,' said the British contractor, 'he's your guy to do all this.'

Now on the second attempt, Zak was able to get within talking distance of a Marine who was closing the gate. He sent a video to Tom, who heard a burst of gunfire, the sobbing of one of Zak's children, and then the video ended frozen on the child's terrified face.

'I never wanted to live anywhere but Kunar Province,' said Zak. 'I served my nation and the American mission in Helmand because I wanted to make Afghanistan a better place for my family to live, not because I wanted to leave.'

But to stay would be fatal, and now Zak and his family were on their third attempt to escape the Taliban in Kabul. Zak knew the stakes first-hand: 'The Taliban hung Najibullah [an acquaintance of Zak's] from a streetlight.'

Before making their third attempt at the airport, Zak knelt in prayer. 'Allah, the Most Merciful, if it is your will that I must die today, for my children to be safe, I will go happily. Please protect my family from the Taliban. Please get them to America.'

But to get there, Zak would again have to pass through Taliban checkpoints. 'I felt as if someone had gripped my heart in their fist.'

On the way to the airport, Zak saw streets deserted save for Taliban in trucks. 'I could not believe they were on the streets of Kabul ... I tried not to make eye contact with them. I did not know how they would respond. I felt like they would know me. Walking toward the Taliban, I realised that the dream of a free Afghanistan was dead ... I heard one shout in Pashto, "Why are you leaving, traitors?"'

Zak used his wits to get by the checkpoint. Realising that the Talib couldn't read what was on his SIV paperwork, Zak pointed to a family in the crowd and said that he and his family had come to see them off, but weren't leaving Kabul themselves. The Talib bought the lie, and waved them through.

After moving through the crowd, and with communication via Tom, Zak and his family were spotted by a Marine officer. Throwing bottles of water to distract the crowd, the US personnel opened a gate so that they could pull Zak and his family through.

'A man shouted at me in Pashto, his face crushed against the bars, "Help us, brother! Take my children with you!"'

Tom's contact, Major Jared Lefaivre, stayed with Zak's family until they were put on a plane. It was a promise upheld by Tom Schueman, made possible with connections on the ground. SIV had failed, but the Marines had not. In rescuing their brother Zak they had lived up to the motto of the Marine Corps, *Semper Fidelis*.

Always faithful.

Promises kept

'I mean, it's an amazing story, really,' Johnny Mercer said of the effort made by veterans. 'I think we genuinely sort of understood the debt that we owed these guys. So if you think of yourself as a young Afghan, you have to make a conscious decision to step across that line, and be part of the future of Afghanistan. And that's obviously a big deal in Afghanistan. I think we're kind of quick to throw that away in the UK. And we're quick to forget that. And I think for veterans and others who've actually been there, you don't forget it. And it's much more real, it's much more authentic, and that authenticity ultimately has a cost to it, which is that you will keep working until you've done everything you possibly can to get these people to safety.

'It was literally just all done on WhatsApp. Well, you save a lot of lives. But I mean, if you're going to do a proper NEO after twenty years of war and rely on a phone, I'd be a bit pissed off. For veterans, Afghanistan was a big part of our lives . . . it was hard to come home and feel like a country that was busy getting pissed at Glastonbury . . . and you're away scrapping . . . it just feels kind of dislocated. You can feel quite lonely at times that you care about a country [that's] quite a long way away, and it's quite hard to tie a link between that and UK security.

'What it did show was, actually, Afghanistan was a very formative experience for a whole generation of us. And people got it. Even though the institutions may try and leave these people behind, with the kind of human character and spirit of a generation of veterans who fought there, [they were] not going to just allow that to take place. And I think that's important, and I think is important for us as a nation, what it speaks about us, but also, how the generations are changing, and how we look after these people.'

Digital Dunkirk should never have been necessary. It existed because government programmes had failed, but into this void stepped soldiers and veterans and civilians who knew that they owed the Afghan people their time, and effort. They were not always successful, but thanks to the actions of those on the ground, they were able to contribute to something that was bigger than themselves.

'I'm not really proud of what I did on tour,' said one Afghanistan veteran, 'but I'm incredibly proud of what veterans did during the airlift. There are many who continue to do it on behalf of our allies. That partnership meant something to us, and still does. My only regret is that we didn't start sooner.'

For Mike Pratt, the war in Afghanistan had never made sense as a soldier. It was only when he visited Kabul in his civilian role that the positives of the war were made clear. 'Kabul was a different world to Helmand. When I was crawling in ditches dodging bullets I couldn't see what the point was, but when I first visited Kabul, it all made sense. It felt like another world. You could feel the optimism.' Though that optimism may have fled Kabul, there was still a chance to give thousands of Afghan allies a new life in the West. This was what drove men like Mike.

'We will remember them' is the statement repeated at Remembrance services to honour and remember Britain's war dead. In the summer of 2021, the same statement applied to Britain's allies and civilians in Afghanistan. Like much of the events of that summer, it was an attempt to avert individual tragedies in a sea of chaos, but much was done with little more than personal connections and will power. Though no longer in uniform, and for some who had never worn one, a sense of duty and compassion dictated that, although the war may be lost, this was not a time to grieve, but a time for action. It was a unique moment in military history, and one for which the participants should be justly proud.

It is a fight as yet unfinished.

9

Running the Gauntlet

Who dares wins.
— Motto of the Special Air Service

Amongst those attempting to escape Kabul were those who had served in Afghanistan's police or military. With the collapse of the Afghan government, those who had served were now de-facto civilians, but civilians who found themselves at greater risk because of their former employment. This was also true for their families, including children. Though they had never worn a uniform themselves, they were in danger of paying for what the Taliban considered the sins of their parents.

Amongst those most at risk were those who had served in Afghanistan's special forces. Fighting alongside their Western counterparts, these units had taken the war to the Taliban in all parts of the country, targeting Taliban leadership. As such, they held out little hope of mercy. In the summer of 2021, a video surfaced that purported to show twenty-two Afghan commandos being executed by the Taliban when they tried to surrender.[1] A Taliban spokesperson dismissed the video, claiming that it had been spliced from several videos,[2] but a number of witnesses corroborated the events.

Many Afghan commandos were in no doubt that their lives were in danger. One of them was Mohammad Dawood, who had served as an officer with Task Force 333, an Afghan special forces unit that operated in all thirty-four of the country's provinces.

'I joined because I wanted to serve my country,' he said.

As the Taliban were advancing in the summer of 2021, 'we were trying to do our work, but then the provincial centre of Logar was taken by the Taliban. We thought that we needed to go to Kabul to support there, but when we arrived President Ghani ran away. Everyone ran. Everything was gone. The Taliban came and took our weapons and sent us away.'

Mohammad went into hiding with his cousins, moving from place to place to remain out of reach of reprisals. 'At night I didn't sleep. I would be watching the door. I knew the Taliban would behead me. Any noise would wake me up. I slept maybe three hours a day during daylight. The Taliban trapped everyone. No one who was special forces wanted to give them their details. The Taliban were trying to find them and not let them into the airport. They hated the special forces. The Taliban were all over the streets. No one knew what was happening.'

In hiding with Mohammad were his wife and five children. 'If the Taliban found my family, they would try and kill them. They don't allow school, and there were no jobs. For six months [after the fall of Kabul] we were hiding every day.'

Mohammad applied to the ARAP scheme, but found it slow. He decided against trying the airport. He didn't have the ARAP approval, and the Taliban were checking the crowds for people who had served with the special forces. 'For months there was no notifications or emails from ARAP.'

During that time the Taliban would launch special operations in Kabul. Mohammad avoided them at all costs, wearing a mask if he ever needed to be in public.

'It was bad luck the Taliban took over. In a wink our country went back twenty years. Everyone knows that the Taliban are cruel and don't allow independent lives. Everything was gone in a minute. It was very sad. Everyone was running.'

Basira Asghari had grown up in Afghanistan's Ghazni Province before moving to a dormitory in Kabul to study. Even with the progress in the country, it was a difficult situation for her.

'I was a very proud girl. I was always pretending to be very happy. My problems were increasing day by day, and this affected me more and more. I had reached the situation that I was away from everyone.'

Basira struggled to find happiness and fulfilment in Kabul, compounded by financial struggles after she had helped to pay for a nephew's education.

'I had no money to pay, I couldn't find a job in Afghanistan. You had to have intermediaries, be from a certain tribe, or pay bribes. Finally, I decided to become a policeman so that I could do my job and help my family so that my brother and sister could study like me.'

But nepotism stood in Basira's way, as did systemic misogyny.

'Women are the most worthless creature in Afghanistan,' she said. 'Women are known as sex slaves, and if a woman works in any office or place, all men want to take advantage of her, and force them to do whatever they want, because all men in Afghanistan see women as sex slaves, especially the woman who was in the army. I was tired for all of the poor people of Afghanistan. The situation in Afghanistan was exhausting and [full of] suffering, but nevertheless I love Afghanistan with all my life, I worship it with all my life.'

This love manifested in a desire to serve, but Basira knew that it would be a struggle.

'I always said to myself, I will fight until I am [no longer] alive, and I will prove to these men that there are girls and women who are not prostitutes and sex slaves, who come to the army like you, either [from] love, or from compulsion.'

After selection and training, Basira became a police officer, and was assigned to a unit at the forefront of the fight against the Taliban.

'In Kandahar province, I started my career as an ACC member at ATF 444, [which] was formed by the British army, and had been under the administration of the Afghan Interior Ministry after 2014. I was appointed deputy commander of ATF 444 after a few months, until the war in Afghanistan intensified so much that even in one day a few provinces of Afghanistan were falling. The districts of Kandahar province all collapsed, and the fighting inside the city deteriorated, and every day we had several martyrs [troops killed in action] and wounded.'

In other provinces, women working in special units had been sent home to stop them from falling into the Taliban's hands. Basira was in no doubt about what her fate would be in such circumstances.

'They raped you and dismembered you.'

Despite these horrors, Basira remained optimistic about her country's hopes. 'We never thought Afghanistan would fall completely. On the other hand, we heard every day that the Taliban raped women and girls. They brutally murdered them, even sent them to Pakistan to buy and sell.'

When Kandahar fell to the Taliban, Basira and other female officers barricaded themselves inside their dorm, and spent a sleepless night wondering what would become of them.

'I said [to my male colleagues], "If you don't stay, at least let us get out and do something ourselves. It's no use sitting here, we can't be here anymore." Then the deputy of the operation found a person whose house was near the square and his family was going to his friends' house in the city. We rented a taxi for 15,000 Afghanis to transport us to Kabul on the way.'

It was a journey full of dangers.

'Everywhere the Taliban were trying and asking where we came from,' said Basira. 'It was 12:00 p.m. when we arrived in Maidan Shahr, close to Kabul, where fighting was going on, and we didn't want to enter Kabul. We spent the night in a car, until the morning, and the war calmed down a little bit. The same day that coincided with August 15th 2021, the Taliban entered Kabul, and Kabul fell, and everywhere it was too terrible and disappointing, the sound of gunfire was heard, the sound of the planes travelling all over the sky in Kabul, people were all on the run and I was like a soulless living person.'

Every sound that Basira heard made her think that the Taliban had found her. It was with relief that she then heard from colleagues about the ARAP programme, and British efforts to evacuate members of 444. Like tens of thousands of her fellow citizens, Basira made for HKIA.

'A few days passed and I had to go to the airport to save my life. There was a very terrible situation, people were [trampled] under the crowd, children were dying, the Taliban beat men and women and shot straight at them. That's the day there was a strong explosion at the airport that left many dead and wounded. I returned home in fear until the airport finally closed completely on August 30th. I couldn't save myself.'

Basira reached out to a former commander for help. While people across the world were helping to evacuate strangers simply because it was the right thing to do, Basira's former officer tried to leverage her situation for his own deplorable benefit.

'He said [there were] two ways [I could pay him]: [have] a relationship with me or give me money. I told him I would pay. I didn't have any money with me. There was a little bit of money in the bank [but] the banks were closed. All our colleagues who were men refused to answer and asked me for a bad job [sexual reward].'

Basira's manager had already been evacuated to the UK. She asked him for help.

'I messaged him, and he replied, "I tried very hard to have a relationship with you on duty, but I couldn't convince you, and you didn't care about me."'

She refused to give in to his exploitative demands. 'He threatened me and said, "If you deceive me, I can beat you to the ground and take you to heaven."'

The situation looked more dire when a Helmandi Taliban took up residence in the house opposite to where Basira was hiding with other would-be evacuees, but Basira didn't give up, using social media and the internet to eventually make contact with a British woman named Pam French, a charity worker at Gulab Sork Foundation.

'If it wasn't for her help and cooperation, we would never have saved our lives,' said Basira. 'We settled in Islamabad, Pakistan, for eight months at the Ramada Hotel, where the British government had provided us with many facilities, but we spent all night and day with fear and worry that they would send us back to Afghanistan, and on the other hand we were worried about our old parents being left alone there.'

With perseverance, courage and the aid of strangers, Basira and her family were eventually evacuated to the UK via Pakistan.

It was not only those who had served in uniform against the Taliban who were in danger. As a woman who had worked at the British embassy, Huria was in danger of Taliban retribution, and certainly of an oppressed future. With the encouragement of British friends, she made the dangerous journey to HKIA, and was soon faced with the reality of the situation:

That was when I really started to feel scared, when I saw the dead bodies. My husband said, 'You are going to kill yourself, myself and our baby. Do you know that you're making a very big mistake?' I said, well, we have to die just once rather than all of our life. They actually moved seven dead bodies from in front of our eyes. My daughter was just looking. They put white blankets on the dead bodies ... my daughter said, 'Mommy, what are they?' And most of these people I could see that on the blankets there was blood. Marks of blood. I couldn't close my eyes. I had to see them.

I saw those seven dead bodies, but then I said to myself that you have to be strong. You need to remember what your mother said. You have to be strong. And when my daughter asked me, 'Mommy, what's happening? Why are they firing? Why are they shouting?' I said, 'Baby, they are playing.' And when she was asking what are they moving, I was saying they are carrying something, it's nothing, you don't have to look at that. Inside I was so scared, but still I was showing a smile to my daughter to give her the energy that we are not at risk. However, I knew that she could be killed. I could be killed.

That was the moment I felt that maybe I can be one of these people. They were killed last night ... My daughter can be one of these people. My husband can be one of these people. But still

I closed my eyes and I just lifted myself and my family to God and I said God is there and he is going to help us from here. You have to be brave.

I text my British friends and I said to them, 'I'm at the first checkpoint and I can see the dead bodies. What should I do? We can be killed.' And then he replied back to me and said, 'This is the only way, you have to make it, otherwise you will be left in Afghanistan. You have made it. You have entered the first checkpoint, so you can make it to the other ones. Be brave. You can make it, and share with me your location. Take pictures if you can, so that we can see how we can help you. How we can send someone to help you. But right now you are so far we can't help you there. You need to come as close to the barriers so as we can see you and do something for you.'

Huria listened, and persevered:

It took us the whole day to make it to the second checkpoint. The Taliban put their cars there to block. Their cars were like barriers. They were not letting people go to the other side. And one of them started to turn on his car and move it, that was the time that I held my daughter tightly and there was a tiny space in front of the car. I moved inside that. The guy was angry and he wanted to push me back on the wall and I screamed and I said, 'Don't do that, I have a baby' and he stopped it. My husband was left behind and I cried and my daughter screamed for Papa. She called her father and I said, 'Stop, you are going to kill my daughter. Stop, I have a baby.'

And that was when he stopped and he said, 'Have you lost your mind? Don't you know that you are not allowed to move to the other part?' I said now I have made it, if you want to kill me, kill me. And I have no one to help me with my daughter. I have no man with me. Let my husband cross that checkpoint and come here with me. He was so angry at me, but he couldn't do anything to me, because I was a woman and my child was crying and everyone was looking at me. The moment when I crossed this checkpoint, other women with children dared to cross.

My husband wanted to come to this side. He fell down. He lost his glasses. Because so many people rushed after I found that place, I lost my husband. That was the moment that I lost my husband. He came back to me and I couldn't recognise him. I said what happened to your face? He said, 'I fell down and so many people were walking on me.'

Despite making it to the second checkpoint, Huria and her family were still far from safety:

By now it was dark. That place was quite stinky. There was so many other people. They wanted to get to these checkpoints and the airport. I started to feel that my daughter has got fever. When I touched her, she started to have a fever. When I was giving her food, she was not having an appetite and was saying, 'Mommy, I'm cold. Mommy, I'm shivering. Mommy, why don't we go back home? What's happening?' She was also scared. She was holding me very tightly.

It was eight at night and my husband said that you can see the containers. You can see so many people are lying down, they are sleeping. I'm not allowing you to go there. It's quite dark and anything is possible to happen. I said, 'The moment when the gate is open, the moment when the British soldiers are on the top of the containers, I have to make it close to those containers.

That's what my British friend told me to do, and if we don't go there, they can't help us here. We are still far from there.'

My husband said, 'I'm not going. If you want to go, go, I just want to go back home.' But I said, 'Well, this is the time you need to decide. If you don't want to go with us, don't go with us, but I am going with my daughter and I have made my decision.' So he said, 'Go, if you can, go, but I'm not going.'

So what happened, it was quite dark among that big crowd of people, but I went there, and one of the Taliban stopped me and said, 'Where are you going, people are sleeping there. There is no space.' I said, 'You don't talk to me. You don't have the right to touch me.' He said, 'Stop.' He just wanted to stop me. I said, 'You can't touch me. I'm going.'

They said, 'Who is your husband? Who are you with?' I said, 'My husband is sitting there and he's scared of you guys, because you're going to kill him. You're going to beat him.' They said, 'We will not do that, but he has to be with you. The gate is not opening for you and you can't make it to that place, you know that. If you think you can go, go, if you think you can find a place,' and I said, 'I'll just go over there,' and he was angry at me.

At that time I was scared and I was thinking they are going to shoot my husband. And they are coming back and they are going to shoot me. But what happened, and I really don't know how this guy was feeling, what made him go to my husband, hold his hand and just bring him to me. He brought my husband there and I looked at him and said, 'Thank you.' He said that it's fine, but stay with him. I really couldn't believe it and he was speaking Persian, he wasn't speaking Pashto, and so I was happy we could understand his language and he could understand mine.

He said, 'If these people see you, they will get you back to sit

there, so if you want to move there move as quickly as possible.'
And I told my husband we have to go there. There was so many
people. Sleeping, and sitting. They were saying, 'Why are you
coming here?' They were saying, 'Oh, you hurt my finger. Oh,
you hurt my feet. Watch out where you are walking.'

Still, I could make it. I could find a very small space. I told my
husband, 'Sit here.' I put my bag down and told my husband to
sit on my bag. There was no space, I had to stand up. I told my
husband, 'Hold my baby.' There was a guy who was sitting and
he said you can sit and I can stand up. He wanted to go to
America. He was a translator. He was a nice guy. There was also
a woman who had a Canadian passport and she wanted to go to
Canada. There was so many people just like us.

Hope lay on the other side of the gate. Huria was close, but time
was running out:

I spoke with my British friends and I said, 'My daughter is dying.
You told me to make it to the third checkpoint close to the
barriers and you told me that you will send the British soldiers
to help us.' One of them wrote back to me and said, 'Sorry, until
the next morning there is going to be no flight and you have to
wait until six in the morning.'

That was the time I went mad and started to regret speaking
to him. I said, 'You guys always said that you are responsible for
our safety and you will do anything to save us. Where is that
promise? There is an ISIS threat, that's why you're scared you
can't come on this side, but at the same time you want to keep
me here? I understand if there's no flight, at least you have to
take us outside this place to a safer place, no matter if it takes me
three or four days, at least I can stay outside of this place. This

place is not safe for me and my family and my daughter is dying.'

I said, 'My mobile battery is low and I may not be able to chat with you further.' He said, 'We are going to do something for you, have patience, we are doing our best.' And then he said, 'Can you stand up and wave your hands? I'm sending someone to see you. Can you see someone in a blue dress?' It was almost ten thirty p.m. and I can see no one. 'Stand up and wave your hands.' I didn't know that he was using the cameras to spot me. I stood up and couldn't see anyone. But when I turned my face, I saw a big camera with a red light and that was the moment the camera stopped at me, and that was the time I waved my hand, and the Taliban looked at me, took his gun, and shot the camera.

Huria and her husband worried that they would become the Taliban's next target:

My husband dragged me down and said, 'Sit down, they're going to kill you.' [The Taliban] couldn't find me in that crowd of people. I was hidden. I turned my back and everyone was saying, 'Do you want to be killed?' My British friends understood that they shot the camera and knew I was really at risk. That was the time they said, 'In ten to fifteen minutes, the guy is going to be there and he will help you.' My battery is going to be dead. I turned off my mobile, because I had one or two per cent left.

Fifteen minutes is gone and no one has come to help us. When I turned on my mobile again, I got a message that he is on the way and he is talking to the Taliban to see how they can help you. My mobile was dead and couldn't communicate further. I said to my husband, 'There is no one and if no one comes in another fifteen minutes, I promise I will leave with you back to home.' My husband says, 'It's not easy to cross the three checkpoints and go back.' I said maybe we can ask a Talib to help us, and he said, 'They can't do that. If they thought you worked with the UK embassy, they will kill the three of us.' We had no choice, but we were still thinking of returning to home, and that was the moment I heard [someone calling my name].

Huria took her chance:

If they want to kill us they will only kill me and I'm taking this risk. And I stood up and I said that I am Huria. The Taliban were calling, 'Huria, Huria, who's Huria?' and I said, 'I am Huria.' I was so scared, my heart was beating very quickly. The Taliban said to me, 'You are three, you are a family of three. Come here.' I said, 'What is wrong, why should I come there?' He said, 'You want to go to England. Your translator is here.'

The other Taliban guys, they were angry. I could hear they were whispering something, but at the same time I could hear the British soldiers. There was a narrow path and I could hear the Taliban say to the translator, 'You cannot come this way, you can only tell us their name and how many people they are.'

I could hear the British soldiers saying, 'Tell them you need Huria and her kid. Tell them.' And they were very angry at these Taliban guys. That was the time when I got some energy and I thought, they are standing there for me. Even if they shoot me, the British soldiers are going to shoot them back. I said to my husband, 'Come with me, we have the British soldiers.' The Taliban guy was looking at us very angrily. What happened was they were just looking at us and we were walking very close to the translator and to the British soldiers. The translator covered me and my husband. He said, 'Come with me, you are safe. There's nothing going to happen.'

I could see the British soldiers pointing their guns at the Taliban. They didn't want them to shoot us. The moment I crossed this narrow path and reached the British soldiers, those brave British soldiers, I burst into tears and started to cry. Started to scream. My daughter was also screaming and I took a deep breath and he said, 'Now I feel like I can breathe.' The British soldier put [his] hand around my shoulder and he said, 'You are safe now, Huria. You don't have to worry. We are here for you.'

Thanks to them, and I was still crying, and the Taliban guy could still see me. And he was saying, 'Shame on you. He's putting his hand on your shoulder. And you are not saying anything. Shame on you. You are leaving your country. Shame on you.'

I looked at him and I couldn't say anything. I had so many things to say back to him, but I didn't feel safe. The British soldier said, 'Huria, you don't have to say anything back. Let's move you from here.'

The British soldiers took us to a safer place. They brought us water. They brought us diapers for my daughter. They brought us biscuits. And we spent the whole night in the Baron. There was a parking place for cars and that was the only space we had to spend the night. The British brought blankets for old people and people with small children. I shared a blanket with two old people. It was so cold, but all I could do was cover my daughter. There was a toilet. I washed my face and my daughter's face and hands. There was other Afghan families. I asked them for paracetamol and antibacterials. A family helped me, and then my daughter fell asleep. The whole night she was sleeping on my lap.

It was a night spent in discomfort, but relative safety:

It was five o'clock in the morning when the British came and checked our passports. Everything. It took us until two o'clock, and then at two o'clock another call came. And they put us inside a car.

It moved us inside the Kabul airport. When I reached there, it was around two thirty and I saw the military plane and it was making a lot of noise. The back of it was open and they were carrying a big car inside it. I said, 'What's happening, why are we brought here?' And then the British guy said that we are going to take you to Dubai, and from Dubai you will have a comfortable plane to take you directly to England.

When I got on the plane, the car was chained in front of my face. The sound was horrible inside the plane. It took us about two hours to reach Dubai. We had about three hours inside Dubai airport, and there we could change our clothes and have a little bit of food. We got inside the other plane and then we made it to England.

Thanks to Huria's courage and determination, her British friends had been able to honour their promise. Huria's family was tired, but alive.

Such tragedy and drama was unfolding at every gate, at every minute. Not everyone was saved. None escaped without an ordeal, whether that was their own, or as witness to the distress of others.

Three lions

The WhatsApp War extended much further than the military and Foreign Office. Civilians volunteered their time and experience, and as Kabul fell, a trio of British women found the lives of a girl's football team in their hands. There were many similar stories, but this one is particularly deserving of a mention.

'The football pitch was our safe zone,' said Khalida Popal, a former local football club player in Afghanistan. 'We were not thinking about the challenges, but thinking about the moment, because football is all about the moment.'[3]

Under a Taliban regime, the future of female players was bleak. Not only would sport be banned under the Taliban, but there was a very real threat to the women's lives.

'We had a few occasions where some of our players' houses were burned down,'[4] Popal told Sky News.

The Afghan national team had been rescued, but regional teams were left behind. The rescue of these women and their families would become a complicated web involving strangers, determination and luck.

Siu-Anne Marie Gill was a British woman and CEO of the RoKit Foundation, a charity organisation 'identifying, engaging, and supporting changemakers who are creating a better world'.

'Two weeks before Kabul fell,' recalled Siu-Anne, 'I got called by Jonathan, the chairman of RoKit, and he said, "Siu-Anne, let's sponsor those girls and get them out, whatever it takes." I had some contacts and I had an idea. We were going to sponsor the girls, give them some money. But first I needed to get some help from a mediator. That's how I found Laura.'

'I worked in the humanitarian field for years in all kinds of conflict zones,' said Laura, who had first-hand experience of

Afghanistan. 'We had been working in Afghanistan for three years. We supported President Ghani as peace advisors in trying to help navigate the Taliban talks. It was hugely challenging. We were deeply involved right until the moment Ghani got on a plane, not that we knew he was going to do that. We'd spoken to him very shortly beforehand and we were definitely given to understand that he was staying. When he did take off, it was clear that [the government] was going to collapse.

'Around that time I got a phone call. It was a Saturday, August the twenty-first. I was at home with my daughter. It was just your average Saturday. I got a phone call from one of the people on our board and she said, "Look, I wonder if you might be able to help. There is a woman who I know and she has twenty young women and girls, female footballers, on a bus in Kabul and they're headed to the Pakistani border. They've got visas for Pakistan, but they need security. How can they get over the border safely?" And I remember thinking at the time, this sounds like a really terrible idea.'

Laura agreed to speak with the board member's friend, Siu-Anne.

'We had a conversation and what I anticipated, I think, was that I'd spend an afternoon making a few phone calls, trying to see if there was anybody who could provide them with security on the ground. I didn't expect it to turn into four to five months of the most unbelievable, heart-wrenching stress. Of feeling like lives might depend on what we were, or weren't, able to do. Feeling like people's entire futures could hang on whether we could keep promises that we had implicitly made to them by asking them to put their trust in us. And it was just . . . I honestly don't know if I would have had the guts to take it on if I'd known what it was going to be, because I'm not an extraction expert at all, but it felt like at no point could you just turn around to these people and say actually this is all too much.'

Siu-Anne, Laura, and later Emily would go on to enable the evacuation of more than a hundred Afghans. What had started as a call to sponsor a team turned into a mission to save their lives.

'Sponsoring us doesn't help us,' one of the players told Siu-Anne. 'Right now we've got twenty girls and you are our only way out.'

'I need to get these girls out on a plane,' Siu-Anne had told Laura.

'I called a friend of mine who I knew was trying to get people scheduled on the Qatari flights,' said Laura. It was during the final throes of the fall:

The first thing my friend in Qatar asked me was, 'Do they have visas?' Blithely I assured her that they did, because that's what I'd been told, but it turned out that they did not have visas, and that was an entertaining phone call to have to make a few days later, once I asked for written proof of the visas to send to Qatar. So then there was a scramble to provide them with visas. To find some assurance that they would be allowed to stay in Pakistan. Meanwhile they did get listed on this flight, thanks to the incredible work of this woman who had been doing sterling work getting people listed on these planes, and they were picked up by the government of Qatar, and driven in a bus into the airport.

It was chaos, and we ended up missing a manifest, and I will never quite get over that. I kept asking for names, and the names were not coming, and eventually I came to realise that the person who was supposed to be sending names was the former captain of the women's national squad. She was a great part in organising this rescue. She'd managed to get the national team out and she was managing multiple lists with multiple extraction partners, and the extraction partners were people with money who could facilitate people getting out.

I didn't have money, but what I had was contacts and knowledge of how the system worked on the ground. Siu-Anne was representing the organisation with the money. As far as I was concerned, the challenge was to try and persuade Qatar that they were a good humanitarian cause and they deserved to be listed.

'The situation was these football girls were totally stuck,' said Siu-Anne. 'They were in all sorts of places. Because the Herat region was the most vilified by the Taliban, they were the most at risk.'

One of the women in Herat was a doctor called Parmilla:

I was the team doctor to the Herat football team. I spoke with Laura. I said that honestly, I'm not a footballer. I played football for five months. I'm a basketball player and I'm a doctor. I'm a gynaecologist. I said what was the truth. She said, 'I'm really sorry, we can't do that. I wish I could do something for you.'

I said that our life is in danger. And we can't have a normal life here. My dad was a colonel. He worked for the army in Afghanistan. If they find out what his job was, they will kill him. It was the biggest problem. My dad worked in districts that were all Taliban. My dad sent my brother to Germany eight years ago. They killed eight of my dad's colleagues.

After two or three days, Laura spoke with Siu-Anne and she said OK, because they are human, we don't care just about football players. It was my aim that one day I could see Siu-Anne just so I could say thank you. It was my biggest mission. My children were twins. They were two and three years old, and they didn't have passports. They said I should leave my children and later they can arrange for them. I spoke with my husband and he said, 'No, you can't leave [the] children here.' So after one week I spoke to Laura and she said, 'You should go to Kabul and we will find someone there to get passports for your children.'

My husband was in Kabul and I was in Herat city. We lived in secret places because we left our houses. All places were full of dead people. You could hear shooting. We didn't know what to do, so we asked for family to provide for us. We didn't get to say goodbye. My dad said they shouldn't kill all of us together, so we were in separate places.

Laura recalled her first conversation on the phone with Parmilla. 'She told me that she'd studied so hard for her medical exams that she miscarried. And that being a doctor was all that she ever wanted, but that she'd gone to the hospital to work that day and they'd sent her home and said don't come out. I talked to this woman every day on the phone. Given all of that, how do you step out?'

It was a heavy burden to carry. 'Your number gets around,' said Laura. 'You'd get the most heart-wrenching messages. Some of them were from mothers who would weep down the phone and they would say to me, "What am I going to tell my daughter? How will she grow up here?" They were desperate. Desperate. I was reading all these messages, and I just started crying on the train, and my daughter was with me, and she said, "What is it?" She wrote me a note and she said, "It's alright, Mummy. You'll get these ladies out and they'll all be fine."'

Abbey Gate and the Baron Hotel, Hamid Karzai International Airport. An artist's impression of the chaos from above.

In the last days of the evacuation, troops slept for only a few hours during chaos. Exhausted UK and US soldiers worked side by side.

The UK evacuated over 15,000 people from Kabul in two weeks. Soldiers had to ensure people had the correct paperwork or they would be turned away.

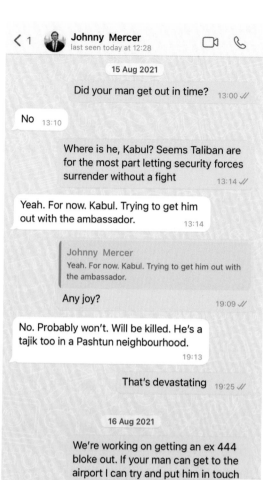

Johnny Mercer
last seen today at 12:28

15 Aug 2021

Did your man get out in time? 13:00

No 13:10

Where is he, Kabul? Seems Taliban are for the most part letting security forces surrender without a fight 13:14

Yeah. For now. Kabul. Trying to get him out with the ambassador. 13:14

> Johnny Mercer
> Yeah. For now. Kabul. Trying to get him out with the ambassador.

Any joy? 19:09

No. Probably won't. Will be killed. He's a tajik too in a Pashtun neighbourhood. 19:13

That's devastating 19:25

16 Aug 2021

We're working on getting an ex 444 bloke out. If your man can get to the airport I can try and put him in touch with the 2 PARA OC on the ground 20:4...

I want you to create a sign that will attract the attention of Paratroopers when you are close.
I will tell you what to write now 19:28

Ok 19:28

Big and bold 19:28

Not that ... message to follow 19:29

OK 19:30

I HATE CRAPHATS 19:30

> You
> I HATE
> CRAPHATS

Should I write this ?? 19:30

Many veterans in the UK helped their former Afghan allies escape in what became known as the 'WhatsApp War'. They helped coordinate with soldiers at the airport gates who would look out for Afghans holding signs and shouting codewords to let them into the airport.

A sewage canal by Abbey Gate that flanked the Baron Hotel was the
scene of mass slaughter when the ISIS bomb went off.

Anthony Tuitt and his team of UN security consultants stayed in Kabul after the fall and worked with the Taliban on a daily basis.

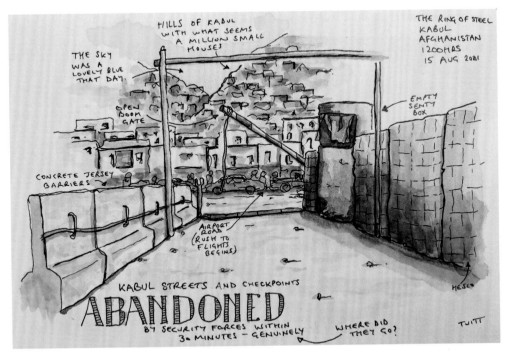

Tuitt's sketch of an abandoned Afghan security checkpoint.

In the chaos, soldiers were also confronted with lost or abandoned children, some of whom had been passed over the fence by their parents in an effort to save them. In some cases, babies were thrown over barbed wire to troops.

A carry team moves a transfer case containing the remains of Marine Corps Lance Cpl. Jared M. Schmitz, who died aged twenty in an attack at Kabul airport along with twelve other US service members.

Scenes of humanity among the horror ... A US Marine calms an infant who has been separated from its parents. Sgt. Nicole Leeann Gee posted this photo on Instagram, captioned 'I love my job'. Just six days later she was killed in the suicide bombing outside Kabul's airport.

Hundreds of Afghans were squeezed into each plane. For a time during the final days, flights were said to be taking off every twenty minutes from Kabul airport. Nearly 40 per cent of all evacuees were moved out via Qatar.

Children, parents and grandparents were among those waiting many days for processing. Many were left behind and faced severe risk from the Taliban. More than a year later, the UK's relocation scheme is still overwhelmed. 'We've got a hundred thousand applicants at the moment,' said Ben Wallace MP in the autumn of 2022.

The last US plane left Kabul on 30 August 2021, hours ahead of the US deadline to complete the chaotic withdrawal, bringing an end to a twenty-year campaign.

The trio of Brits worked diligently, writing letters and making calls to anyone who may be able to aid them with the evacuation of the at-risk women and their families. 'I rang up the FIFA people to help me,' said Siu-Anne. 'They said no, you're on your own, fuck off. When FIFA heard I was getting people out on a plane, they said, "You know we were a bit rude to you, but do you think you can take four of our people?"'

'Laura has been amazing,' said Siu-Anne. 'None of this would have moved without me insisting. I had to put my name on the line. If I fucked up [I'd be getting fired]. That sounds really harsh, but we were under so much stress by this point, it was very much like, do not bring any disrepute on our company.'

It was money that got things moving.

'We had a blank cheque,' said Siu-Anne. 'That was the only way to be sure to get these girls through.'

Siu-Anne and Laura advised Parmilla to move to Kabul.

'I travelled by airplane with fake identification and bribes,' Parmilla recalled. 'When we arrived at Kabul, we didn't know we were going to travel to Pakistan on the same day. It was too difficult for us. I couldn't see my dad in that time. I didn't say goodbye. We didn't have money. I called my brother in Germany. He and his friend sent some money for us. We took a taxi to the Pakistan border, but the border was closed. We didn't know what to do.'

'We had two flights that got missed,' said Siu-Anne. 'There was a crossover with another group, and these girls put their names on both lists, and when it came to a US list, they jumped on it. At one point we only had five people left to go on the flight. My first reaction was five people's lives are better than no lives, but Laura said, "I can't do that, the Qataris won't clear the flight."'

'I was getting videos of girls driving up to Kabul through this absolute chaos, arriving as the flight was taking off,' said Laura. 'So we did miss flights.'

These drives took place over many days on awful roads. The Kandahar highway was blocked with checkpoints.

'We did eventually list them, and we did eventually get them manifested, and we did eventually get them on the bus. About one o'clock in the morning, I got a phone call from one of the girls, saying that they had been forced off the bus. The bus had been stopped and they'd been forced off by the driver. They got word saying that they couldn't go to the airport. I think what the Qataris had got wind of was the attack that was about to happen, because we'd been hearing chatter that there was going to be an attack. The girls, luckily, did not get to the gate. They were left in Kabul. Then there was the ISIS attack.'

It was an attack that claimed the lives of as many as 170 civilians, and thirteen US troops.

'The airport was effectively closed at that point,' said Laura. 'If I could have got them on a plane, I would have. Then there was an agonising decision process of, how long do you keep them in Kabul? It's not safe, but if we tell them to go home, how can we ever get them back again? It was not clear when the airport would reopen. It was not clear if the Qataris were going to be able to list them. Then the challenge with the visas came up again. The Americans finally left and it was clear that [the] route of extraction was over. From then on it was going to be a much slower, much more Taliban dependent process. It wasn't clear to me what the best route was.'

'I feel instinctively I can do this,' said Siu-Anne. 'We have all the ingredients on our side. We just need time on our side. I was in touch with the team captain. I was left with five people willing to get on the plane, and the five girls were absolutely frantic. You can imagine the stress on me. We're going to have to go the hard choice, which is to go the overland route. I've never dealt with extractions, or that world. I took what my mum and my grandma said and I said, "We just go." We can do this if we have a team. It's not going to happen without a team. And I said we have the biggest thing on our side, which is a bunch of girls who are willing to give their lives to come over here, and we have the finance, and that was the key point.'

Laura looked into private companies for the extraction, some of whom were charging $65,000 per family to drop them into Eastern European countries. She described the evacuation situation as 'a black comedy'.

'Then there was the Hasidic rabbis,' said Laura. 'My understanding was this. There were these two remaining rabbis in Afghanistan. One of them died and the other was still there, and when the shit hit the fan in August, a special forces guy, a businessman, maybe Mossad, who knows, he came down to try and extract this guy. What I heard is that he said, "I'm not going," because his Israeli wife was trying to divorce him, and as long as he stayed in Afghanistan, he could keep defying her. The guy who had come to extract him started running extractions with this Hasidic community in Brooklyn, and you could not make it up. They managed to get a whole bunch of people out. You needed to call up the rabbi and beg him to be worthy enough to give your money to him.'

People were shepherded through drug smuggling routes and 'rat lines' into neighbouring countries, but these were not options that appealed to Laura.

'The list is growing and growing. I asked Siu-Anne, do you know anyone in Pakistan who we could lobby somehow?'

'The girls were stuck in Kabul,' said Siu-Anne. 'And I said to them, call all your families, call all your friends, call anyone, because we now had a plane to fill. If we've lost most of our list to the Americans, it doesn't matter. I'm going to make the most of this moment and save as many lives as possible. That's how the list grew to 133. I then lobbied to the Pakistan government with a letter that I [also] wrote to the British prime minister, Boris Johnson.'

Siu-Anne wrote letters to several more politicians and agencies. 'There was a newspaper leak from one of the embassies with my name and loads of people's names that had been given to journalists, so that's how they managed to find my name and seek me out. I got a few death threats on my phone. It was people who were objecting to us helping these girl football players. I thought, who are you to tell me that I can't save these girls because you are choosing in your life, as a male, you've chosen not to respect women. That fired me up even more.'

Laura continued to look for ways to get visas for Pakistan. 'I ended up on a call with the owner of Leeds United Football Club. He said I want to help, and he put us in touch with a young Pakistani guy who used to be on the Pakistani football team, and he now runs an NGO called Football for Peace, and on his board is the former vice president of the Pakistan Football Federation. He is very well connected inside the government and he said, "I can get them visas."'

Laura began writing letters, to which the Pakistani organisation and individuals put their names. Leeds promised to host them and RoKit promised to fund them. 'In the end, they were able to get thirty-day humanitarian visas to enter the country. It was a huge relief. Like everything that happened in this extraction it was a relief, but it came with a sting. Originally they said only the footballers could come in, but not their families.'

The Taliban were not negotiated with, but they would need to be faced on the road to Pakistan.

'People were crossing quite a lot for medical treatment,' said Laura. 'There was no question that we thought they would be denied entry so long as they had visas, and getting there, through the checkpoints and everything, well, that was going to be a case of the drivers and everybody doing their thing.'

'I thought, the quicker I get this over and done the better,' said Siu-Anne. 'The less people I get involved the better. I lobbied and finally the Pakistan visas came through. I got eighty-nine to take them over the border. The Qataris helped provide buses coming out of the Pakistani embassy. There were three small mini buses. Eighty-nine went on passes, and when they came out on the other side, we had 133. The girls had snuck in extra friends and family members who weren't on the list. What I had to deal with was trying to keep them separate, so that they wouldn't taint the other group, and take the other group down. You can imagine the crossing was pretty intense.'

'I was being told that they were being denied entry by Ali,' recalled Laura. 'Who the fuck is Ali? I got sent a post-it note with the name Ali, and a phone number. It turned out that Ali was a Pakistani border guard who hadn't had authorisation from the government. So they got all the way through the Taliban, they exited Afghanistan, and they were being denied entry. And the guy who had granted permission, his father had recently died, so he was at the funeral and his phone was switched off. The other person we'd been dealing with was on a plane. I didn't know who to call. In the end, I called Mr Naveed, from the Pakistan Football Federation. He called the current vice president, who'd just emerged from a meeting with Imran Khan.'

A series of calls was then made within Pakistan to allow the girls and their families across the border.

'The most heart-thumping moment was waiting for the girls to cross into Pakistan,' said Siu-Anne. 'All the phones went silent and for the next three hours we heard absolute silence. The border guards beat them. They were threatening them with beating.'

Parmilla and her family had arrived at the border and found it closed. 'All night we were awake. We couldn't sleep. We said goodbye, maybe for always.'

The next day, they tried to cross the border into Pakistan. 'It was the worst event in my life. We were shaking. We couldn't speak. We were afraid. We worried they would kill us. Taliban with sticks and cables were staying there. They hit my husband. I will never forget that.'

With courage and luck, Parmilla's family crossed the border.

'When we passed the border, we took a car and we went from Peshawar to Islamabad. In that hotel we were in the first security bubble in three months. People had lots of sicknesses and mental illnesses. I will never forget that night. It was two o'clock. I called Siu-Anne and said no one would help us. She said, "You shouldn't think about money. I will call them and you should take the child to the hospital. We will provide for everything that you need." She was like an angel for everyone. They accepted our signature and my husband's signature, so we wrote prescriptions for everyone. Every kind of sickness. We had one man who was in a very bad situation, and we provided his prescription. Every time I called for Siu-Anne, she was available.'

'We paid for their hotel,' said Siu-Anne. 'We paid for each one of them individually. It was all about the finance that was being piled in. This started off about sponsorship, but turned into a humanitarian mission.'

Siu-Anne told the UK government, 'If you won't help, I'll go to Sky News.' Such urgency was well needed. One of the girls had told Siu-Anne, 'If you do not save us, we will shoot ourselves in the head before the Taliban get us.'

Such desperate messages were common. 'Emily' was a female chief of staff in the Cabinet Office who was 'moonlighting with evacuees', as Mike Pratt had put it. Emily 'operated in the shadows', working with Laura and Siu-Anne to rescue the girls' team.

'I had had quite a few messages on LinkedIn saying "please help" from complete strangers,' said Emily. 'If [the requests] come through from a trusted contact, then you automatically trust what they're saying, and the ask was, "Emily, can you please help?" There are girls on the ground who have missed the evacuation. They know they're not going to get in, but they know they're going to be killed by the Taliban. We have got some specialists on the ground helping them. Where we need help is advising them with the bit where it gets to the British government, how to navigate that, how to work with the British government. At the moment they've been told that's not going to happen. If they don't get sponsored by the British government, we're running out of time.

'When I came in, they were either just going over the border to Pakistan or had just arrived,' Emily recalled:

They had a very short space of time. Laura was leading the international negotiations and we were frantically scrambling to get sponsorship, so there were letters going out to MPs and people to help navigate that. We were having these meetings and it was

Siu-Anne, Laura, and myself. There was no rule for how this should be done, as it had never been done before.

We were all going 'fuck'. Failure on this is the death of these girls. You've been given a task, which you didn't ask for, you've never done, isn't officially above the line, and there is no option to fail. I also can't compromise my security and job, and identity, so I'm having to do this in the margins, pulling every lever I can and having to just use everything I've got to try and make this successful, whilst thinking, well, the stakes of getting this wrong are higher on every side. It was incredibly stressful.

It's almost like a baton change. I got given the baton by my contact, so I know he was trusted, he then passed the baton to me, going, 'Emily, can you please take the next step of this,' and I knew that I needed to hand over the baton on my side to people somewhere in government, probably in the Home Office. That was my relay leg. But you also know that you don't know, and you don't need to know, the people either side. It's a very trusted chain on a need-to-know basis.

The first message was, 'Do you know people with access to a helicopter to help evacuate them out of Afghanistan?' The answer was, 'Yes, I do.' I contacted some ex-special forces guys who I knew had gone into private security and had access to this, and had also put out publicly, 'If anybody needs evacuating, give us a call.'

I've said before, the one thing you need in a situation like this: cash. And a lot of it. You need contacts who know what they're doing. And you need a bit of luck. I was starting to put the right people in contact together. At the same time the girls had been moved just across the border, and then it very [quickly] switched to getting them into the UK. We hit a lot of brick walls. And it was really terrifying, because we were running out of options, and the bit of luck that finally got to us at the end was that there was a press release saying that the Home Secretary had sponsored them, and we knew she hadn't.

I said, 'Brilliant.' I had my contacts on the ground in the Home Secretary's office feeding back to me what was going on, clearly on the quiet. We would get the press absolutely on it by doing a counter release saying we thank Prime Minister Boris Johnson, we thank the Home Secretary, the British government. We put the press release out confirming that they had supported it and that the girls were now on their way to this country. What that did was back the British government into a corner where they couldn't now go back on that, because it was out publicly in the press.

The awful thing is, you can do all the work on the ground, and success can come down to a well-timed letter in a minister's inbox. And I knew that the Home Office comms team would be flagging this up. I knew that this story was high on the agenda for both the Prime Minister and Number 10, and the comms team would pick it up as a positive news story.

I knew the advice back to [Priti Patel] would be, well, you now have to see it through. We knew what she needed at that point was a good news story, so I gave her a good news story, and she just ran with it. When it then got confirmed, and she did come out with an official statement, when that came out, we were in tears. We've made it happen. And the team went back to the girls in Pakistan saying, 'You've won the jackpot.'

This was a group of women in the UK helping women who were complete strangers.

'They didn't know who we were,' said Emily, 'and that didn't matter, and it didn't matter that when the press release came out that our names weren't on it. It didn't matter. We'd saved their lives and the irony was that, because of work, I couldn't tell anybody about this. It would compromise me.

'I've still never met those girls. Part of me wanted to be on the ground, and just seeing them. The people who wanted media coverage nearly undid the whole thing. When the newspaper report came out, saying Kim Kardashian's done this [as reported in the media],[5] I mean we were just howling with laughter. The reality was that it had been desperate, over crap coffee conversations at Victoria Station, and phone calls at one o'clock in the morning, and the reality was so unglamorous.

'Where did Kim Kardashian come from?' Emily laughed. 'I'm sure she wasn't on our WhatsApp groups. The whole thing was very, very surreal. It was all in the shadows.'

But it worked.

'Everything was OK because Siu-Anne was with us,' said Parmilla. 'Siu-Anne got all 133 visas just three days before we were all going to be deported back over the border. Every day we were crying, because some days they were saying they would deport us back, they would send us back to Afghanistan. So we knew that if they sent us back, they would kill us. We waited one month for airplanes.'

'I want to make it very clear that I never wanted my name to be associated with this,' said Laura:

I was just one piece. What I was able to bring was the understanding of the ground, and diplomacy. There was a complicated coalition of people, all of whom, in their different way, were doing this for humanitarian reasons, but for other reasons as well. Sometimes these interests diverged and they needed to be brought to a place where they could find common ground.

I didn't want to be doing it. It was exhausting and stressful and traumatising. I felt like I was in over my head and that I might end up inadvertently screwing up the lives of countless other people. It felt like a terrible, terrible weight of responsibility.

I think everybody did their best under a shit set of circumstances. I think what Afghanistan turned into was the Wild West after the departure of the Americans. You saw governments failing, fundamentally, and private individuals stepping up, but it did become an industry of a sort. And sometimes, there were times where I felt uncomfortable, because it felt like there was a very delicate balance between doing things to save lives, and doing things to be seen to be saving lives. And I think that we got to that point where that delicate balance looked a little bit shaky to me. Not necessarily with this extraction, but certainly with a lot of the stuff that was going on.

It was chaotic, it was desperate, and some of it seemed to be done without a thought for the future. But, at the end of the day, people were desperate to get out. They were desperate to get out by whatever means possible, and you look at things like refugee camps in Uganda, and all of this stuff, and you've got to ask yourself, like what was better at the end of the day, and how do you make those judgements? And who am I if they should choose to escape or stay put in an untenable situation?

I think it was a shame, in our extraction, that everybody fell out as dramatically as they did. I think a lot of that was about feeling that other people were taking the credit that was due to them. And, that's one of the reasons why I'm super glad that my name was never part of anything, and I don't want it to be part of anything, because it's good to just be very clear about why you're doing things.

Regardless of the reasons, the girls and their families were evac-uated to the United Kingdom. They are safe from the Taliban, and free to live lives of their choosing.

Three determined strangers had made it happen.

Lost children

Tony was a former soldier now working in Afghanistan as a UN security advisor. At the time of the Kabul airlift, he had spent a cumulative seven years in the country.

'I got back into the country on the fourteenth of August. The Taliban were making gains mostly in the countryside in the rural areas. What we thought was gonna happen, and what most people thought, is there'll be a standoff outside the edge of town, on the edge of Kabul.

'My understanding of the situation on the fifteenth of August is the Taliban were coming in along the Jalalabad road, and the reports coming from Jalalabad along that road were faster than was actually possible. So they clearly were there already. One minute they're in Jalalabad. Next minute, they're in Sarobi. Then they were at the city gates. My understanding is the president went to the airport, spoke to the Americans or the guys who were there, spoke to the Taliban and asked for some form of deal. I think they were going to offer fifty per cent of the provinces to be split.'

The Taliban were reported to laugh at the deal.

'At which point, [Ghani] made a decision to disappear. Word spread that he had disappeared pretty fast. And then that's when we saw everyone, every man and his dog, or anyone who was anyone in Kabul, go to the airport. And, as is well documented, people booked onto flights were kicked off. If you have money, you got a seat on the aircraft,' Tony continued:

Then Kabul went very quiet. It was very eerie. We knew the Taliban were at the city gates, which are about, I don't know, four or five k's east of us. It's all a bit strange as the Taliban are coming, the Taliban are there. And then it was silent. We didn't know what to expect. Then, all the military and police disappeared within the space of half an hour. One minute they were there and the next minute they weren't. And then you'd have convoys of people rushing to the airport.

And then again, it was very eerily quiet. I understand the Minister of the Interior spoke to the Taliban and said, 'Look, there's a vacuum here, you need to come in.' The Taliban were reluctant. Their plans were to sit on the edge of town and have a chat for a couple of weeks and then have some sort of negotiated takeover. So they were asked to come in and when they walked along the road from the east, they looked a bit weary. They didn't come in like a fighting force.

There was this fear from the government, or the previous government, that there would be civil unrest, or they didn't know what's going to happen. So if your city is there, you need to come in and police it. So the Taliban were a bit reluctant. So they hadn't planned to come in that day. And that's why you see [...] it's the low level, rural fighters [going into] the palace and they look a bit lost, because it wasn't supposed to happen. They were planning for a proper takeover. And then a grand takeover of the palace and having it all glamorous and media friendly. But that wasn't the case.

So it's all a bit strange. The UN were panicking, saying we need to evacuate. It was UNICEF, who were the lead, along with a couple of other UN agencies like WFP [World Food Programme], and UNHCR [United Nations High Commissioner for Refugees], who were saying, 'We've actually got a job here, there's a humanitarian requirement for us to be here, we can't just look after ourselves, we need to do something.'

My team and the other agencies, we set about looking at the situation, look at what had happened before. When the Taliban had taken over, we hadn't seen mass killings, we hadn't seen mass persecution of the population. It had gone relatively peaceful. And that's probably due to the fact that Taliban had limited numbers, and they're almost like a blitzkrieg.

This meant that the Taliban did not have sufficient forces to hold down all areas if they rose up against them:

When I was fighting, I was down in Lashkar Ghar when they were pushing close onto it. A lot of the population were heading into northern and southern Helmand into Taliban held areas because they were safer, and that's probably down to two reasons. One is because the actual conflict was focused on the government-held areas. So there wasn't any fighting in the Taliban areas. And secondly, I hate to say life was a bit simpler and a bit fairer under the Taliban in some places. Although I don't agree with their methods. It was just one system they're dealing with, whereas with the government forces and the government, that's where you had the corruption. It's a bit more complicated. So we've seen people go into those areas and be okay.

A lot of the NGOs came into the UN compound, which seemed a bit strange, because they're normally very standoff-ish from the UN. They look down on us, and they feel like they're the pure humanitarians. There's a thing called Saving Lives Together, which all NGOs sign up for. And so, as the UN is, when the shit hits the fan, the UN will help NGOs.

So it's a written agreement between all those down to the sort of lowest levels. So they press the button on that, they come in. And the bulk of the evacuations who I evacuated were NGOs, actually, they were the type of people I would expect to stay.

There was one night there was massive celebratory fire. I'd never heard anything like it in my life, and I think there was something like five people killed in Kabul alone. From that moment, I think it's well documented, the Taliban said no more celebratory fire. So that proved they were able to have some form of security control. And there was a feeling of calm across the city.

Along with Rob, a colleague, Tony saw an opportunity 'to do something good':

We're seeing on the news there are lots of kids around the airport and in the airport. We also knew we needed some sort of liaison with the military inside. Rob and I were having a beer and we thought, fuck it, we know people inside, we can actually do something about this. We can get something working. So we came up with this plan of taking Rob to the airport, Rob and I in two vehicles, drive up to the gates where the US Marines were, get his vehicle inside and set up firstly a liaison point between the UN and the military. And secondly, established child-friendly space to look after the kids.

Eventually the UN management signed off on it. They said, okay, if you think you can do it, do it. Rob, myself, and a guy called Alistair, who is an interesting character. He was an officer in the Kiwi military. He left that, came to UK, worked as an IT consultant for Guinness, joined 10 Para as a Tom, and then got accused of impersonating a private soldier because he hadn't resigned his commission properly. And so we came together and we went to the airport. The plan was to drive in.

When we got there, we realised that that was a no go. There was no way we could get the vehicles up to the gate. So Rob and I decided to dismount. There's a video of this on my Instagram feed. We walked up to the gate and the Afghans were looking at us a bit strange. We eventually got to the gate and there was just a huge pressure, people were sort of having to push back and make sure we didn't get crushed against the gates. US Marines were a bit surprised to see two white Westerners pop up out the crowd. We said, 'We need to get the vehicle through,' and they said no can do. So Rob and I made a snap decision. We went for the forty per cent solution. So we decided to throw Rob over the wall.

We chucked Rob over the wall. He's a big-ish guy. And there's probably a 15 foot drop and there was a US Marine at the bottom who is going to catch him. Now Rob claims he floated down like a feather. The US Marine who caught him deserves a Medal of Honour. But Rob jumped over. All he had was a UN T-shirt and those brown camera vest things. He jumped over, he's in the airport, and he came across a 2 Para bloke in one of those pickups.

So he got a lift and he went up to the TOC [Tactical Operations Centre]. He's Canadian. He'd served with a few units in the Canadian military in Afghan and he saw some of his muckers from one of his former units and Australians at the TOC. Yeah, so we had comms in there. I then had to walk out of the crowd. This is where it's interesting. So all the media coverage, and the chaos in Kabul, it was focused on about two or three hundred metres around the airport. Everywhere else in

Kabul was completely normal. There were Taliban on check-points, but not many. It was very bizarre.

When Rob was there, we were able to establish proper comms between the UN and the military. And then we took another convoy in. I think the one I was in was fifty armoured vehicles. We drove in convoy to the airport, went through the front gate, all the people around the airport, were all sat down and organised by the Taliban. They're all sat down. They're all on the road. The Taliban had gained control outside the airport and wouldn't let us in at first, so I have this massive convoy behind me. There's another Brit bloke with me, a guy called Frank, who was known as the Taliban whisperer, fluent in Dari and Pashto.

He jumped out the car. I followed him. It was quite an eerie experience walking up with all the Afghans sat down, there's loads of Taliban around us. They had arranged all of the trollies from the airport as a barricade.

It wasn't Tony's first time coming face to face with the Taliban. During COVID, he had been with the UN in the Taliban-held towns of Sangin and Musa Qala:

There was a bit of umming and ahhing. I thought, oh shit, they don't know we're coming, but eventually we got let in. As we drove down the main road, past the aircraft, the car park in front of the terminal was just surreal. You had the Taliban right up to the edge of the car park. Then in the car park, the 82nd Airborne and a couple of Paras, and the only thing separating them was one strand of barbed wire.

Rob was with the 82nd Airborne, and he walked towards the barbed wire, and the 82nd Airborne were like, 'Hey, hey, what are you doing, how are you going to get across that wire?' And Rob said, 'Watch.' He put his foot on it, and stepped over.

Tony and the other security advisors dropped off their passengers. 'I was chatting to the troops while I was there and they was asking me what it was like outside [the airport]. I told them it was quite normal. Meanwhile, not to make it sound sexy or exciting, but there were gunshots in the distance. They said where am I going, and I said, "I'm going back," and it was one of a number of times I was offered a seat on a flight.'

Tony declined it. 'I'm not suicidal. It's just that I knew we were perfectly safe there at the time.' He would not leave Kabul until 10 October, over a month after the final military flight had left Afghanistan.

'There was a real desire to process these kids. It wasn't a proper facility. It was a makeshift place. In fact, it became the triage point for the casualties on the bomb blast.'

Tony estimates that up to a hundred children passed through their makeshift operation.

'Some went to Qatar. As the operation was drawing down, so some units disappeared, it was really left with the Brits and the Americans, we didn't know what's going to happen. The inner cordon was starting to shrink inside the airport. The Taliban weren't sure if they could control the airfield after the suicide bomb, and there were reports of other suicide bombers in the airport as well. They turned out not to be true, but that information was going around. It was felt that as soon as the Americans and Brits left the airport would be chaos, and Rob was there with the child protection team and a few kids.

'I couldn't get in the airport with other vehicles to get them all out, so I designated an RV point. Alistair and I moved to that point. Rob did some rehearsals, and he got eleven people in one armoured vehicle. Met up with us. Took them back to the UN compound, where all of those children were relocated with their families. There was proper verification. We didn't just hand them over. It all worked out fine.'

The men who had stayed in Kabul 'to do something good' had lived up to their promise. Thanks to the work of Tony, Rob and others, the lost children were reunited with their families.

Others would not be so fortunate.

10

Tragic Endings

History will judge the United States not by the decision to withdraw from Afghanistan, but by the appalling manner this withdrawal was executed, communicated and planned – twice.

– Mir Sadat, American author and National Security Advisor[1]

The war in Afghanistan had no shortage of misery, and the last week of August 2021 was no exception. Western servicemen and Afghan civilians were killed in the final days of an abandoned cause. The fall of Afghanistan is made up of millions of individual tragedies – the loss of an education, the breakup of a family, the death of a loved one – but amongst this backdrop of unimaginable hardship, two events stood out to the world. One was a suicide attack by the Islamic State (IS-K), and the other was the retaliation against them.

The American-led mission would not end in peace, but with the same violent death that had been the war's inception: a suicide attack, and death from the sky.

Abbey Gate

Suicide bomber threats were a regular occurrence at the gates to HKIA. The gates were thick with people, huge crowds making the perfect cover for a suicide bomber. For the Marines and soldiers trying to seek out such threats, there was a good chance that the first time they knew about a bomber in the crowd would be when he detonated his vest.

The threat of these bombings came not from the Taliban, but from the terrorist organisation IS-K, which views the Taliban and the American-led coalition as its enemies. According to the *New York Times*, IS-K was 'Founded in 2015 by disaffected Pakistani Taliban, [it] is smaller, newer and embraces a more violent version of Islam than the Taliban. In 2016, a year after it was founded, IS-K was at its peak size, with about 3000 to 4000 fighters, according to analyst estimates. That figure was cut in half after the group was targeted by American airstrikes and Afghan commando raids.'[2]

War correspondent Hollie McKay reported on the Islamic State both in their war in Iraq and Syria and in Afghanistan, and she has seen the power they are gaining in parts of the latter.

'Some of the Taliban's intelligence leaders even told me that they no longer refer to the Daesh [as IS is known colloquially] by such names, and instead use the term "rebels". Yet, the situation on the ground tells a starkly different story. Especially in and around the Nangarhar capital of Jalalabad, bodies are being decapitated and strung up for all to see on a daily basis, often with a stamped letter warning that if anyone comes to collect the dead, they will be in trouble.'[3]

Such mutual enemies perhaps explain another reason why there was so much willingness between the Taliban and US-led forces to work alongside each other at the airport. By 26 August, the ceasefire had held, enabling thousands of Afghans to be processed through the gates, and onto aircraft.

'On the twentieth of August, we emplaced the chevron, which consisted of six shipping containers at Abbey Gate,' said

Brigadier General Lance Curtis, the lead investigator into what would become known as the Abbey Gate bombing:

> The chevron is named because of the shape ... the chevron is in place for at least two reasons: vehicle-borne IED threat mitigation, and also, it enables processing at Abbey Gate.
>
> From the 20th through the 22nd of August, the gates were closed at HKIA. This is because the intermediate staging bases were at capacity. On the 25th of August, East and North Gate closed permanently. Now, we'll explain the reasons for that. East Gate was more challenging to process, given the geographic situation of the gate. At North Gate, there were vehicle-borne IED threats, and that was a leading cause in the decision to close North Gate.
>
> From the 25th through the 26th, we tracked the imminent threat streams at Abbey Gate and some of the other threat streams across HKIA. There were at least four imminent threat streams that occurred between the 25th and the 26th at Abbey Gate, and what we found is that leaders took the appropriate measures tied to these imminent threat streams. They would lower their profiles, seek cover, and at times they would even cease operations at the gate for periods of time.
>
> At 16:00 on the 26th, Gulf Company changed out 4th Platoon with 1st Platoon. This was an hour earlier than scheduled, but this was because of the high OPTEMPO [Operational Tempo] that was occurring, and also, the sensory overload. This demonstrated that leaders were keeping their fingers on the pulse of the situation on the ground.
>
> At 17:00 on the 26th, Brigadier General Sullivan, who was the Joint Task Force crisis response commander, was at Abbey Gate. That was thirty-six minutes before the blast. He was there

for a meeting with the Brits and the Taliban. The 82nd Airborne Division commander, the 24th MEU commander were also at Abbey Gate on the 26th of August. The 2nd Battalion commander was physically on the ground at the time of the blast, and he was wounded, and then we had multiple company commanders who were also on the ground at the time of the attack.

At 17:36 and 52 seconds on the 26th, we have the actual attack.[4]

On the day of the Abbey Gate bombing, Major Danny Riley was in HKIA's pump house that supplied water to HKIA. 'It had underground wells, but the workers had left. The place was flooded and the Yanks were trying the switches. There was a massive boom, and sparks, and all the power cut. I said, "Alright, let's get the engineers in to look at this."'

Danny had just come from the pump house to the SPMAGTAF (Special Purpose Marine Air-Ground Task Force) ops room, when they got the news about Abbey Gate.

'The commander looked like a traditional US Marine. I saw him get the information on his guys. The numbers kept going up. I knew it was Jeff's company who'd been hit.' Jeff [a US company commander] and his men had been crucial in the operation to install the chevron. The US Marine had shared dangers with Danny, and this had formed a strong bond. Now, Danny waited with the Marines to learn of the fate of their friends and comrades.

'We didn't know what the casualty ratio was, so we sent runners to the hospital to count uniform types.'

Eventually it became clear that all of the military casualties were American. 'If the detonation was different by a couple of degrees, it would have been a different story.'

As liaison officer, Danny had called the British bomb disposal officer forward to the SPMAGTAF ops room. 'Our EOD guys went in once the casualties had been moved. We were all expecting some kind of secondary attack. It was deadly silent in the ops room. I think because I'd got on well with them, and told them how great their guys had been on the chevron op, after the IED blast they were happy for me to come in and help. It was tense. It was quiet. No one could comprehend how one IED blast had caused so many casualties. We thought it was double reporting, but it was bang on after about twenty minutes.'

Danny visited the site of the blast to observe the aftermath, and the reason for the high amount of casualties became clear. 'It was density. He [the suicide bomber] stood on a wall and literally shredded heads.'

In the year following the attack, witness testimony emerged from the ranks of the Marines, claiming that the suicide bomber had been spotted hours before the attack. On the afternoon of 26 August, two Marines thought that they had matched a person to an intelligence threat warning, and asked for permission to engage. They were denied, apparently due to too many civilians being in the area.

The suspect was lost to sight in the massive crowd. Hours later, a powerful explosion tore through the crowd, killing and maiming civilians and US service personnel. What was already a hell became a house of horrors, as hundreds of people were caught in the blast, shredded by shrapnel and tossed by the powerful blast.

'That's a hard thing to deal with,' said the Marine who had spotted the suspect from the tower. 'That's something that, honestly, eats at me every single day.'[5]

The 24-year-old Marine, Sgt Tyler Vargas-Andrews, suffered catastrophic wounds in the blast, losing an arm, a leg, and large parts of his intestine.[6]

Among the crowd of civilians was 'Jon'. A former translator, his occupation had already led to him being shot eight times by the Taliban. Now that the regime was back in power, Jon and his family were trying to escape Kabul. In desperation, Jon waded through a canal filled with fetid water. As Jon reached out to hand US Marines his documents, the suicide bomber detonated his device. 'There was people's flesh all over my face, all over my body.'

The *Washington Post* reported that: 'Multiple gunmen then opened fire on the civilians and military forces.'[7] This is recalled by several witnesses. The DoD interviewed 100 people for their own report, and came to a different conclusion.

'The investigation found no definitive proof that anyone was ever hit or killed by gunfire, either US or Afghan,' said General McKenzie. 'This conclusion was based upon the careful consideration of sworn testimony of more than 100 witnesses, and especially those witnesses in observation towers, both American and British, who were in locations unaffected by the blast and that had commanding views of the scene before, during and after the explosive attack. This conclusion was also confirmed by the findings and analysis of medical examiners and explosive experts, a review of all available physical evidence, and a review of all available video evidence, including an MQ-9 unmanned aerial vehicle, which began observing the scene about three minutes after the attack. At this point I want to acknowledge that the investigation differs from what we initially believed on the day of the attack. At the time, the best information we had in the immediate aftermath of the attack indicated that it was a complex attack by both a suicide bomber and IS-K gunmen.'

A soldier of 2 Para disputes this. 'We'd been at Abbey Gate about thirty minutes before the bomb went off,' said the soldier. 'We were getting scoff and we didn't hear it, but someone ran into the scoff house shouting, "Stand to, stand to!" The Pentagon said there was no firefight after the bomb, but that's bollocks. As we were running out, there was a massive weight of fire going down. We were told there was gunmen trying to break in. The Yanks said they saw them. I didn't. As far as I know, there wasn't any gunmen bodies.'

The lead investigator for the Pentagon, General Lance Curtis, reported, 'This was not a complex attack. It was a single blast, and it did not have a follow-on attack. There were a series of crossing fires to the front of the service members on the ground that created the illusion that there was a complex attack, but there absolutely was not. There were no gunshot wounds. We have universal agreement between the Armed Forces Medical Examiner's Office, and also, the medical providers on the ground. There were absolutely no gunshot wounds.'

Whatever had caused the injuries, the wounded and dead numbered in the hundreds. 'The injured started coming in,' said a 2 Para soldier. 'I helped a medic work on a teenage boy. His abdomen was swelling from internal bleeding and his face was totally fucked. He looked like he'd been thrown from a blast and smashed against a wall. I don't know if he lived or died. We were giving emergency first aid, and then they'd be taken to the field hospital. I didn't go to the site of the bomb. The NCOs went out there, to the canal. I think they did it to shield the lads from the carnage, which pisses me off. We could have done it.'

Private Fahim of 3 Para recalled his experience of that day.

'I'd been at Abbey Gate every day, but on the day of the bomb, I was a hundred metres away when it happened. It looked like something from a movie. There was a flash, and a wind. There was meat everywhere. Heads. Hands. Pieces of bodies. I ran to Abbey Gate. I had to walk over bodies. I could hear and feel the bones and meat. People were crying over their loved ones. A husband found a piece of pink garment and recognised it. His wife's body was in two pieces. He started screaming. All the dead were in different positions. Someone held my hand and wouldn't let go.'

When Fahim heard that the Marines had suffered casualties, he hoped that those he had come to know would not be among them.

'There was one Marine that I talked to every day, but I didn't know his name. You get to know faces. He was just such a nice guy. He was one of the dead.'

Abbey Gate, already a place of desperation and fear, had been turned into a vision of hell.

'This isn't something that I want to talk about,' Fahim said calmly. 'That day was a nightmare, and that's it.'

Captain Aaron Nunkoosing was another 2 Para witness to the blast:

Just before the bomb went off, I was getting out twelve or thirteen people from the British Council. I said, 'Make sure you're all in, don't highlight yourselves yet. We'll wait for the right moment and then we'll pull you out as a oner, because if we make this take an hour it's going to be really hard. Let's be efficient.'

There was a guy with a British accent and he was looking at me saying, 'Brother, brother, get me out.' He was about my age. I said, 'Mate, just stay calm, just stay there, don't worry. Honestly, mate, you're probably better coming back tomorrow.' And he was like, 'Brother, they're going to kill me.'

I could have pulled him out, but I didn't because I didn't want to ramp up the crowd. And I genuinely thought we would get him later. And it was probably about thirty to forty minutes after that that the bomb went off. I still don't know the fate of that bloke. I think three Brits died in that crowd, and I trawled the newspapers afterwards, and I'm pretty sure it wasn't him, but I don't know if he got injured, and that's definitely one that's played on my mind.

I was probably just under fifty metres away from the edge of the blast when it happened. The two Paras in front of me, they got blown down. I still don't know how I didn't. I saw people go down in front of me, and I saw people and body parts go up in the air. It felt like slow motion.

Where it happened, that's where I was trying to pull out the British Council guys. I'd gone over to some of the US Marines and I said, 'Hey guys, do you mind if we pull these guys out here?' and what saved my life, and the lives of about three or four other Brits, was the fact that the Americans said, 'Hey, no, sorry man, can you move down fifty metres or so?' Something as simple as that. And for the next thirty or forty minutes we were just guiding the British Council guys through the packed canal and away from the Americans' location so that we could get them out.

2 Para and the Marines had known that there was a danger of such attacks:

We had J2 [intelligence] of a suicide bomber inbound. I was conscious of this and wanted to get the British Council party out sooner rather than later. I was getting incredibly frustrated, because as we got them out, I realised one of the individuals was not on the nominal roll I had been passed, and I was having a real go at the only English-speaking member of the group just as the bomb went off.

I remember the loudest bang I'd ever heard in my life and reacted by drawing my pistol and almost wincing, because I thought that we were about to get fired on as well, but then getting malleted by this woman as she ran away from the explosion and knocked me down. The bomb didn't knock me down, but this woman ran through me and that knocked me down! And I just heard one of the guys screaming at me, 'Boss, boss!' As soon as he did that, I knew I was supposed to start extracting and we started pepper-potting back. I could feel the crowd coming at me and thought I was about to get trampled. I was about to start firing warning shots.

One of the junior Paras was throwing people aside to stop their group from being overrun:

He let off a few rounds. Everyone just dropped and hit the floor. That calmed everything down and allowed us a split second to extract. I told the twelve from the British Council to follow me and I was running with them back towards the gate at the Baron, where a 3 Para sergeant was shouting at me, saying, 'No civvies, no civvies!' So I had to drop them where they were. The CS gas was hitting us. It was chaos. I left the twelve outside. I would eventually, with Colonel Dave's blessing, go back to get them. They didn't think that we were coming back for them.

The casualties start coming in, and I genuinely thought a good friend of mine, Corporal Sales, was dead. As I got in, the boss put an arm on my shoulder and said, 'Aaron, what's happened?' And like an idiot I turned around to him and said 'IED', as if he hadn't just seen it. He asked if there were any British casualties. I said, 'Sir, I think Corporal Sales was there.'

Not long afterwards, I saw Corporal Sales come back through the front gate of the Baron. I said to him, 'I've been looking for you, I thought you were dead,' and he said, 'I'm not, I'm here.' That was a great feeling, because Corporal Sales has been a mate of mine for many years, but then the casualties start coming in.

In the investigation into the Abbey Gate bombing, General Curtis gave an overview of the medical facilities available at HKIA.

'There were four medical capabilities ... The first one is a hospital that is at Camp Alvarado, in the upper left there. This was run by 1st Brigade of the 82nd, and they had one surgical team of four. The highest-level medical capability was the main hospital ... This was a facility that was originally run by the Norwegians, but it became a joint facility. At any given time it remained a coalition flavour, in that you would have seen Norwegians there and frequently Brits and Germans as well.

'This had eight surgical teams of four, a very robust medical capability. And it was sometimes referred to as a Role 2 enhanced and this was because it had additional capability, think a CT scan. There were two Shock Trauma Platoons. The first was at the East Gate in a hardened facility. And that was run by the 2nd Battalion, 1st Marine Regiment. The second was run by the 24th MEU in very close proximity to the main hospital.'

'I didn't hear the bomb go off,' said a US Navy nurse. The first thing that she and her team knew about it was when someone with wide eyes came running into the Joint Operations Centre, and told them that there had been a blast at Abbey Gate. Within minutes, casualties were arriving at the aid station. The first of hundreds.

'We had a makeshift field hospital set up by East Gate, as close as we could to Abbey to support our Marines. It was an abandoned security building and we used conference tables as our patient exam beds. The Role 2 was established by a Norwegian medical team about ten minutes from Abbey Gate. It's where all the surgical teams were, and where the casualties ended up.

'We only had two emergency medicine physicians to do damage control resuscitation and buy some time to get a surgeon. Our team saw six or seven of the Marines as they stopped at us en route to the Role 2. Two of the Marines were very critically injured and would likely have been triaged as expectant at the Role 2.'

Expectant means that the casualty is expected to die. Therefore, they usually forgo care so that those with a better chance of survival can be worked on by the limited number of surgeons.

'There were four or five surgical teams at the Role 2 from Britain, Norway, the US Army, and US Air Force,' said the US Navy nurse. 'Had there not been so many, there's no way some of the injured would have survived.'

But not all pulled through.

'Some of those that passed made it a few hours, but there's nothing that could have been done. I know of at least three that died instantly. I don't know the official number, but the air evacuation the next morning took I think something like sixty injured people. Some were very critical. It was about an equal amount of civilians and US service members.'

Looking back on the events of that day brings her a mixture of emotions.

'I think about the many Afghans we couldn't treat, or those who received subpar care because of the lack of supplies. I think about the pain I saw in the Marines' eyes after the blast, and being so overwhelmed in triage that I couldn't give them the support or care that they needed. The common theme of "I could have done more" is really heavy.'

It is a common feeling among military members, but the efforts of the nurse and her teammates were not in vain.

'There are a few that survived because of the actions of our medical team. Mangled, dealing with a new body, or paralysed. A hard life, but alive.'

'The medics were incredible,' said Captain Nunkoosing of 2 Para. 'And it was C Company – I think it was C Company – incredible. They ran out, secured the area. The boss was out. The ops officer was out. Securing it so the guys could treat casualties. And those medics, those young girls and boys, they did an incredible job. They really did do an incredible job. I remember this baby getting brought in with the dad. The baby had all holes in the back of him. The dad, I had to search him and he was sitting there shaking. And then I just put an arm around him, and we were doing that the whole time.'

Despite the horrors of that day, Nunkoosing believes that the Paras were able to prevent an even greater tragedy.

'We knew there was a threat of it. I am convinced to this day that they were trying to hit us with a vehicle IED at the back gate, and a suicide IED at the front. That vehicle IED never happened at the back, and the reason I felt that was because we were getting a threat warning of a gold Corolla VBIED [vehicle-borne improvised explosive device] making its way to our location a couple of times.

'I was at the back gate trying to get someone else out, and one of the platoon commanders, Charlie Rendle, he just started shouting down to me, "Aaron, Aaron! Gold Corolla! Gold Corolla!" So I relayed that to the commander at the back gate, and he just shut it down. That Gold Corolla went away. Then, later, it tried to get in on the back of a civilian logistics resupply into the hotel. It was trying to get in on the back of that. Again, we shut it down and it went away. It's just a feeling, and it was never corroborated. Maybe someday someone can piece together the bits.'

Thirteen US service personnel died in the Abbey Gate attack. Each one left a family behind. Their hopes for the future ended in a country far from home. They died alongside more than a hundred Afghans. They were strangers to each other, born in different cultures and to different languages, but the US service personnel had placed the lives of strangers above their own. In doing so they paid the ultimate sacrifice, and gave their lives so that others may live.

These are their names:

- Marine Lance Cpl. David Espinoza, 20
- Marine Sgt. Nicole Gee, 23
- Marine Staff Sgt. Darin Taylor Hoover, 31
- Army Staff Sgt. Ryan Knauss, 23
- Marine Cpl. Hunter Lopez, 22
- Marine Lance Cpl. Dylan Merola, 20
- Marine Lance Cpl. Rylee McCollum, 20
- Marine Lance Cpl. Kareem Nikoui, 20
- Marine Cpl. Daegan Page, 23

- Marine Sgt. Johanny Rosario Pichardo, 25
- Marine Cpl. Humberto Sanchez, 22
- Marine Lance Cpl. Jared Schmitz, 20
- Navy Hospitalman Maxton Soviak, 22

We will remember them.

The aftermath

On the day of the bombing, Warrant Officer Lee Bowden was commanding his EOD team from the Joint Operations Centre (JOC). The news of fellow Marines suffering casualties was a blow, but not one that was unexpected.

'On my first deployment, my team leader had told the Marine infantry unit that if they didn't get continuous eyes on a certain stretch of the highway, it was going to get used for IEDs. He said, "It's going to take this battalion losing men before they take this seriously." And I felt the same way with the gates at HKIA. We knew there was a suicide bomber threat. When it finally happened, I was stunned, but not surprised.'

In the wake of an explosion, secondary devices are of high concern. A secondary device is placed specifically to target the people who rush in to deal with the casualties from the first explosion. It is difficult to recover from one blast, and harder to recover from two. Particularly if the medical teams and commanders have been caught in the secondary explosion. While it is a soldier's instinct to rush into such a situation, team leaders like Bowden have been trained and taught to remove emotion from the situation so that they can deal with it in the most rational way.

When asked about how he felt about sending his men into

such carnage, Bowden replied, 'Every EOD tech knows that they're going into a tough job, and we accept that. About ten minutes after the bomb went off, someone from 2/1 came into the JOC and said, "We need EOD at Abbey Gate." I said, how much? And he said, "Everything you've got." I give kudos to 2/1 to recognise that it was better to have enablers and not need them, than leave the call too late.'

Bowden's team's first priority was the search for more bombs.

'When my teams arrived there, they swept for additional threats, such as searching bags for secondary devices. Some of the casualties had weapons and kit on them, including grenades, and these needed to be made safe. Once these immediate concerns were dealt with, my guys did what they could to facilitate the Casualty Collection Point by pulling in more med gear wherever they could find it.'

Overseeing the operation from the JOC, Bowden had a natural concern for his team's safety, but he had no worries about their ability to work through the situation and aid in the fallout of the bombing.

'I had full trust in my guys to be able to operate independently of me. Growing up I played soccer, and I had a coach from Zambia. He said that it was his time to influence his players during practice, not game time, and that's what I adopted with my men. The twelve of them were some of the best EOD techs I ever worked with, and they made my job very easy.'

Like many others, Bowden's team performed admirably that day. Eventually, casualties were cleared from the gate, and the area was made secure, but the EOD team's work was not done.

'The next day I went to Abbey Gate to do a PBA [Post Blast Analysis]. We weren't expecting to find much, as there's rarely much that can be exploited from a suicide device, but we made a solid assessment of where he was, how he orientated himself and the composition of the device, which we think was about 20lbs of military commercial explosive.' This analysis was based on the intensity of the blast, and the distance that fragmentation had travelled and buried itself into permanent objects.

'There were small ball bearings in the device, and it was likely carried in a backpack or under his clothes.'

The device claimed more than 150 lives. What had made it so deadly?

Based on his suspicions and analysis, Bowden reckoned that 'being on a ledge put [the suicide bomber] above people and gave the device an airburst effect. With so many people packed in tightly between the blast walls, the pressure and frag were more deadly. That entire area was a channel that would have enhanced the Blast Over Pressure.'

This would cause all manner of internal injuries that would prove fatal without immediate trauma care. 'I think a lot of the Afghans will have died from their wounds.'

Photos and footage following the blast show Afghan casualties being taken away in wheelbarrows. Without the attention of a surgeon, many may have succumbed to the effects of the blast wave.

'We linked in with British EOD who had done the initial Post Blast Analysis. They had components that they thought could have been part of the device, but we were able to discount them. They were pieces of a Marine's radio.'

Such discoveries could be gut-wrenching, but those emotions needed to be placed aside.

'Post Blast Analysis is detective work. We take witness accounts and look for physical evidence. As we were doing this, the Taliban were watching. As an EOD tech, I'd never had any close-up interaction with them before. We fight a faceless enemy, and interact with their IEDs. Because of that impersonal aspect, and because the ability to compartmentalise is essential to EOD, I didn't have an emotional reaction to seeing them. You can't be emotional in EOD. You have to use the logical part of your brain.'

For other soldiers, such emotional detachment was not possible. Paratroopers are known for their toughness, but they are not automatons, and the aftermath of the suicide attack weighed heavily on all.

'We were very lucky,' said one 2 Para soldier. 'Our blokes had just been there [at Abbey Gate], and one Tom was blown off his feet.'

One British officer felt as though there was an unnecessary post-mortem of the IED incident, and unwarranted criticism directed at the response of the US troops, who had apparently opened fire at what they believed was a follow-up attack.

ProPublica reported that 'military investigators found that "several Marines returned fire" after the blast. What they were shooting at and who, if anyone, they hit, remains unclear. "There's wide variation of thought on where the firing origin-ated and who was actually doing the firing."'[8]

'CS gas was going off,' said the British officer. 'There was smoke and dust. It was unfair to criticise the Americans. They were trying to do the right thing in chaos.'

The same was true of some of 2 Para's junior soldiers. 'A lot of our blokes were first to deal with the mess. It changed every-thing, then. The attitude became "let's get out of here".'

Another 2 Para soldier disagreed. 'We left the day after the bomb. I didn't want to go. I felt like there was more to do, and even though it was shit, I was enjoying it. When the platoon sergeant said, "We're going home," everyone just kind of stared at him. We weren't happy.'

For a US Marine in 1/8, Abbey Gate was the moment when 'the mood turned dark. People stopped going out. Our building was the only place we considered secure.'

News of the casualties was a gut punch. Many of the company knew those among the dead.

'The next day we were sent to the blast area. The Paras were there. My friend saw something in the dirt. It was a patch that had belonged to one of the fallen Marines. We took it to his command so that they could get it back to his family.'

In the months following the attack, it was reported that the suicide bomber had been released from prison only days before, freed from the abandoned US base at Bagram.[9]

For Western nations and their leadership, the suicide bombing was the sign that time was up. The Kabul airlift was almost at an end, but before the final aircraft left the runway, there would be one more violent tragedy seen around the world.

'An honest mistake'

The Ahmadi family had hoped to leave Kabul and start a new life in America. They believed in the American dream, but they would soon find themselves on the end of an American reality.

Thirty-eight-year-old Zemari Ahmadi worked for a US aid group. He believed in the new Afghanistan and in America, but that would not be enough to save him: Zemari had just pulled up at his home when his thirteen-year-old son ran out to greet him. Seconds later a missile tore into his car, blowing them apart. Eight other members of the family were killed in the blast, including six more children.

'Collateral damage' has long been one of the most overused, and misunderstood terms of American-led war. It is a sanitised way of saying civilian casualties, which in itself is a sanitised way of saying 'innocent people torn limb from limb, burned alive, or choked to death on their own blood.'

There is a danger that, because of the very real and meaningful acts of the troops during the airlift, that the real face of the war in Afghanistan is forgotten. That we forget that Operation Enduring Freedom was not a humanitarian effort, but a war. A brutal, twenty-year war that claimed the lives of tens of thousands of Afghan civilians, many of them dying from bombs dropped by US and allied aircraft.

In the weeks that followed 29 August, the world would be reminded of this. The events of that day, and the whitewash that followed, would encapsulate all that was wrong with the American-led mission in Afghanistan: failures of intelligence, a reliance on air power, the death of civilians, and finally, often a lack of accountability.

The drone programme has long been criticised for its high number of civilian deaths, and lack of liability when they occurred. Leaving aside the fact that the drones often violate the sovereignty of other nations, this assassination programme, far from being the clinical operation that the US government pretends it to be, has killed as many as 1750 civilians.[10] To the author's knowledge, not one drone operator, nor the officers who oversee them, have been criminally charged for these deaths. By contrast, both the US and British have punished troops for killing civilians and wounded enemy combatants on the ground. This is not the case with the drone programme, which holds a privileged, untouchable position.

The strike on 29 August was said to be the prevention of another suicide attack at the airport. That had been carried out by IS-K, but it was the Ahmadi family who would suffer America's wrath.

Given the political temperature following the deaths of the US Marines, there is a feeling that America had to strike *someone*. The idea that the US Military could leave Kabul without striking a blow in retaliation was unfathomable. After all, the attacks on 9/11 had led to twenty years of war in Afghanistan, predominantly against an enemy who had not planned nor carried out the attacks. Given that track history of revenge, it would be naive to think that America would not engage in retaliation before its last soldier left the country. Did this lead to rushed intelligence? Was information made to fit a target, rather than a target fitting with the information?

In a Pentagon press conference, Lt General Said, the USAF Inspector General, said that the killing of the Ahmadi family was down to 'execution errors, combined with confirmation bias and communications breakdowns. That assessment was primarily driven by interpretation of intelligence and correlating that to observe movement throughout an eight-hour window, in which the vehicle was tracked throughout the day before it was ultimately struck. Regrettably, the interpretation or the correlation of the intelligence to what was being perceived at the time, in real time, was inaccurate. In fact, the vehicle, its occupant and contents did not pose any risk to US forces.'

This mouthful of jargon is the military's way of saying that 'we messed up and killed a family.'

'There was intelligence available,' continued General Said, 'that correlated the Corolla to particular locations, and the way it was interpreted is this was the Corolla of interest. Now obviously incorrectly, in hindsight, but it didn't stop there. When I'm talking about confirmation bias, the initial correlation I think if you all saw it in a classified setting, would be reasonable to conclude that that should be a vehicle of interest, right. And I think that would be very, very reasonable given the information that you're having, that you're receiving and you're trying to assess.

'But what transpired over eight hours – cumulative, right – is the observed pattern of movement, the observed behaviour and activity, that all has to aggregate and connect with intelligence to see is it reaffirming that this is truly the vehicle of interest to reach a point where you're so confident that you're going to strike it … Human nature, we all see it, right, everybody knows what confirmation bias is, when you're consciously or subconsciously start to perceive something and you go that is a suspicious person, every activity they take thereafter and you start seeing it through that lens.'

One reporter asked Lt General Said when it was evident that there were children at the compound:

General Said: So the first time we have confirmation of kids
    was at the two-minute timeframe.
Question: Two minutes before the impact?
General Said: Before the trigger pull.

Another reporter asked the officer if the attack at Abbey Gate had influenced the strike. The general agreed that it had.

'It was believed that the method, or at least the container that had the explosives in it [at Abbey Gate] was a computer bag. So, the fact that on that day, on the 29th, we're watching this white Corolla, we saw an exchange of a computer bag. It wasn't lost on people to go, "You know what, that's what was used to contain the explosives three days prior." And that is potentially indicative of, here we go again, another computer bag that contains explosives,' explained General Said, outlining what could have been in the heads of the strike team.

'True, I can understand that. But [it] could also be just a computer bag. And as it turns out and we can affirm it, it *was* a computer bag, right? But you could see that correlation of "I've seen this movie before".'

In the 'movie' that the strike team were seeing, a family was condemned to death because a white Corolla was seen in an area of interest, and a man was handed a computer bag. It is perhaps worth noting that there are close to 500,000 Toyota Corollas in Kabul,[11] a high number of them white, and that computer bags are predominantly used for the transportation of computers, not suicide bombs.

Given that the intelligence was already being stretched, at best, it is worth looking at the actions of the man driving the car. Mr Ahmadi was not driving for the airport, which was four miles away, or approaching coalition troops. He was getting out of his car, being greeted by children, and going into a house, and yet this was deemed by the generals to be an 'imminent threat'.

The only thing that was imminent was the death of an innocent family, blown to pieces by an American missile. Ten human beings, seven of them children, were condemned to death because Zemari Ahmadi was driving a white Corolla, and carrying a computer bag.

It is worth asking: what would happen if there was a suspected suicide bomber on US soil? Would the US Government sanction a drone strike in a busy residential area, based on the most flimsy intelligence? If not, then why is it acceptable to do so in other countries? What does that say about the value America and its allies place on human life outside of their own borders? The passport you hold should not determine how much your life is worth.

There are some who will make the argument that 'it is better to be safe than sorry', but this is a woeful argument on many levels. First, it places Western lives above Afghan ones, as though there is a difference in human life. Secondly, the Western soldiers and Marines were at the airport because they had *chosen* to be there. They volunteered for a dangerous job, and they did so knowing that they would be risking their lives for the lives of others. Soldiers and Marines don't want 'better safe than sorry'. If they did, they would never have become soldiers and Marines in the first place.

Does that mean that there should never be pre-emptive action?

No, and mistakes will always happen, so long as there is war, and the fog of war. But there was no immediate threat here, and the evidence to launch a missile was lacking. Facts were made to fit a narrative, and things that should have been obvious – such as children at the target – were either missed or ignored.

During the investigation that followed, it was claimed that the drone operators had not seen the three children that came out to greet the man as he left his car. Given that there were six drones on target, this seems unlikely. Lt General Said himself said that he could see the children on the footage, and he was not a trained operator.

And what of the survivors? Almost three weeks on from the attack, a father who lost a toddler said that no one from America had contacted the family to apologise.[12]

They were evidently not invited to the video teleconference given to reporters by General Kenneth McKenzie, commander of US military operations in the Middle East. 'At the time of the strike,' he said, 'I was confident that the strike had averted an imminent threat to our forces at the airport. Our investigation now concludes that the strike was a tragic mistake.'

'Honest'. 'Tragic'. But not 'unacceptable'. The general did not 'fall on his sword' by resigning. His words amounted to a shrug of the shoulders. The truth of the matter is that these deadly 'mistakes' *are* acceptable, both to the Pentagon and to the White House. They are made all the time, and nothing is done except to say 'oops' in an official sounding way, and offer up some money.

The Pentagon said that it would compensate the Ahmadi family members that survived the terror of their attack. For victims of American missiles, money is supposed to be enough, but for American casualties, such as those that died on 9/11, a twenty-year war was deemed the appropriate compensation. A war where 48,000 civilians have been killed in airstrikes across America's seven major conflict zones.[13] In the compensation paid for these innocents' deaths, about $5000 is the going rate for a child's life.[14] By comparison, a Hellfire missile costs about $100,000.

The drone and air campaigns are big business. Until the damages for fatal mistakes hit careers or budgets, there will be little appetite to change the situation as it stands. The Ahmadi family were not the first to be killed by an American coalition 'honest mistake', and they won't be the last. Often the ones to pay the price are the people 'we're here to help'. In any organisation where there is no accountability, people will over-reach and act recklessly. The events of 29 August are a clear demonstration of this. If a mistakenly fired missile could have cost officers their careers, then perhaps they would not have authorised it. And so, instead of a mistake being paid by the military member with rank and pay, it is instead paid for in innocent civilian lives.

They had believed in the new Afghanistan. They had joined the cause, supported America, and yet the Ahmadis were killed by an American missile fired by an American operator. As with the larger war itself, no one was held accountable for this tragedy. The killing of the Ahmadi family was, in all ways, the perfect encapsulation of all that was wrong with the American-led mission in Afghanistan.

By contrast, the actions of the troops involved with the airlift showed a different side of the war: that there was never a lack of effort or bravery by those who were deployed there. Despite the flaws of the war, it attracted many who placed their own lives and safety below that of strangers, and that must be lauded, valued and never forgotten. Because of the risk taken by the service personnel at HKIA, tens of thousands of Afghans were able to escape the Taliban, and start safer lives out of reach of the cruel regime.

11

The Final Airlift

Per Ardua Ad Astra: Through Adversity to the Stars.
— Motto of the Royal Air Force

The achievements of those on the ground could not have been done without the work of the RAF, USAF and the aircrews of allied nations. Airmen and women ferried in troops, took out civilians, and then came back for those who had been defending HKIA and enabling the evacuation. They did so by flying over terrain occupied by the Taliban and terrorist groups, flying into an airport that the world was watching, but which did not have a functioning air traffic control, and had been at times overrun by civilians and armed men. The Royal Air Force has a distinguished history, but if the Battle of Britain belonged to the fighter pilots, then the RAF's 'finest hour' in the Kabul airlift was made possible by the aircrews of its transport fleet.

Flight Lieutenant Robert Manson was one among them. He joined the RAF during the peak of British involvement in Afghanistan, but by the time that he completed his four years of training to become a C-130 pilot, UK forces' role in the country was coming to an end.

'I always expected to go to Afghanistan but, by the time that I became a pilot with the air mobility fleet, the British pull-out from Helmand was already happening. I had a real chip on my shoulder about not going. I took part in other operations around the world, including humanitarian missions, but I had this feeling like there was a hole in my heart. Afghanistan was the war of my generation, and I'd missed it.'

Like many of those who would deploy on Op Pitting, Manson was on leave when he got the call.

'My boss called and asked me if I wanted to go on something interesting. I'd been watching the news, so I could figure out what he meant. It was obvious it was Afghanistan. I ran it by my wife, but she wasn't keen for me to go. I was on leave and I was about to go on operations soon anyway. I turned the job down, but my wife could soon see that we'd made a mistake. I went from really enjoying our holiday to just moping around the place, tracking the planes in and out of Kabul on an app. I felt like I'd blown my chance to ever go out there.'

It was the sheer complexity of the airlift that would give Manson a second chance. 'I got a call to go out and take over the C-130 detachment as lead planner. Up until then, Syria, Iraq and Afghan ops were all being planned through one man, but the continuous changing nature of what was happening in Kabul just made this impossible, and so I came in to take over the Kabul side of things.'

Arriving in the Middle East, Manson found an airbase packed to the gills with aircraft and personnel that were part of the mission. It wasn't long until he was taking off from the desert in the cockpit of a C-130, a workhorse of British campaigns.

'Our flight simulators are great, and before missions we'll fly the profile so that we've seen what the terrain looks like, but none of that was possible for Kabul. There just wasn't time, and things could change.'

Manson describes the first time that he entered Afghan airspace. A moment he had waited twelve years to experience.

'My first flight was on a moonlit night. We were flying by Night Vision Goggles and the sky and mountains looked amazing. Our radios were very busy,' Manson remembered, referring to a high volume of radio traffic from other aircraft, and those talking them down at HKIA.

'The flight plan brought us in from the south-east, and then we'd turn at five nautical miles' distance to make a westerly approach. This brought us over the Red Desert and close to the mountains, but I wasn't worried about them with all of the light that the NVGs were picking up. They were easy to see. What was a problem was the air traffic control situation, which was non-existent.

'This was a very unique situation. All of the Afghan controllers had left, so there was one USMC JTAC [Joint Terminal Attack Controller], who was controlling everything without the help of radar, and just by moving paper planes around a board. He was great, but there's only so much you can do for air traffic control without radar. That put a lot on the pilots. On a later run, we had a US plane cut in front of us to land. I don't think they'd seen us, so we had to come around again. On the first run, nothing like that happened, but we could see streams of tracer fire going up into the air. It looked like it was celebratory. Nothing accurate.'

An accidental bullet is as damaging as an intentional one, but Manson had to weigh up other risks.

'There was only one runway at HKIA, and people and vehicles were crossing it all of the time. And then there were other aircraft taxiing, or taking off and landing. Any collision would have been catastrophic. Not only in terms of loss of life, but it would have closed the runway and ground the entire operation to a halt. For that reason, I felt that not being seen was a bigger danger than small arms fire, and so I made the decision to come in with all of my lights on. This was counter to the usual SOP [Standard Operating Procedure], but it was based on the situation at the time.'

Still, small arms fire would continue to pose problems to Manson and his crew.

'On our second sortie, there was tracer going up right at the end of the runway, and right through the area where we would have to fly if there was some reason why we couldn't land.'

Such a reason soon appeared: a convoy of vehicles driving across the runway.

'We were three hundred feet from them and they were still crossing. At the end of the runway, there was still fire going into the air. I was sure it would hit us, so I didn't want to break off from landing until the last possible moment. The convoy was still crossing. At a hundred feet distance to them I judged they would be out of the way, and committed to the landing rather than fly into the tracer.'

A 'Wild West' is how Manson and many others described the situation at HKIA. US special forces had commandeered a fire truck and, according to one of Manson's colleagues, drove it right below his wing. Without a proper air traffic control, the situation on the runway was perilous, but Manson was highly impressed with the efficiency and organisation of the ground element.

'A "follow me" vehicle would lead you to a spot, and there would either be passengers or equipment waiting to go. We'd load and get straight back out. This could be as little as fifteen minutes for passengers, or up to an hour if it was equipment, which obviously does not move itself.'

Like many who were part of Operation Pitting, Manson had never seen the secret plan himself. 'It felt like it was being made up on the hoof,' he said, though not disparagingly. 'The blokes on the fence really did so well. Because they did their job, they kept us safe. There were no incursions when I was there. The American JTAC was great, too. Different nations were doing their own thing, but everyone was doing their best. Naturally, we were getting in each other's way. We would report to the JTAC what our approach and distance was, and he'd use paper planes on a board to keep track. It was very rudimentary, but it worked.'

Manson had waited twelve years to come to Afghanistan. Due to COVID restrictions, he wasn't able to talk to the locals face to face. The pilot's first experience of meeting Afghans was watching them board as refugees into the back of his aircraft.

'They all looked wiped out. Knackered. Most of them had their whole lives packed into a carrier bag. I was struck by the number of kids. My sister had a five-month-old baby, who was about the same age as one of the children on the flight. I got quite choked up thinking about how different their lives were.'

The pilot needed to set his feelings aside to see the people to safety.

'Once we got airborne there was a sense of relief, and then they all went to sleep. Kids were sleeping in all kinds of positions. Only one person was awake.'

Manson landed the aircraft in the Middle East, and moved from the cockpit to the tailgate so that he could see his passengers disembark.

'There were lots of smiles, thumbs up and waves. Usually in air mobility we don't see the direct effect of what we do, so this was very gratifying.'

Manson and his crew continued to bring people and material out of Kabul until finally, there was only one more mission to be flown.

'A C-17 had taken most of the remaining Paras, so there was just one more flight of British military kit and equipment to do. We were on one-hour notice to be airborne, which meant that we just had to fire up the engines. We were using an encrypted civilian app to work out the timings.'

The fewer troops were at the airfield, the more precarious the situation for those left behind, and so Manson wanted to waste no time in getting out to them.

'What I didn't know was that, because it was a historic moment, the rest of the flight had come out to send us off. I just saw people in front of the aircraft, and they had to run to get out of the way.'

Later that night at HKIA, Manson's aircraft was loaded with men and equipment. Much of Britain's men and materials had come in and out of the country in aircraft like this one, but this would be the final sortie of the twenty-year war. As they taxied to the runway, Flight Lieutenant Manson felt obliged to broadcast a transmission 'for everyone who had been there'.

'This is the last UK aircraft to leave Kabul,' he transmitted. 'Thank you for everything that you have done. For everyone that lost their lives here, we will remember them.'

It was a quiet flight back. The end of an era. For those in the rear of the aircraft, their jobs done, it was a time of reflection. By the time that Manson landed his aircraft, the Defence Secretary had made the public statement that the last British aircraft had left Kabul.

When they landed in the Middle East, there was no *Top Gun* moment for Manson and his crew. The mission was over, but no one felt like celebrating. 'We had a beer, then went to bed.'

What had been a bustling airbase soon became a ghost town. The RAF held a C-130 and C-17 on standby in case of an emergency at Kabul, but once the Americans had pulled out, it was time to go back to Cyprus.

'In Cyprus we had to isolate for COVID. Some of the aircrew there dropped us off some beers. We got smashed, and then I slept for eighteen hours.'

The rest was well earned, and well needed. After his COVID isolation, Manson was straight back into the air. This time, supporting operations in Iraq and Syria.

'I didn't have time to process anything ... It was a strange feeling, but it was one of those things where you push emotions to the back of your mind to do your job. You process afterwards. Mission first, emotion second. And of course, when it's done, there's a massive sense of relief.'

Not only relief, but no more hole in his heart. The man who thought that he had missed out on the British mission in Afghanistan had flown the last plane out of Kabul.

Precious cargo

'Each time I've been in Afghan has been as some sort of draw down,' said Sergeant Andy Livingstone, a loadmaster in the RAF. 'I never really came into contact with the civilian population.'

This would change dramatically on Operation Pitting, which would come with new challenges and new dangers.

'Going back in [to Kabul] it was not so much the ground-to-air threat. The threat was a complete breakdown in air traffic [control]. We were very much aware of other aircraft that weren't necessarily under active control, and we were doing our best, using common frequencies, to avoid collision.'

Livingstone had been at HKIA as recently as the early summer.

'The feeling [of being in Kabul] was completely different. It was pretty sad seeing what had happened. Previously, Afghanistan had felt like not quite a functioning country, but it had an international airport, air traffic control. It seemed like it was working. Flying over Kabul, especially during the day, it looked like any normal city. And then, into Pitting, it was just back into a warzone again. The airfield was in a mess. The country was in a state of disintegration. Going back in there was a sense of failure. Over the space of a month a functioning country had fallen, and back into the hands of a people who, as a country and as a coalition, we thought we'd got the better of.'

Andy recognised that, no matter how many people the UK evacuated, 'there was going to be a lot, lot more who'd have a very hard time.'

Most of the A400M fleet's experience was military freight and passengers, not civilians. Carrying refugees, particularly children, would present new difficulties to be overcome. 'They didn't know what it was like to be on a plane. They didn't know how to act or what to do, and they didn't know what was going to be on the other end. Seeing two hundred people lined up at the back, with often just plastic shopping bags.'

The language barrier was another factor, particularly when it came to giving safety briefs to the passengers, many of whom were incredibly fatigued after their experiences of clearing the gates into HKIA.

'We kept the engines running, because we wanted to get them away as quickly as you can. You've got the noise, you've got the wind. People were coming on with serious injuries. Blood down their clothes. The amount of children who were in an absolute state, bandages and everything, it was just incredible to see. It's something that you'll never forget.'

Livingstone and other crew members soon realised that they would need to implement the old military adage of 'improvise, adapt, and overcome'.

'Usually we've got fifty-six sidewall seats and we can fit maybe another fifty down the centre, but a hundred or so just wasn't going to cut it.' The crews found new ways of creating 'seats' using cargo strapping as seat belts. 'We sat as many people as we could on the floor. Comfort wasn't our priority.' Livingstone and the crew members assured their passengers that the flight would only last a few hours. 'Everyone was terrified. No one had a clue. It was chaos, but the planning and the chats that we'd had as crews beforehand certainly helped.'

Family dynamics were another challenge. 'In most cases the family patriarch led the way with his family with him. The vast majority of all our passengers were women and children.' On his second flight, Livingstone and the crew took out two hundred children. 'They all wanted to sit together. They all wanted to be together. And when you're trying to fit two hundred people in a plane that's seventeen metres long inside, it just isn't going to work.

'As a Western male, if you see a pregnant woman you're going to offer her a seat.' Livingstone and his crew would witness the patriarch of the family taking the place for himself and 'pushing her onto the floor. We tried to get Dad back out of the seat, and say no, no, she's clearly the important one here, but it would never happen. The dads would be sat along the sides with the eldest son, and mothers and children were on the floor. No matter what we tried it was never going to change, and that was a struggle. That was really difficult.'

'We're all pretty friendly guys,' said the loadmaster:

We've all done a bit of humanitarian [operations]. We all really want to do that. The best way to manage them is to make them feel safe.

Trying to convince the air transport security guys that they could chill, and not have to stay rigid to the SOPs, sat there with a weapon in hand and helmet and body armour, because that's just threatening to these families and kids. And we got there. The amount of money we spent on sweeties and biscuits and crisps. We didn't eat on the plane. We ordered food, as we usually would, but any food was all given out. We tried our best to help. More often than not people were fucked. It was honking.

Being a dad, you know how these kids are feeling, and how resilient kids can be, because they can't understand the gravity of what's happening. It was actually really easy to bring them around from being really terrified by taking the helmet off, getting rid of the long weapons, and offering a smile and sweeties. Just little things. Anything that we could do to make things fun for them, because that's all you can do.

I wasn't able to fix what had happened up until they got to the aircraft, and what happened after the aircraft, so that's what we tried to do. This could be a good thing, knowing that, realistically, they were refugees, homeless and with absolutely nothing. It wasn't really until after the op, seeing my own kids, that things really hit hard. I just couldn't imagine being a parent in that position.

There was an older woman who came on in a wheelchair. Her son wouldn't strap himself down or do anything than hold onto the wheelchair, even though it was secure. He just wouldn't leave his mum. He was holding onto the only thing he had. The first thing she did was get her handbag out, and she was just handing out sweets to every kid around her.

Andy gave his sunglasses to a young boy, and his older brother took them for himself. 'I thought, that's fairly normal.'

Livingstone recalled an incident on one flight out of Kabul:

Most of the time we flew with medics, but on that trip we didn't. That family were first on. It was a teenage son, a teenage daughter, Mum, Dad and the baby. The daughter was proper fucked. Passing out, coming back, passing out. Looking ill. It was exhaustion. Me and one of the flight engineers were trying to get her to come around, and whilst we were doing all of that something fell, and when I looked around it wasn't a bag, but a child. Mum hadn't noticed, because she was hanging out, but Dad just looked at her and it reminded her that she'd dropped the baby. She scrambled down and picked it back up.

It happened a second time and the reminders got more physical from her husband, so I stepped in at that point. I tried to strap the baby to her with the seat belts, but she was just too fucked to keep herself up and awake, and so I picked the baby up. Dad didn't have a clue what was going on. I doubt he'd ever seen anything like a man holding a baby. Mum didn't protest either. She shut her eyes. I was fine. There was nothing else to do, so I was just going to sit with the baby, let her be alright. There was no crying, but the dad woke the mum up eventually and said no, have her back.

I can't remember if it was the same trip or another one, but I remember there was another baby and they pulled out a changing bag with nappies and stuff. And they pulled out this bottle of milk and it was yellow. It wasn't fresh. I went up and pulled the top off and it was stinking. It was rancid. They were about to feed it to them, because that was all they had. I sent the bottle upstairs to one of the pilots and he was devastated, because he's another dad.

Little things like that hit you like a fucking train. What would have happened to that baby after drinking half a pint of fucked milk? And what sort of desperation from the parents would make them think that was OK? We got her some fresh milk, but it was just, what the fuck?

Coming home

'We felt guilty we were leaving,' said Stuart Ramsay, a British journalist who had been in the thick of things in Kabul and at HKIA, 'myself, my producer Dominique, Sky colleague Martin, and Toby. An easy exit for a group of journalists guaranteed safety by our soldiers and our governments. I'll take the jibes and the scorn for leaving. But I will say this: if we hadn't been there, nobody would have seen any of the scenes of horror and desperation that have engulfed this entire operation, none of the incredible work by the British military, and the Foreign and Home Office staff.

'It was the strangest sensation . . . walking and joining the line with refugees; watched on the whole time by armed soldiers. They were all uniformly courteous to us and they were, to be fair, to the evacuees. But it felt demeaning to me, and if I felt it, what did the men and women, young and old, proud of their Afghan heritage, feel? I watched as an elderly couple, holding hands, looked back at the Afghan mountains looming over the airport. Mountains that are the very essence of this country. It seemed to me they were saying goodbye, one last look at their country. They clutched each other for a moment and turned. They will never come back.'[1]

Will the same be true of the soldiers who served there?

'Flying out, we were packed pretty tight in a C-17, but we were happy to be done with it,' said Sergeant Stumpf, who had been deployed to Kabul months before the Taliban's rapid advance. 'It was certainly a relief to finally be getting out of there. Granted, by that time we were such a small group [about 175 people or so], so we didn't have the muscle of the other forces on the ground that were there by the hundreds [and] thousands. But I think subconsciously I would have wanted to stay until the very end. Just being so close to the absolute end after the previous ten months was a bit of a change.

'Of course, the day after we landed in Kuwait is when the bomb went off at Abbey Gate. A lot of guilt was felt by most of the guys. I know there were some medical folks [actual trauma/ER people] that flew out with us. I can't imagine how they felt, knowing they could have helped if they'd stayed back.'

'Leaving was weird,' said Major Steve White of 2 Para. 'I was knackered. We went four days without sleep, but I had a feeling we'd done something special, and we'd left a shit situation with pride and honour. Every minute that we held on meant an extra extraction. The guys got that, and there was never any need for rousing speeches. We gave it everything we had. We couldn't have left anything more on the field.'

Inside the C-17, men sat silently, legs intertwined, any conversation drowned by the hum of the engines.

'One soldier had a brother killed on [Operation] Herrick,' said White. 'He felt like, now he'd been here too, it put some of his demons to rest.'

'I was exhausted,' said Aaron Nunkoosing, 2 Para's adjutant. 'I think a lot of us, we were at that point where we wanted to do more, we wanted to keep getting people through, but we were fucked. On one hand we were happy to leave, because we knew the situation was untenable. But, on the other there was also this massive, massive feeling of "we could do more". It was a bit of a conflicting feeling.

'We'd also just done the ceremony for the thirteen [US service personnel killed in the Abbey Gate attack]. We lined the road as the thirteen coffins went by, and we realised how lucky we all were. A moment, or a step in the wrong direction, and that could have been British soldiers. It was that feeling of we've done something awesome, something good, but we don't know if anyone back home will appreciate it. There were lots of emotions: we are fucked, it could have been worse, it's time to go, holy fuck, there's still a load of people back here, what's going to happen about them?'

Lee Bowden, the leader of a USMC EOD team, recalled his experience of leaving Kabul. 'I left with the last of my teams on the thirtieth. There was a mix of units on the flight, and we sat between each other's legs. It was cramped and surreal. I hadn't reconciled what had happened yet.'

'Some of my Marines had gone through training with the guys who died,' said Captain Sam McGrury of 1/8 Marines. 'They were pissed off.'

On 29 August, Sam handed over control of North Gate to the 82nd Airborne. His company left Kabul the next day, Sam boarding the flight after his men. 'I hate flying and I thought that we might get shot at, but I was too tired to care.' He lay down on the tail ramp and fell asleep.

'We were the last Marine infantry company in Afghanistan,' Sam recalled with pride. The last of thousands of US Marines who would leave a piece of themselves in that country, returning home different men than those who had departed. Hundreds of Marines had died in the twenty-year war, with thousands more injured. 'There was definitely a feeling of what did we do this for? But that came later. I brought all of my Marines home, and I could tell they were proud of their achievement.'

Soldiers who had been living on adrenaline now found themselves with long days filled with boredom.

'They flew us back to the UK and we went into COVID isolation,' said a 2 Para soldier. 'Everyone was snapped. We were kept in a hangar for five days and not even allowed to our [barracks] block, which we could see from the hangar.'

There was an awareness by the Army that the efforts in Kabul would have taken a heavy mental toll.

'After two days everyone got TRIM, but it was too early,' the soldier said, referring to the practice of Trauma Risk Incident Management. 'No one had processed what had happened yet. I don't think the mass TRIM got done again in later months.'

The paratrooper had been moved to join the Army in part because of documentaries about Afghanistan.

'One good thing did happen while we were in the hangars. Ross Kemp came to visit us.'

The appearance was remembered fondly by other 2 Para soldiers. 'Ross Kemp came by,' said Josh. On the efforts of the British forces, he was rightly proud.

'It felt like we'd improved the lives of other people. It was a team effort. 2 Yorks were grafting. And the RAF were flying in crap conditions. I didn't ever consider that my life was in danger there, although I suppose that it was. It's just the job.'

As 2 Para and other units left Kabul, the situation became more precarious for those left behind.

'How are we going to get out?' one US Marine wanted to know.

The answer was to work 24 hours a day to build layers of defences through which they could fall back, and stem the tide of people who would try to follow them. They laid wire, built gates, and welded shipping containers together to form barricades. There was even a plan to lay a burning bus across the road; a tactic borrowed from Mexican drug cartels.

'We had a broken arrow scenario, which was to get yourself to any plane, by any means, and get on.'

HKIA was awash with equipment that the Marines did not want falling into Taliban hands. 'It was anarchy in the base,' the Marine remembered. 'We were breaking into buildings, destroying stuff and smashing cars. When else are you going to be allowed to drive cars into walls? We found loads of equipment that was waiting for the ANP. Helmets, body armour, weapons sights, etc. Some of it was taken home. We also traded stuff with the ANA, Germans and British Paras. We started taking the Afghan flags off of vehicles and buildings. The Taliban would destroy them, and we wanted to keep it intact and alive. One ANA soldier gave me his Velcro flag patch and a full-size folded flag.

'The Army were the last to leave. It was a photo op for a general, and that pissed us off. A three star general was the last to get onboard. The last boots off the ground should have been Afghan.'

After overcoming their exhaustion, there was time for the Marines to reflect. 'We couldn't understand why so many fighting-aged males were not fighting the Taliban, or leaving their families. How can the same culture that produces such warriors also produce men who would use women and children to get over razor wire?'

Still, the Marine was in no doubt that they were leaving a country in a worse state than they had found it. 'We got to a point of hoping that the Taliban would change.'

In Kuwait, the Marines underwent COVID quarantine and mental health assessments. There was a general worry about what would happen when the unit got home and went on leave.

'We were pretty much told not to talk about it.'

Major Danny Riley had been the liaison officer between the British and American forces.

'I got on that plane confident that the 82nd had security. There was lots of time for reflection. It was a good effort. It was not Helmand or Basra, it was a very different experience for me, but in terms of what we'd achieved I was proud. I felt like I'd played a part in something amazing. We played the hand we'd been dealt, but a couple of months more would have helped a lot. We were working to the Americans' plan, which is OK, because we're the junior partner, but we need to be careful about our hubris. When I asked for something from the Americans, they always provided it. I was always happy to go out with them, and I can hold my head up high, because I helped get hundreds of Americans out.'

Despite being proud and full of praise of the combined effort, Major Riley recognised that things could have gone very differently.

'We were lucky. We were on the ground without radios and ammunition. 2 Para were utterly fatigued. It was a success, but it was a rocky success. In my head I thought it was going to be a mixture of Helmand and Basra, all in that little area, but it wasn't that. If we'd have got there a few days earlier, we could have had outer cordons, better security and given the people more confidence.'

Coming back from a deployment is often a difficult transition, and Op Pitting was no different. Major Riley recalled that 'when we landed the RAF clapped us off, which was quite embarrassing really, but also quite telling. I went on the lash for a month solid. I genuinely don't know why, because it wasn't as messy as anything I'd done in the past. I still haven't balanced myself from it. I just can't comprehend it, but that's fine. That's how it goes.'

Flying into the UK was a homecoming for the British troops, but for the Afghan evacuees it was an arrival in a new and alien place. Huria had worked at the British embassy in Kabul, and had escaped her beloved home with her husband and young daughter.

'When the plane landed in Birmingham airport, we had to spend six to seven hours inside the place because other Afghan families came before us and their passports were not checked. They were still in the queue and they were not allowing us to get off the plane, because they had to get done with checking those people. It was quite stinky. Children were farting. Old people were complaining. Everyone was kind of depressed and tired. They just wanted to get off the plane. After six hours, they took us off the plane and they took us to a big terminal. It was quite cold. This is my first time in England. When we entered the terminal it was so cold and we didn't have anything except our clothes. We had nothing.'

Parmilla and her family, who had been aided in their escape by three British women, recalled a similarly tough flight to the UK. 'We didn't have water on the plane. Our children were crying. We were all thirsty. We had all sick people on that airplane.

They said we should have had it with us. My twins were crying for water.'

Mohammad Dawood had been part of the Afghan special forces. Like Parmilla, he would escape via Pakistan. After six months in hiding, living on frayed nerves, Mohammad received an email to say that his ARAP application had been approved, but he would need to cross the border in order to get to the UK. 'A family friend drove us as we hid,' he said. Like thousands of others, he would only escape Kabul long after the fall of the Afghan government.

The military endeavour at HKIA was a Herculean effort. The US airlifted 124,000 people. Britain took out more than 15,000, including 2200 children. Families were saved, yet torn apart. New lives could begin, but challenges remained. For Afghanistan, for its people, and for those who served there, the escape from Kabul was not a final act, but the latest chapter in a long story of war and suffering.

12

The Aftermath

It is no use saying, 'We are doing our best.'You have got to succeed in doing what is necessary.

— Winston Churchill

One year later

Operation Pitting was a humanitarian mission. That is, it was launched to save and protect human lives. Those who deployed as soldiers, Marines and airmen did so voluntarily and with great courage, but there was no such choice afforded to those that they would be evacuating: tens of thousands of Afghan civilians were running for their lives.

There is a danger that, in recounting military operations, the civilians are forgotten. Compartmentalisation was a necessity for those on the ground, lest they be overcome by the enormity of the suffering they were facing, but the reality is that those civilians who escaped Afghanistan were not a number, but living, breathing human beings with hopes and dreams that were dashed by the Taliban's advance and re-capture of the country. More than a hundred thousand civilians were airlifted from HKIA, and more escaped through Pakistan. They left behind lives that they had built, and people and a land that they loved. None took the decision lightly. People do not attempt to climb onto the landing gear of an aircraft unless all hope has vanished.

For every person who escaped from Kabul, though, many more were left behind. For them, the collapse of the country was the end of one struggle and the beginning of another.

'Since the Taliban came back to power, nearly a million Afghans have lost their jobs,' said Nelufar Hedayat, a British-Afghan journalist, and host of the Kabul Falling Podcast. 'Under the former government, Afghanistan's economy had been largely dependent on international aid with 43 per cent of its GDP coming from foreign donors. When Kabul fell, Afghanistan's economy was suddenly isolated, with disastrous consequences for ordinary Afghans. Afghanistan is now experiencing one of the worst famines in its history caused by the economic crisis and compounded by a long drought and harsher than usual winter. Desperate families burned furniture to stay warm. Some have sold their daughters to survive.'[1]

'My heart stopped beating,' said Gul, recalling the moment she discovered that her husband had sold their daughter into marriage. 'I wished I could have died at that time, but maybe God didn't want me to die. [My husband] said he wanted to sell one and save the others. "You all would have died this way," [he said.] I told him, "Dying was much better than what you have done."'[2]

Mercifully, with the help of the community, Gul's family were able to secure a 'divorce' for their daughter for a payment of around $1000. Others have not been so fortunate. As the situation in Afghanistan shows no signs of improvement, the sale of children is a practice that is likely to continue.

'According to the World Food Programme, 92 per cent of the population doesn't have enough to eat,' said Hedayat, '1.1 million children are acutely malnourished and 4.7 million more children, pregnant women and nursing mothers are at risk of a similar fate. To make matters worse, this June an earthquake hit the provinces of Paktia and Khost, leaving 362,000 people in need of humanitarian assistance. Meanwhile, broad and punishing US sanctions have further severed Afghanistan's economy from the rest of the world.'[3]

'It is a dilemma that the United States and much of the international community will be forced painfully to reconcile with,' writes reporter Hollie McKay. 'Either recognise the new Taliban regime and release the funds that could stop innocent Afghans from starving to death, or pariah the country and hold out for a longer game, in the hopes the regime eliminates terrorism and values human rights.'[4]

The freezing of assets marked for Afghanistan has proven catastrophic for many.

'Afghanistan's intensifying hunger and health crisis is urgent and at its root a banking crisis,' said John Sifton, Asia advocacy director at Human Rights Watch. 'Regardless of the Taliban's status or credibility with outside governments, international economic restrictions are still driving the country's catastrophe and hurting the Afghan people.'[5]

Foreign aid assistance is essential, but large amounts of aid are being blocked by the US government.

'Six months after the fall of Kabul, President Biden issued an executive order that seized the seven billion the Afghan government had in US banks,' said journalist Nelufar Hedayat. 'Since then, other countries and institutions worldwide have done the same, effectively cutting off the Taliban government and the Afghan people from international banking. The Biden administration decided that half of the frozen funds would be set aside for the families of 9/11 victims, who had previously filed lawsuits against the Taliban.'

It is worth remembering that no Afghan took part in the 9/11 attack, and a study by Brown University found that more than 70,000 Afghan and Pakistani civilians had died as the result of the war that followed. Afghanistan has paid its 'compensation' in blood.

'The other 3.5 billion dollars of these reserves are still earmarked for Afghans,' said Hedayat on the Kabul Falling podcast,[6] 'but on August 15th, the one year anniversary of the fall of Kabul, the US said it did not plan to release that money to Afghanistan central bank anytime soon. Officials say they're concerned the funds could flow to terrorists. The announcement came just weeks after the Biden administration said the US had killed Ayman al-Zawahiri, the leader of al-Qaeda and an architect of the 9/11 attacks, in a drone strike. He'd been tucked away in a safe house in a wealthy neighbourhood in downtown Kabul, that's now reportedly home to numerous Taliban officials.'

Al-Zawahiri's death undermined Joe Biden's July 2021 claim that America had rid Afghanistan of al-Qaeda. While there is some legitimacy to the worry that released funds could flow to the wrong people, much as there was a legitimate case for taking military action following 9/11, it is ordinary Afghans who are paying the price in both instances.

'People have nothing to eat,' an Afghan humanitarian official told Human Rights Watch in July 2022. 'You may not imagine it, but children are starving . . . The situation is dire, especially if you go to the villages.' He said he knew of one family who had lost two children, aged five and two, to starvation in the last two months.[7]

More than 90 per cent of Afghans have been suffering from some form of food insecurity since the US coalition left the country.[8] In September 2022, the US announced that it would begin a slow release of the frozen reserves earmarked for Afghans. 'The Afghan Fund will help mitigate the economic challenges facing Afghanistan while protecting and preserving $3.5 billion in reserves from Da Afghanistan Bank [DAB], Afghanistan's central bank, for the benefit of the people of Afghanistan,' said Wally Adeyemo, United States deputy secretary of the Treasury.[9]

For many the aid will come too late, if at all. After twenty years, the civilians in Afghanistan are still caught between the US Government and the Taliban.

'We will stay hungry and build our country,' said Mujahid, a Taliban fighter with a degree in Social Care. 'We don't expect support.'[10]

Food is not the only concern. For many minorities in Afghanistan, both the present and future are bleak. There is little hope that the Taliban will respect individual rights, particularly of those they find guilty of breaking Sharia law. 'We are gay boys, but we cannot even share our problems with our families,' said one young Afghan man. 'My father or uncle will kill us. Or the Taliban will kill us. We are humans; we have rights, we have a life to live. But how?'[11]

Also at risk are those who fought against the Taliban, many of them afraid to even venture outside of their homes. Cut off from the outside world in almost all ways, their mental health is eroded daily in an effort to protect their physical bodies. In 2020, many Westerners had a taste of what it is like to be confined in their homes. Imagine, on top of this, the very real threat that at any time a death squad could turn up at your door. Assurances of an amnesty from the Taliban mean little when people have been disappeared, or been found murdered.

'Earlier this month, the decimated bodies of four Afghans – two women and two men – were discovered in Mazar-e-Sharif, the capital of the northern Balkh province, several days after being reported missing,' reported Hollie McKay.[12]

One of the dead was a prominent women's rights activist. It appears as though the victims were lured from hiding by someone posing as part of an evacuation effort. Such scams usually cost families their money, rather than their lives.

'Several Afghans have come forward with chilling tales of having been contacted via WhatsApp under the guise of being a US evacuation authority and collecting the exposed individual's private details, documents and identification cards,' wrote McKay.[13]

As some seek to flee the country, others are grudgingly optimistic about Afghanistan's future under the Taliban. Haider al-Abadi, an Iraqi politician who has written about Afghanistan, said that: 'if it [the Taliban] is able to turn the page on the history of violence and oppression ... there are arguably opportunities for the Taliban to create a more positive future for the population under its control ...

'The Taliban also has the benefit of operating a quick and efficient judicial process – which, of course, in the past has been manipulated and used as a vehicle for violence and terror. But if it harnesses these efficiencies and implements justice on a local level, it may be able to build trust among communities that have been fighting for years against the tide of bureaucracy and red tape. If Taliban members themselves partake in corruption, however, the people will see through their fragile veil of religious legitimacy immediately.'[14]

Many already have, thanks to the Taliban's longstanding tradition of punishing them. When asked if there would be continued persecution of minorities in Afghanistan, such as the Hazaras, the Taliban spokesman Suhail Shaheen answered, 'We promised just freedom to them and as a basis of our Islamic rules, because they are also Muslims, but maybe some differences in the jurisprudence of religious jurisprudence. But they are Muslims and we have no discrimination against other ethnicities, all ethnicities living in Afghanistan, they are brothers to each other. So they are like all ethnicities, like different flowers in a garden. So we want a national unity of the country.

'At that time, there were commanders, our military commander was among the Shia people, very famous commanders we had in that war, and [Ustad] Akbari, the leader of Shia, he had joined our forces. He was with us. Now we have a policy that we do not have any kind of discrimination against the Shia people. They are Afghans. They can live in this country peacefully and they can contribute to the reconstruction, prosperity and development of the country.'[15]

Under the previous, Western-supported regime, women were allowed to work jobs and hold positions in government. On 18 August 2021, the Taliban's spokesman made assurances that this would continue. 'The women have a right to education and to work so they can hold different positions and jobs right now. The doctors who have started serving. The teachers have started teaching. And also in other fields, the women are working. The journalist women, they have started working, by observing hijab. So, yes, women can do their job – only they should observe hijab.'[16]

Despite these assurances, in the following month it was reported that women were only being allowed to do work that men could not do, such as cleaning bathrooms.[17] At the time of publishing, it seems as though the Taliban – and other forces inside Afghanistan – do not intend for women to return to the workplace or the classroom.

'They want to prevent us from getting education, but they cannot,' said Ms Haidari, a witness to a brutal bomb attack on an education centre. 'No one can stop us. We are not going to give up.'[18]

The attack took place in September 2022 and claimed the lives of fifty-three people, most of them young women.[19]

'The attack on civilian places shows weakness and hostility toward the people of our country,'[20] said Abdul Nafi Takoor, the Taliban spokesman for the Interior Ministry.

Perhaps this sentiment is a sign of a rift in the Taliban. Some of their officials have called for girls to return to school, perhaps recognising that this would ease America's reluctance to release aid. Time will tell if the words are anything more than a ploy, and as Afghanistan fades from the headlines, it remains to be seen what will happen to the rights of minorities. What is clear is that they will not be silent. Whether this will result in greater rights, or greater suffering, is as yet unknown.

For those looking for a silver lining in the country's situation, it is perhaps to be found in the fact that the feared mass reprisals have not been forthcoming. Tony, a UN security advisor, remained in the country until October.

'In the immediate aftermath of the takeover, security was good. IS-K didn't really do much. The Taliban were trying to do the right thing in controlling the airport and controlling people. Their methods were perhaps quite a bit strange, as in there's lots of firing to control crowds, but they were trying to control the city.'

Tony offers some insight as to why support for IS-K may be growing:

> Throughout ISAF and Resolute Support there was always this talk about we don't like night raids, we don't like the way international forces are doing these raids. Very soon, the Taliban were doing exactly the same to defeat IS-K. And all of a sudden they'd just become the government and they had the same problems, were conducting the same type of operations as the army was before, so it's like, what changed? And then when they started wearing a uniform, it's like, if you didn't know any different, you'd just think no one had changed. So again, this was the space where IS-K grew. People became pissed off that the Taliban were then conducting those types of raids, which then pushes the community away, and gives space for the people against the Taliban to operate.

The UN security advisor stayed in Afghanistan for some six weeks after the last US flight left Kabul:

> It all went a bit strange. The international military left and there was just this void. It's quite strange being in a country where there's no flights in and out and you're not sure what's going to happen. I went back up to Jalalabad by road. Into Paktika. We did Kabul to Kandahar. Kabul to Mazar. Everyone was a bit numb. There wasn't mass panic. There wasn't mass hysteria. There was almost an acceptance of, okay, this is where we are. There was a massive increase of Afghans dressing traditionally.

As part of his role for the UN, Tony was often face to face with the Taliban:

Kabul became a massive melting pot [of Taliban]. The Taliban is not a homogenous group. Outside the UN compound, they provided security, but there was an argument between them because we had the Helmand Taliban, we had the Taliban from Paktia, we had Haqqani Taliban there as well, so they were very different groups. In the early days it was very much whoever turned up somewhere first gained control and ownership of the area, and so because the UN was one of the very few locations where internationals still were, there was prime kudos associated with that. And they were perfectly fine. They didn't come into the compound. But then ultimately as time went on, more and more roles became more formalised and organised, and a lot of the Haqqanis' blokes became the de facto escorts and guards for places.

They'd all ask us, were you surprised how quick we took over? Yeah, of course we were. We weren't expecting it. But then I'd ask them, were you surprised that you took over so fast? And they paused, they'd start chuckling, and then they'd say, 'Yeah.' So in terms of this being a failure, the Taliban didn't even know they were going to take over, so if they didn't know, how could anyone else?

Chatting to them, they obviously weren't all sweetness and nice smiles. There were some very hardcore blokes kicking around, who'd give you evil stares. Conversely, you'd spend some time chatting to the escorts, the low level soldiers, they're just normal blokes. There would be some who approached us and ask, 'Can you get us a job for my wife?' Or, 'Are there any opportunities? Do you need other security advisors?' And some of them were like, you'd talk to them about their hopes, some had been to university. Some had been to university in the West. Some wanted to go to university, but the underlying thing was they just wanted to earn some money, and the majority wanted to earn some money so they could afford to get married.

As much as I hate to say it, we'd have a bit of banter with them as well. And they were generally OK people. They were genuinely interested in what we were doing. The day I dropped off the child protection team at the airport, I then went to a girls' school just on the edge of Kabul, and this is after they'd taken over. So we went there, and we had the Taliban in tow, and there was normality in this little village. It was very surreal.

It isn't great that they took over, but we need to remember that the Afghan government were propped up and had an awful lot of support and money from the Western world, so when the Taliban took over that money stopped, everything was frozen, so the Taliban were put in an impossible position. And I know I sound like a Taliban supporter, but I'm not. They had an impossible task. They had all these problems to fix but they had no assets. That was probably the biggest fear in Kabul after the takeover, and once the military left, it was more an economic thing.

Tony is unhappy with the actions of Western governments in the aftermath of the war:

They've forgotten the normal people on the ground, and I just feel ashamed of how the West let down the Afghan people, massively. These stupid games, and it's always the people at the bottom who lose out. They're striving to make a normal life, and a normal living, and they're just being fucked around. To them it doesn't really matter who's in charge as long as they've got access to food, a bit of education, shelter, and maybe a bit of fun. But it seems to get lost, and people are playing petty games.

And then, in terms of the media, what was being reported didn't reflect what was going on on the ground. The focus was all on the airport. So there was a lot of pressure to get people out and Afghans played it, and I don't blame them. I would have done exactly the same if my family were there, but you could argue a lot of people who came out didn't need to come out. There was a good meaning from outside the country that was informed by the media pictures that they were seeing. And also with the media, you see it with everything, there's probably about a two or three month life cycle behind any story. So by the time I came out in October, Afghanistan had really died in the news. No one was interested. It's just sad.

The war in the country may be over, but the situation is as cruel as ever.

Government

The Kabul airlift was the end product of twenty years of policy, and for those who worked within government or the military, it is hard to look back on the event without reflection on why it was ever needed.

'I don't think we ever really thought seriously about the nature of the country we're in and what we were trying to achieve there,' said Ambassador Sir Laurie Bristow. 'I mean, a close relative asked me when I agreed to take on the job, what do you think you're doing? Why are we still there? And how are we going to leave? And, those questions, I think, summed up for me the failings in that campaign. So, never clearly articulating exactly what we were there to achieve, and how we are going to bring it to an end. And in the end, we brought it to an end in a way that was just awful really, so we achieved nothing of what we might conceivably be setting out to achieve.

'I think that if there's one thing that needs to come through the telling of this story, though, it's about people doing the best they could, playing the hand they were dealt to the best of their ability. And whether it's the military doing their stuff in Helmand, or the Operation Pitting team, please make sure you get the contribution of the Home Office guys in there. You're given a situation where you don't have any control over the strategic gains or how you got here. What you've got to do is deal with what's in front of you. And that, I think, was something that the whole of the Pitting team need to be very proud of, actually. And it's got kind of tainted in the general smatter.'

Like many, Bristow has mixed feelings about the future of the country.

'If you look at the human impact on, particularly women and girls of what's happened, basically, the Taliban coming back to power. I think, sort of stepping back a bit, the diplomat in me, rather than tactician, thinks long. So first of all, Afghanistan is falling from the headlines. And the anniversary was really telling; it just disappeared almost instantly, partly because of other things happening. Ukraine and so on. But I think the underlying point here is that the reasons for us having an interest in Afghanistan have not gone away. So state failure, internationally mobile terrorism, narcotics, who is it turning up in the channel in little boats? What are the things that the public, the voters, are interested in? And what are our tools for addressing them?

'This is one of the points I was trying to make on the *Today* programme. One of the reasons you have an aid programme is because it's intrinsically linked with your national security, or it is if you do it right. The other thing that really interests me is, it

is way too early to tell where it comes out, it's a whole generation of young Afghan men and women who know something
different. That's not going to change anything anytime soon,
because the men with beards are in charge.

'This story isn't over yet,' said the former ambassador. 'This
is where I do open myself up to optimism bias. But I think
that the thing I would add to that is, I think, if we've learned
nothing else over the last twenty years, it's that you can't do it
for them. You can create conditions where people can make
genuine choices, but you can't do it for them. And you
certainly can't democratise a country through counterinsurgency. I mean, one of the huge mistakes, tactical, verging on
strategic mistakes, you kick people's doors down in the night,
they're not going to love you, and they're not going to love
the government you're propping up. And again, this is not
rocket science.'

Nick Fishwick, who worked in Kabul for the Foreign
Commonwealth & Development Office wrote that: 'When
Western troops overthrew the Taliban in 2001, the assumption
was that (a) the "Afghan people" would be sick of the Taliban –
their brutality, their technophobia, their misogyny, their bigoted
version of Islam and their incompetence as rulers; and therefore
(b) that Afghans would welcome the establishment of a government committed to democratic elections, human rights and the
rule of law. (a) may have been correct – we don't know; (b) was
at best hopelessly naive.'[21]

Ben Wallace, the British secretary of state for defence, and an
army veteran himself, praised the efforts of those involved in
Operation Pitting. 'I think it went off pretty amazingly. And
mainly built, not only on the military command here, but on the
men and women who were on the ground and managed the

incredibly difficult situation. To the extent that almost no other army could have done that.'

Still, the operation was a close run thing.

'There was fear,' said Wallace. 'We had a contingency plan, which involved moving assets elsewhere. I would speak directly to my Qatari counterpart, because there are two parts of the Taliban. There was the political team in Qatar and then there was the military team. If you wanted to make sure you got some assurances, you need to speak to the military Taliban. And so I would go direct to my Qatari counterpart to get assurances. So we got quite a lot of assurances from him via Qatar. But we didn't know.

'We very quickly became the conduit of the international community, apart from America, and controlled all of that. The Baron Hotel, etc. But I think that the most worrying bit was, when, if, you lose control of that perimeter and the whole thing falls. You can't take planes off. I think that was the scariest bit. And we did, we moved some assets. We were worried at one stage. ISIS suddenly became more worrying than the Taliban. But I think the real question was going to be the final day as well. The last plane out. Are they going to get mortared? Are the Taliban going to say goodbye? But they didn't. I think the Taliban knew that they'd won.'

On how Op Pitting affected UK/US military relations, Wallace said, 'I think militarily, fine. I think it was an issue that we weren't really sighted much in the Pentagon plan. The Trump plan. And you can get angry, but we don't have a military that has the enablers that we need. It's a simple fact of life. And if you want to do something about that, we better do something about it and invest in a bigger military, or bigger enablers. Because what happens is, you take the US for granted.'

'We maintained strong professional relations as best we could throughout,' said Dominic Raab, the Foreign Secretary. 'I think there's a looming and unanswered question mark about what the US's posture was. But again, I feel there was a lot of wishful thinking, not just in the UK military circles, but across NATO about this. The US government's position was decided in February 2020, it was backed cross-party during the course of the US presidential election, and the US commitment to the "Forever Wars" was over. I think the idea that they would go back on that, there would be some hedge or some hybrid approach, I thought was crazy. And that has triggered lots of questions.

'It's heartbreaking to lose the gains that people sacrificed so much for,' said Raab of the war. 'At the end of the day, smart strategy and policy requires you to reconcile your ends to your means, and we didn't do that. Could Pitting have been organised more smartly? And better? You know, that's a question for the MOD and Ben Wallace. But actually, I think in fairness, it was very difficult getting decisions out of the US.

'We wanted the USA – our allies wanted – a commitment to something at least approaching a conditions-based approach, and some extension based on that, and I always thought it was pie in the sky thinking that the US's allies were going to shift on this. President Biden had been clear he was sticking to the broad timeline. And once that was gone, there was always a risk of a more chaotic situation.'

Despite this chaos, much was accomplished.

'I think getting seventeen thousand UK nationals and Afghan workers out between April and August was a pretty heroic achievement,' said Raab. 'I've got every admiration for all of the military effort on the ground. But I would also be absolutely trenchant in defending the diplomatic and the Home Office staff, who were trying to do the same too.'

As both a member of parliament and a veteran of the war in Afghanistan, Johnny Mercer felt strongly about what had been achieved in the country, and what had not:

The complacency around the resettlement programmes for those who work with UK forces was awful, and has cost lives. I mean, guys have been lynched in the night because we didn't get them out and that is unforgivable.

I think it comes back to everything around veterans, which is just empathy. What is it like if your kid died there, and Afghanistan still looks exactly like it looked twenty years ago? What is that like, it's not something you sit down and think about for an hour. It's there every day.

Every day there'll be wives in this country who get up and try and get their kids to school, without a dad in the home who died in Afghanistan. What does that actually feel like? And what does that feel like to watch the country collapse into a pile of rubble? You personally have sacrificed. Not only that, but the guys who've suffered in mind and body since they've come back. One guy told me, 'I lost my legs in Afghan and my life's completely different, every fucking day. I can't play football. Was it worth it? No.' And that's how he feels.

Just efforts to understand and empathise with that is all I've ever asked for veterans, I don't want free shit. I don't want a special deal. I just want people to, if we're going to commit to this stuff as a nation, to understand what it's like to ask the generation of young people from lots of different backgrounds to go to scrap and sacrifice in a war that is a long way away, and not well understood.

When it came to the UK Government's decision to leave Afghanistan, Mercer believed that it came down to a lack of commitment:

> You have to do things properly, you have to, if you're going to commit that much to a mission, I think, even two and a half thousand troops out there for an indeterminate period of time, in order to support what is a very embryonic, still a very embryonic Afghan state, then you have to be patient. We just didn't have the willpower to do it.
>
> The way we let ourselves down was just by being in complete adherence. The Americans are not thinking of this as our stand-alone mission. You speak to a mum who's lost her son out there, she didn't give a fuck about the American flag and the American mission. This was about her son signing up to join the UK military to fight for the UK and so on. So for the UK ministers to go, 'Sorry, the Americans are leaving,' makes her pain ten times harder, and I saw that viscerally in terms of conversations with these people at the time, and it made it a lot harder for veterans as well. Because a lot of veterans are like, 'What was the fucking point?'
>
> Everyone knows that we were on the same mission, but we will do things differently. And it's just a massive cop out, a cowardly cop out, to say the Americans are doing this, so we're off as well.

Mercer is not alone in his criticism of the UK's response. A report by the Commons International Development Committee found ministers were too slow to provide help to humanitarian workers and Afghans.[22]

The committee's chairwoman, Labour MP Sarah Champion, said that: 'We are deeply grateful to aid workers – be they British,

Afghan or of other nationalities – for all they have done for the people of Afghanistan. The work that they do is phenomenal. But we are ashamed that the government did not give them the support that they needed during the UK's withdrawal, or now, during the complex task of delivering an aid programme under Taliban rule.'[23]

Outside of politicians, few people will try and make the argument that the withdrawal was anything more than cutting losses. Politics being what it is, this was set just before the twentieth anniversary of the 9/11 attacks. In order to fit this theatrical timeframe, service people were put at greater risk, and thousands of Afghans were left behind. In a war that had seemed aimless, it seems particularly cruel that its moment of focus should come at the expense of those who had supported the American-led mission, and bought into the dream of a new Afghanistan.

If al-Qaeda's aim on 9/11 was to draw America into a war that they could not win, then they were successful. The deaths of leaders like Osama Bin Laden may be of some solace to the West, but it is worth remembering that 'martyrdom' is what jihadis seek. Bin Laden's death elevates him to a kind of sainthood amongst the followers of his doctrine, many of whom were not alive at the time of 9/11. The newest cadres of jihad have grown up in a world where America and its allies are constantly at war in Islamic countries: is it a surprise that so many are radicalised?

In the last two decades we have seen the American-led West support, then essentially walk away from wars in Afghanistan, Iraq and Libya. Trust is an essential component of diplomacy. Can we expect a nation's people to throw in their lot with the cause of 'democracy', given these recent examples? Perhaps their country's leadership will, for the riches that come with being a government allied to the West, but without the support of the population, insurgencies will simmer, boil and eventually overflow. The only answer to contain that appears to be more violence, and we see the results of that policy at work all over the Middle East. Brutal dictatorships fall, only to be replaced by at least an equally brutal civil war.

Many will decry the move of some governments from intervention to isolationism. Perhaps this break is necessary. A revaluation of strategy certainly is. It is laudable to put one's own blood and treasure at risk to aid another, but such a risk should be justified in the results, and these have been lacking. Spending trillions of dollars, and losing thousands of lives, should not be acceptable when it leaves more war and misery in its wake.

No doubt decisions and justifications will be mulled over for decades, but what is politics and strategy to some are lived experiences to millions of others. When all is said and done, it is their lives, their voices, that matter.

Civilians

More than 100,000 Afghans were evacuated to the US during the Kabul airlift. There they found a mixture of hope and further challenges.

'Until the end of December, they didn't help me at all,' said Tariq. 'That was a nightmare, finding a house. I tried to reach out for them so many times, but they were really unresponsive at the beginning. I believe people went through much worse here in the United States, comparing to what's in the airport in Afghanistan. When I reached the US I thought, I'm settled. Everything will be good. But then the worst thing begins, the life here in the USA was even worse, like living in the camp and the military base and those things.'[24]

An email was leaked from one US Central Command official, describing the refugees' temporary housing in the Middle East. 'A humid day today. Where the Afghans are housed is a living hell. Trash, urine, faecal matter, spilled liquids and vomit cover the floors.'[25]

Others were more optimistic about their new situation. Shaima was also evacuated to the US. 'I'm really hopeful to receive my bikes and continue my cycling activities to be a professional and successful cycling coach in the future, or to be a role model for other Afghan girls who are living in a really hard situation. I love to participate in Olympic 2024 and be a champion.'[26]

Some escaped the war, but not its touch.

'When I wake up, I feel like I'm in Kabul because the noise outside is the same as Kabul,' said Fatima, who has won a fellowship at Columbia University. 'And the light is as bright as Kabul, but the room is not the same. And it takes me a while to figure out where exactly I am. And my body is so exhausted that just two days ago I had a panic attack and I couldn't move for five hours. This is what war does to people. Take your inner peace away, turn you to kind of a robot, if I can say. Sometimes you have no emotions, no feelings. Sometimes you are a ball of anger. Sometimes you feel like a ghost, that nobody sees you. Nobody cares about you. Nobody knows what is happening to you. And nobody asks, how are you doing?'[27]

'We will try our best,' said Abdul, who is twice a refugee, having fled the Soviet invasion as a child. 'The way the Americans' government, the American nation, my boss, everybody, I want them to be proud of me. I want to do something on behalf of myself and my family, so that the Americans will be proud of us, not be regret of bringing us. This is something I want to do.'[28]

Jeff Phaneuf works with No One Left Behind, the organisation that aids in both evacuation to, and resettlement in, the United States.

'It's difficult, because you get a home that's foreign to you and you've got to find a home, you've got to find a job, you've got to get your kids into schools. The refugee resettlement agencies in the US provide about three months of resources for people when they first arrive, and that's a small amount of money for rent, and that's not going to cover a home that can suit four or five children. Many of them live in hotels at first and then eventually have to rent an apartment. It's hard. These are people who have gone through incredibly difficult circumstances just to get here, and then they get dropped in the US with limited support.

'That's where groups like No One Left Behind come in, where we give things like rental assistance, we do no-interest car loans, we help with food and clothing and furniture and try to help these people get set up for success, because that is hard, and if it weren't for groups like this a lot of these folks would be in very difficult circumstances. We also see people who have very high qualifications, but because their law degree or medical degree doesn't count in the US, then they can't get the jobs that they're qualified for. A lot of those folks take jobs driving for Uber, or DoorDash, or things like that. It's hard for them to get the credentials they need to go back to their professions.'

The same is true in the United Kingdom, which took in more than 15,000 evacuees.

'It was lockdown when we came here,' said Parmilla, who had been a doctor in Afghanistan. 'We had positive tests for COVID. We were in a small room and not allowed to come out. It was a culture shock. Everything was different for us. Nothing was clear. After nearly one year we are still living in a hotel. It is still a bad situation. We are four people in one room.

'Me, my husband and my sister, we are all doctors. We take the train to go to Manchester. We have classes. Most of the time we are at the hotel. We don't know what we should do. How can we find places on our own? Some people can't speak English. How can they find houses? It is really difficult for us. We left everything behind. Most of them have mental problems now. Maybe people think we enjoy being in a hotel, that we have a good time. But we are people who had everything in Afghanistan. We left everything behind.'

Parmilla's father was a colonel in the Afghan National Army, and at great risk of reprisals.

'If my dad is alive now, if we are safe, it is because of Siu-Anne. I know what she did for everyone. I asked her, how do you feel that you saved all these families, all these humans? I couldn't forgive myself, maybe for all of my life, because I couldn't kiss my dad goodbye.'

But through the work of Siu-Anne, Laura and Emily, Parmilla's family was able to join her in the UK. 'I made a promise to Parmilla that I wouldn't leave her dad, and when I found a gap, I went for it,' said Siu-Anne.

Nuria, who had worked at the British embassy, was one of those who escaped Kabul. She and her family are free of danger from the Taliban, but life in a new country has its own difficulties.

'My daughter is safe. Her future is safe. But there are still financial challenges. Other problems. If I didn't have a security issue, I would have never left my country. I had my beautiful palace, I had my car, I had my job, I had my family members.

Financially I had no problem at all. The challenges I currently have, they will take some time to adjust myself to the situation because I am not used to this situation to rely on government. There are challenges, but I am happy. The government is helping us. They are not letting us starve. We are grateful to them.

'You have to build everything back from scratch. I already had everything built. Here it bothers you mentally that you have to start from scratch. Otherwise I have a good feeling, but I also miss my country. I miss my family members. After three months when I left for England, they moved to Germany. It's been one year and I haven't yet seen them.

'My daughter is going to school. She has learned the English language. She's good, however she still remembers her beautiful room, her toys, her cousins, and she is feeling alone. She says, "Mommy, why can't we go back to Afghanistan?" and I show her the videos where those young girls were killed in Afghanistan. She's missing her friends, her teachers. But I show her, and I say in Afghanistan we don't have peace. People are killed. You are safe here. It's very hard, but I'm happy.

'In Afghanistan every single day you felt like, even if there wasn't an explosion, I felt like one is going to happen. I felt that we are not at peace and at any time it's possible to happen to me or to my family members. Especially when I took her to kinder-garten. It's not easy. But we have to go through all these chal-lenges for the happy future of our daughter.'

It is a future that is unlikely to involve her homeland.

'I'm not hopeful [of going back to Afghanistan]. When I was five years old, I remembered that was the time when I started to experience war in my country. And now I'm in my forties.'

Mohammad Dawood had served in the Afghan special forces. Though ARAP was slow, it did eventually allow Mohammad and his family to move to the UK via Pakistan. 'I'm so happy now and grateful to the UK government. I am happy with the way of life. My kids are going to school, learning English and knowledge. They have a bright future. I am grateful.'

Basira Asghari had served as a police officer with TF444. After being failed by her commanders – who would only offer help with evacuation in return for sexual exploitation – Basira and her family were eventually evacuated via ARAP, and with the aid of the Gulab Sorkh Foundation.

'We are so grateful to the government of Great Britain for accepting us, for helping us and providing all the facilities,' said Basira. 'The British people are very kind and philanthropic, and we are very grateful to all the British people, especially Mrs Pam French.'

On the future of Afghanistan, Basira believes that the Taliban's days are numbered.

'I think the Taliban government cannot continue and the crisis and conditions in Afghanistan are facing a disaster. Due to the negative attitude of the people of the world to the events in Afghanistan, legitimacy to the Taliban government was not achieved on the international stage. I also predict the gradual fall of the Taliban, given the internal differences between the Taliban and the incompetence in managing people's affairs and the welcome of the younger generation to the Resistance Front. This painful incident reflects the incompetence of the Taliban government, and poverty and hunger are rampant among all Afghans, and they do not pay any attention to protecting the lives of all Afghans, especially the people of the Hazara tribes.'

Basira had to overcome much to become a female police officer in Afghanistan. 'I have always served honestly and fought against those who consider a policewoman a sex slave, to prove that not all women in society, especially women in the police, are like this. While I [was] humiliated by my colleagues for being a millennial and a girl, we were able to resist and stand up.'

Basira is an inspirational figure, and while she and her family were able to reach the UK, thousands more ARAP-qualified Afghans are still trapped inside Afghanistan and Pakistan. The UK's effort to live up to its promise of a safe life in the West is still ongoing.

'We've got one hundred thousand applicants at the moment,' said Ben Wallace, 'which are just the symptom of everybody who can't use any other schemes. They apply to every scheme, which is not helpful to the genuine ARAPs. Because, how do you start with that list? We try and use people to at least guide us about people we know. Pick them out of the haystack. But everybody just wanting to leave Afghanistan is now applying to ARAP. And that's not going to work.'

At the time of writing, more than ninety staff members of the Ministry of Defence were still processing these applications. Since the end of Op Pitting, more than 3600 Afghans have been brought to the UK.

'We will carry on,' said Wallace. 'And we are doing it overtly and covertly with countries in the region, and we bring people out, and we pay for them to come here. We do all of that.'

On those who have made it to the UK, but are still in temporary housing, Wallace said, 'There is some group in the hotel, I think a tiny minority of them, who've been offered and haven't taken accommodation. And I'm just in the place of trying to mandate that you offer it, you leave, you go to these places, because my problem is, if we don't get a good throughput on ARAP, they will be lumped in with all the other issues. And I don't want them to be lumped in with asylum seekers and channel crossers, because that is where the Home Office starts to shut things down. And we end up in a really difficult position. So we're trying to pull through the ARAP people who are here because they deserve to be here, they helped us, and it's really important.'

It is a problem and a sentiment shared in the United States. Jeff Phaneuf, of No One Left Behind, continues to work to bring at-risk families out of Afghanistan:

I think that we left Afghanistan without a plan to take care of the people who worked for us. We left Afghanistan, where there are now probably about 200,000 people who are qualified to come to the US on a visa because they worked for us, because they supported us, because they often fought in combat alongside US troops, and there wasn't a plan, and that to me is the biggest shame and the biggest takeaway.

We could have done this better, and it's something we've done recurrently. We did the same thing in Vietnam. And it's funny how the narrative repeats itself. In Vietnam, the American officials refused to have a mass evacuation plan for our allies, because they were worried that it would signal a lack of confidence in the Vietnamese military to continue the fight, and you hear that from American officials here. So instead we created a massive humanitarian disaster ...

I've been reading a lot about Vietnam, because I think understanding that history helps us understand what happened here, and they were worried about this self-fulfilling prophecy, where we signal that we don't trust them and we're going to get our people out, and then that therefore hastens the demise. And I think that in both instances, we see the demise of these countries came quickly anyway, so all we've done is fail to prepare and fail to plan.

For me, what's really heartbreaking is to hear from the Afghans that I'm still working with a year later, that they still believe in the idea of America, that they still believe in the mission that the Brits and the Americans, and the Aussies, and everyone else in the NATO coalition in Afghanistan fought for. That it was a dream for them. They believe in that still. Even though we left them in such an awful set of circumstances.

I was talking with an interpreter last week who's still in Afghanistan. He fought with the US Army. When Kabul fell to the Taliban his passport was at the US embassy in Kabul, because it was just waiting to get the final stamp for the visa. When the embassy withdrew, they burned all the documents including this guy's passport, and those of his sons and wife. And so he was left without the documents to get out. Because of that he's now spent over a year waiting. He was about to complete his visa and is still waiting now to get out, and that to me is pretty unconscionable.

The takeaways for me there are, if we're going to have a visa programme, we need to fix it so it works, because right now the US government's bureaucracy is creating more harm for our former allies there than even the Taliban is, and that to me is just so unacceptable, and we need to fix that.

The troops

For many of those who were at HKIA, it is a difficult time to look back on.

'It's heavy most days, but especially now,' a US Navy nurse said on the first anniversary of the airlift. 'It still feels so fresh. I'm hoping I can get there eventually, to only feeling pride. There are pieces that I am incredibly proud to be a part of. So many from the deployment are struggling with getting adequate mental health care. From who I've talked to, the need isn't being met. When we got back, there was this knee-jerk reaction to getting people support, but it quickly tapered. I don't think many were ready to talk about it yet. There is significant moral injury.'

According to the Moral Injury Project: 'Moral injury is the damage done to one's conscience or moral compass when that person perpetrates, witnesses, or fails to prevent acts that transgress one's own moral beliefs, values, or ethical codes of conduct.'[29]

The US Navy nurse feels as though both she, and the United States, failed to live up to their moral codes.

'Like many others who were there, it felt like we were being forced to be the bad guy. I can remember a young girl who came to us for medical care begging at me for her life, because I had to take her back out of the gate once she'd received care. We had no authorisation to push people through the process. You aren't sure if you sent them to their death or not.'

Such dark days are hard to re-live, but she takes great pride in her comrades, and what they were able to accomplish. Particularly how they kept one Marine alive after the suicide attack with very little equipment or support. 'I think all of us feel that heavy weight of feeling like we could have done more, but our presence made a difference in a very big way for at least one person. And to see him fucking killing it a year into his recovery makes it worthwhile.'

She is equally proud of the US forces at large.

'The way the military responded to what was a shitshow really was amazing. No one knew what to expect and it was so out of control, to put it lightly, that it's amazing that they were even [able to] accomplish what they did. In the same vein, I don't know if it's the military, but why the fuck did we wait so long? It was a self-imposed, arbitrary date. We knew for months this was coming. I've seen it said multiple times, but a battalion S4 could have fucking planned that better. Coming from my limited scope and understanding, I really think the Department of State was the source of most of the problems. There are so many unanswered questions. I know I'm a nurse with limited scope, but what the fuck?'

Sergeant Stumpf, of the 10th Mountain Division, is hopeful for the future for the families who were able to escape Kabul.

'I think that in twenty years' time maybe the fruits of our labours will start to show. Afghanistan itself is a whole different story, but I guess I hope that the people who made it out, regardless of where they ended up, I hope they become productive members of their societies, and can live and thrive without having to look over their shoulders. If that happens to those folks, I'll be happy with that, I guess. Looking back, I'm still angry about the whole thing. I think history may be kind in that we were all able to get a lot of people out. It was an impressive feat in and of itself, but it shouldn't have had to happen like that in the first place.

'There was never an efficient plan set in place to vet people way back when we knew we were leaving. It just seemed like a major problem that people in charge on the civilian side just kept kicking down the road as someone else's responsibility. Then all of a sudden, you have thousands of desperate people and families clamouring to escape. It didn't need to be like that. I'll also never understand why the powers that be decided to shut down Bagram airfield and focus on HKIA. Bagram was the better option on so many levels. Not using it was an absolute blunder. I understand using HKIA for government folks and embassy personnel, etc., but no one on the ground thought closing Bagram was a good idea.'

'A year on, I try and block it out,' said Warrant Officer Lee Bowden, USMC EOD team leader. 'Not the deployments, but the picture of the war. Was it worth it? And questions like that. I look at the deployments for what they're worth. They shaped me into who I am today. I couldn't be more proud of what my team did, and I would love to serve with any one of them again. What the Marines did as a whole was amazing. They made the best of a shitty situation.'

One of these Marines recalled his first few months at home.

'The public didn't care. It was rough for the first few months. It took me about six months to come down. Guys were drinking a lot. Some secluded themselves. A close friend of mine really struggles with it. Our hierarchy are getting better at dealing with us now. I think they know a lot of us are going to leave the Marines soon, so they leave us alone. The guys that want to re-enlist are scared about asking for help. A lot of us are trying to walk the line between getting help, but not burning the bridge for future employment.

'A lot of officers wrote their own awards,' the Marine said. 'There were a lot of Bronze Stars. Some of the enlisted have started getting them now, but in the first few months it was all officers.'

Though bitter about some aspects of the operation, he is proud of what was accomplished by his fellow Marines, and thinks often about the Afghans who weren't able to leave the country, and who now live under the fundamentalist regime.

'I think we all want the best for Afghanistan. If that means doing business with the Taliban, then so be it. It's the civilians who will pay the price if we don't.'

'I look back on it with lots of pride,' said Captain Sam McGrury, A Company commander in 1/8 Marines. 'The Marines were able to overcome stress, tiredness, dehydration and hunger. They overcame human nature. It would have been incredibly easy for them to resort to behaving like Cro Magnon, but they kept their ethical balance, and that was amazing. I think that any infantry officer or junior enlisted would have found a way to get it done, because that's what we do.'

Sam doesn't blame his commanders for not putting the Marines into HKIA sooner. Far from it. 'I feel like our generals were chomping at the bit to get us in there.'

Back in the UK, British soldiers were also making the adjustment from operational life.

'We went on summer leave,' said a 2 Para soldier. 'I was angry. Looking back now, I was a dickhead. I started not liking civvies. I'd done all that and they hadn't. I was angry at their ignorance. They had no concept of what's going on. Things were all good for them in their world, so nothing else is happening.'

This is a common experience felt by many returning soldiers, as is a feeling of regimental pride.

'The experience made me feel a stronger connection to the Reg, and more committed to it,' said the young paratrooper. 'It was a funny situation out there, because it almost felt like every man for himself. You had to use your own initiative. We had two brand new blokes in our platoon, but they settled straight in and earned their place. There's definitely pride in being the last British troops out there. I look back on the whole thing positively and with pride.'

As part of the RAF's transport fleet, Sergeant Andy Livingstone had been part of the crews that evacuated both civilians and troops.

'One of the most humbling trips was bringing our blokes and girls back. Most of them were absolutely fucked, but after a hard day you brew up, you get some scran, and you're good to go. Absolutely super-human, and it was an absolute pleasure to bring those guys home and with no casualties, and to chat and hear their stories. They'd seen some shit. The most satisfying troop withdrawal that I've ever done was bringing them out of the action and bringing them back home.'

The crew that Livingstone was part of had brought out two hundred children on one flight.

'As a dad, I wasn't sure what effect it had on me until after the mission was done. I was completely unprepared for the amount of children. Probably the worst part, and this probably sounds fucking mental, was seeing people in their best clothes. It was almost as if these kids were going to a christening or a wedding, or some sort of event, because it was their very best. And I suppose I could only think, what would I have done in the same situation? And I suppose, if all you bring is what you're wearing and a shopping bag, then you bring the best that you've got.

'It was a complete contrast to what was actually happening, where there was essentially a conflict going on outside the walls, and still explosions going off, still people doing crazy things whilst everyone's wearing their best clothes. You just don't expect to see that. It doesn't add up in your mind when you think of conflict, and think of a war. It was awful, and thinking back on that was crazy.'

Livingstone has no doubt about the importance of what he and his squadron were involved in.

'Ultimately, it's probably the most important thing that I'll ever do, in any context. We were the first flight in after the explosion [at Abbey Gate], and having the opportunity to save

317

some lives is not something that many people will ever get the opportunity to do. There's a feeling of pride [in the squadron]. All of us who'd done it felt incredible about what we were doing, because we were helping. As soon as the Op was called, everyone wanted to do it. Everyone involved, and I mean everyone from 2 Para, who saw so many horrible things. Even the old and bold probably hadn't seen everything like what was going on in those queues and in that processing.'

Livingstone praised the efforts of the RAF's support staff.

'The air movement guys who did processing and stayed there every single day, working twenty-four hours a day to get through as many people as they could, those are heroes. The movements teams were incredible. They deserve knighthoods. Even the engineers where we were based at (our base in the Middle East). Small team. Ten guys. They worked night and day to make sure that the aircraft we had was ready. Every single person who was involved dug the fuck out for those people. I don't think any of us will do anything better. And it's also proof that we are expeditionary.

'Morale [in the forces] is pretty low because we don't have a war to fight, and that's what armed forces are for. We all join up to go and fight the fight, so it was really good to know that we all could – with no notice, with what we had, and the diminishing forces that we've got – that we could just go and absolutely smash it. Every [aircraft] crew absolutely nailed it. It was just outstanding that, as a tri-service organisation, we absolutely nailed it, but coming out of it, I don't think that we'll ever see anything like that again. Not that you wish it to happen again, but ultimately, we're a better armed forces for it. I'm a better operator for it. And the squadron's a better squadron for it.'

'Initially I just wanted to put it behind me,' said 2 Para's Aaron

Nunkoosing. 'We didn't want to overstate what we'd done, because there probably was an element of guilt about leaving a lot of people behind. I would say the first month or two, you put it to the back of your mind, because you've got to do the next thing. Around Christmas time, it started to play on my mind a lot more.'

This feeling came from spending time with his own child. 'I think a lot of people were like that. Also you have a bit of booze and you stop and get into your thoughts a bit. I kept in contact with Ed [who worked with him on extractions]. I think the memory of those couple of weeks became a big part of both of our lives, we will always have that. I know Ed continued to do work afterwards for people who were still there.'

Aaron has kept in touch with many of the families that he helped to escape.

'You end up having relationships with these people. You've seen them in their most desperate of times, and you have a shared hardship. It was a really shit time for them, and I think we'll have that relationship forever. I saw Abdul recently, they have very little, but his daughters bought a gift for my son.

'You've got to be careful not to overplay it, because it wasn't a combat operation. It very nearly was, but it wasn't. We joined the Parachute Regiment for combat operations. We're airborne infantry. So it's not necessarily the thing we joined for, so you have to be careful not to overstate it. It was a very small thing in the twenty years [of operations in Afghanistan]. It's one of those things where I look back at the regimental charter of the Parachute Regiment, and there's a bit which states that we seek to be "a force for good". And it felt like we'd lived up to that. I've never been prouder of that blue DZ flash on my arm. There's immense pride that comes with working with these kind of people.'

'The Escape from Kabul' was a unique moment in the lives of many, and the memories of it will be carried forever by those who were there. Some will understandably want to draw a line under the experience, but for Private Fahim of 3 Para, the work wasn't finished when he left Afghanistan.

'Op Pitting didn't stop for me when we left Kabul. My phone wouldn't stop ringing. I'd given my number to people who couldn't get through the processing. I basically turned into a home office worker, helping with people's ARAPs, and things like that. A year later, some of these people are still getting through.'

In conducting interviews for this book, the work of Private Fahim was recognised from the junior ranks to 2 Para's Commanding Officer. Six months after Op Pitting, Private Fahim was rightly recognised officially for his efforts.

'In March 2022 I was recognised in the Queen's Honours list, and awarded a Mention In Dispatches. I wasn't expecting it, and some of the most deserving didn't get recognised. To be honest I felt honoured and lucky, but I was one amongst many on Op Pitting.'

Winston Churchill said that 'a medal glitters, but it also casts a shadow'. This was something that was felt by Fahim. 'I was being awarded for something that was a tragedy. I respect it, and I'm pleased, but it's not something you celebrate.'

Everyone had their role, but few were as critical to the mission as the Para who had grown up beneath Kabul's mountains. Many think about the Afghans that they left behind. For Fahim, who had grown up under the Taliban, this was his country, his city, and those that were not evacuated were left to a life that had been worth fighting for.

'What keeps me going is knowing I maxed out and did all that I could.'

The same can be said of the military effort on Op Pitting as a whole. From aircrews to the infantry, an impossible task was achieved because people not only rose to the challenge, but went above and beyond the call of duty. No matter what criticism can be levelled at the Afghan mission, Britain can be rightly proud of the achievements of its forces in Kabul. The mottos of the Parachute Regiment and the US Pararescue Jumpers apply to all who were involved. They were 'ready for anything', and risked their lives 'so that others may live'.

Their efforts, and the plight of the Afghan people, must never be forgotten.

Acknowledgements

Every book requires a collaborative effort, but the writing of *Escape From Kabul* in particular relied on the generosity of an immense number of people who kindly gave their time to recount their own stories in verbal interviews and written testaments.

We are indebted to Lieutenant Colonel Dave Middleton, Major Steve White, Major Aaron Nunkoosing, Private Ahmed Fahim and those soldiers with whom we talked from the Parachute Regiment. To Flight Lieutenant Robert Manson, and Sergeant Andrew Livingston of the RAF. To Major Danny Riley of the Royal Engineers. To Major Thomas Schueman, Captain Sam McGrury, and Warrant Officer Lee Bowden of the United States Marine Corps. Our deepest thanks are also due to several serving military members who gave interviews on condition of anonymity.

We are grateful to Ambassador Laurie Bristow, Johnny Mercer MP, Dominic Raab MP and Ben Wallace MP for granting us interviews. Thanks are due to Hollie McKay and Antony Tuitt for their compelling insights into Afghanistan.

To Mohammed, Basira, Rabia, Zak, Parmilla and the Afghan Women's Football Team, we are honoured to include your stories in this book and wish you the very best in your new homes in the UK and the US. Thanks to Mike Pratt, Jo Pratt, Siu-Anne, Kitty, Claire and Jeff for your recounting of your own amazing efforts during that time and onwards.

This book also drew upon books, articles, documentaries and interviews which are part of the public record. We are grateful to have been able to cite these works. A list of these sources can be found in the book's endnotes.

We are deeply grateful to Evangeline Modell for her keen eye and insights, to Rupert Lancaster at Hodder for commissioning the book, to Barry and Tom for their edit, to our agents Jo and Rowan, and to Liam Hipple for the sketch.

Lieutenant Colonel Bayard Barron at the Ministry of Defence facilitated the correct permissions in the most painless of ways and was beyond helpful. Thanks too to Pete Quentin, Tom McShane, Lieutenant Colonel Robert Philipson-Stow, Captain Mark Hankey RN, Charles Heath-Saunders, Charlie Lort-Phillips, Dickie Haldenby, Simon Davey, Pam French from the Gulab Sorkh Foundation, and all the others – both military and civilian – who helped in so many ways.

It was a great honour to tell the stories of some of those who were in Kabul, and of those who were involved in the evacuation process, often from their own homes. It is a project that has strengthened our pride in the members of both the UK and US forces, given us a deeper understanding of the challenges faced by those escaping Kabul, and inspired us with the courage of all.

Finally, we are grateful to you, the reader, for giving us your valuable time. We hope that we have done justice to the incredible people who made this work possible.

Levison Wood & Geraint Jones

Picture Acknowledgements

First plate section

p. 1: (top) © Spencer Platt/Getty Images; (bottom) © The Picture Art Collection/Alamy Stock Photo.

p. 2: (top) UK MOD © Crown copyright 2002; (bottom) Source: US Department of State. Image in the public domain.

p. 3: (top) Source: Taliban media/Badri 313. Image in the public domain; (bottom) Source: Department of Defense photo by US Air Force Staff Sgt. Jette Carr/CC BY 2.0.

p. 4: (top) © Zabi Karimi/AP/Shutterstock; (bottom) © Aaron Nunkoosing.

p. 5: (top) Source unknown; (bottom) Photograph by LPhot Ben Shread. UK MOD © Crown copyright 2021.

p. 6: (top) Source: Twitter (@laurie_bristow, 28 August 2021), used by permission of Laurie Bristow and Dan Blanchford; (bottom) Source unknown.

p. 7: (top) Photograph by LPhot Ben Shread. UK Mod © Crown copyright 2021; (bottom) Source unknown.

p. 8: top) © Marcus Yam/Los Angeles Times/Getty Images; (bottom) Source unknown.

Second plate section

p. 1: © Liam Hipple

p. 2: (top) Photograph by LPhot Ben Shread. UK MOD © Crown copyright 2021; (bottom) photograph by Stuart Ramsay © Sky News.

p. 3: (top left) Used by permission of Johnny Mercer MP; (top right) Source unknown; (bottom) UK MOD © Crown copyright 2021.

p. 4: © AKHTER GULFAM/EPA-EFE/Shutterstock.

p. 5: Both images used by permission of Anthony Tuitt.

p. 6: (top) © Alamy/US Army courtesy photo; (bottom) © Kaster/AP/Shutterstock.

p. 7: (top) Source unknown; (bottom) Courtesy of Defense One.
p. 8: (top) © Marcos del Mazo/Alamy Stock Photo; (bottom) Source unknown.

Source Notes

Chapter 1: The Forever War

1 https://www.nbcnews.com/investigations/us-left-78000-afghan-allies-ngo-report-rcna18119
2 https://www.migrationpolicy.org/article/us-government-rush-evacuate-afghan-allies-allocate-special-visas
3 https://www.wartimeallies.co/_files/ugd/5887eb_6334755bb6f64b0
09b629f3513a16204.pdf
4 Ibid.
5 Ibid.
6 https://www.theguardian.com/world/2021/aug/27/british-nationals-left-behind-kabul-describe-feeling-abandoned-uk
-officials
7 https://www.militarytimes.com/news/your-military/2016/07/06/a
-timeline-of-u-s-troop-levels-in-afghanistan-since-2001/
8 https://holliesmckay.substack.com/p/dispatches-from-afghanistan
-talking
9 https://www.mirror.co.uk/news/world-news/british-army-fired-
46-million-5475716?utm_source=linkCopy&utm_medium=
social&utm_campaign=sharebar
10 https://watson.brown.edu/costsofwar/
11 Major Adam Jowett, *No Way Out* (Pan, 2019), p. 126.
12 Nick Fishwick in: Brian Brivati (ed.), *Losing Afghanistan* (Biteback, 2022), p. 209.
13 https://commonslibrary.parliament.uk/research-briefings/cbp-9298/
14 Ibid.

Chapter 2: Pandora's Box

1 https://online.ucpress.edu/as/article-abstract/37/2/111/23411/
Afghanistan-in-1996-Year-of-the-Taliban

2 https://digitalarchive.wilsoncenter.org/document/113260.pdf, p. 2.

3 https://kabulfalling.com/episodes/why-i-fight-a-taliban-fighter-
speaks-from-afghanistan/transcript/

4 http://edition.cnn.com/2015/07/29/opinions/bergen-mullah-omar/

5 Ibid.

6 Ibid.

7 https://www.forbes.com/sites/bowmanmarsico/2021/07/08/the-
war-in-afghanistan-a-polling-post-mortem/

8 https://www.reuters.com/article/uk-afghan-operation-dam
-idUKBAK16060620080902

9 https://kabulfalling.com/episodes/why-i-fight-a-taliban-fighter-
speaks-from-afghanistan/transcript/

10 https://www.npr.org/2021/08/18/1028780816/transcript-taliban-
spokesman-suhail-shaheen-interview

11 https://holliesmckay.substack.com/p/dispatches-from-afghanistan
-talking

12 Ibid.

13 https://www.npr.org/2021/08/18/1028780816/transcript-taliban-
spokesman-suhail-shaheen-interview

14 https://www.gov.uk/government/speeches/the-prime-ministers-
opening-statement-on-afghanistan-18-august-2021

15 Ibid.

16 https://www.aljazeera.com/news/2020/9/2/afghan-negotiators-set
-to-fly-to-doha-as-prisoner-release-resumes

17 https://edition.cnn.com/2021/10/06/politics/kabul-airport-
attacker-prison/index.html

18 https://www.npr.org/2021/08/18/1028780816/transcript-taliban-
spokesman-suhail-shaheen-interview

19 https://media.defense.gov/2012/Aug/23/2001330098/-1/-1/0/
Oper%20Frequent%20Wind.pdf

20 https://www.history.com/news/vietnam-war-refugees

21 https://www.whitehouse.gov/briefing-room/speeches-remarks/
2021/07/08/remarks-by-president-biden-on-the-drawdown-of-u-s
-forces-in-afghanistan/

Chapter 3: The Downfall of a Nation

1 https://holliesmckay.substack.com/p/dispatches-from-afghanistan-from
2 https://www.aljazeera.com/news/2021/9/8/ashraf-ghani-apologises-afghans-says-fled-ensure-peace
3 Brivati, *Losing Afghanistan*, 'The end of the forever war', p. xi.
4 https://www.aljazeera.com/news/2021/9/8/ashraf-ghani-apologises-afghans-says-fled-ensure-peace
5 https://www.transparency.org/en/cpi/2020/index/afg
6 https://www.bbc.co.uk/news/world-asia-59230564
7 https://holliesmckay.substack.com/p/dispatches-from-afghanistan-from
8 https://www.journalofdemocracy.org/articles/the-collapse-of-afghanistan/
9 https://www.whitehouse.gov/briefing-room/speeches-remarks/2021/08/16/remarks-by-president-biden-on-afghanistan/
10 Jowett, *No Way Out*, p. 85.
11 https://watermark.silverchair.com/milmed-d-11-00086.pdf
12 https://www.telegraph.co.uk/expat/expatnews/6635393/Fifteen-per-cent-of-Afghan-army-are-drug-addicts.html
13 https://www.theguardian.com/uk-news/2020/aug/24/rise-in-number-of-british-soldiers-being-sacked-for-drug-use
14 https://www.nytimes.com/2015/09/21/world/asia/us-soldiers-told-to-ignore-afghan-allies-abuse-of-boys.html
15 Ibid.
16 https://www.nytimes.com/2018/09/21/world/asia/afghanistan-security-casualties-taliban.html
17 https://www.washingtonpost.com/world/2021/12/30/afghanistan-security-forces-deaths/
18 https://www.theguardian.com/world/2015/dec/22/mothers-of-british-soldiers-waste-fall-of-sangin-helmand?CMP=share_btn_tw
19 https://www.npr.org/2021/08/18/1028780816/transcript-taliban-spokesman-suhail-shaheen-interview
20 https://www.voanews.com/a/pentagon-downplays-7-billion-in-us-military-equipment-left-in-afghanistan/6549546.html
21 https://www.state.gov/briefings/department-press-briefing-august-11-2021/
22 https://www.reuters.com/world/asia-pacific/taliban-fighters-capture-eighth-provincial-capital-six-days-2021-08-11/

Chapter 4: Ready for Anything

1 https://publications.parliament.uk/pa/cm5803/cmselect/cmfaff/
169/report.html
2 https://www.aljazeera.com/news/2021/8/12/afghanistan-taliban-
kandahar-prison-police-ghazni-live-updates
3 https://www.army.mod.uk/media/5219/20180910-values_standards
_2018_final.pdf
4 https://www.army.mod.uk/news-and-events/news/2021/07/last-
commanding-officer-in-afghanistan-reflects-on-20-years-of-deployment/

Chapter 5: Serve to Lead

1 https://publications.parliament.uk/pa/cm5803/cmselect/cmfaff/
630/report.html
2 https://www.thetimes.co.uk/article/british-embassy-left-details-of-
afghan-staff-for-taliban-to-find-pr7vh5db0

Chapter 6: The Fight for the Flightline

1 https://variety.com/2021/tv/news/sky-news-stuart-ramsay-
afghanistan-taliban-1235045469/
2 *Escape from Kabul*, documentary, HBO.
3 https://af.usembassy.gov/security-alert-u-s-embassy-kabul-
afghanistan-15/
4 *Escape from Kabul*.
5 https://theintercept.com/2022/09/13/afghanistan-air-force-taliban-kabul/
6 *Escape from Kabul*.
7 Ibid.

Chapter 7: The Gates of Hell

1 *Escape from Kabul*, documentary, HBO.
2 Ibid.
3 Ibid.
4 Ibid.

5 Ibid.
6 Ibid.
7 Ibid.
8 https://migrationobservatory.ox.ac.uk/resources/commentaries/afghan-refugees-in-the-uk/
9 https://www.realcleardefense.com/articles/2017/03/21/green-on-blue_attacks_in_afghanistan_the_data_111015.html

Chapter 8: Digital Dunkirk

1 https://www.gov.uk/government/publications/afghan-relocations-and-assistance-policy/afghan-relocations-and-assistance-policy-information-and-guidance.
2 https://publications.parliament.uk/pa/cm5803/cmselect/cmfaff/169/report.html.
3 Ibid.
4 https://www.thetimes.co.uk/article/ex-forces-chiefs-condemn-failure-to-protect-afghan-interpreters-5z2kvqrzl
5 https://publications.parliament.uk/pa/cm5803/cmselect/cmfaff/169/report.html
6 Ibid.
7 Ibid.
8 https://en.wikipedia.org/wiki/2021_Kabul_airlift
9 Major Tom Schueman and Zainullah Zaki, *Always Faithful* (Harper-Collins, 2022), p. 260.

Chapter 9: Running the Gauntlet

1 https://www.cnn.com/2021/07/13/asia/afghanistan-taliban-commandos-killed-intl-hnk/index.html
2 https://www.npr.org/2021/08/18/1028780816/transcript-taliban-spokesman-suhail-shaheen-interview
3 Sky News.
4 Ibid.
5 https://news.sky.com/story/kim-kardashian-and-leeds-united-help-afghan-junior-womens-football-team-arrive-in-uk-after-escaping-taliban-12471716

Chapter 10: Tragic Endings

1   https://www.atlanticcouncil.org/blogs/new-atlanticist/experts-react-the-us-withdrawal-from-afghanistan-is-complete-whats-next/
2   https://www.nytimes.com/2021/08/27/world/asia/who-isis-k-afghanistan.html
3   https://holliesmckay.substack.com/p/dispatches-from-afghanistan-exclusive
4   https://www.defense.gov/News/Transcripts/Transcript/Article/2924617/general-kenneth-f-mckenzie-jr-commander-us-central-command-holds-a-press-briefing/
5   https://www.washingtonpost.com/national-security/2022/08/24/kabul-airport-bombing-afghanistan-evacuation/
6   Ibid.
7   https://www.washingtonpost.com/world/2021/08/28/afghanistan-airport-attack-videos/
8   https://www.propublica.org/article/report-u-s-marines-returned-fire-after-suicide-bombing-but-no-enemies-were-shooting-at-them
9   https://edition.cnn.com/2021/10/06/politics/kabul-airport-attacker-prison/index.html
10 https://www.brookings.edu/articles/biden-can-reduce-civilian-casualties-during-us-drone-strikes-heres-how
11 https://leftlanenews.com/2010/08/27/corolla-accounts-for-90-of-all-cars-in-afghanistan/
12 https://www.nbcnews.com/news/world/relatives-afghan-family-killed-u-s-drone-strike-call-compensation-n1279499
13 https://airwars.org/news-and-investigations/tens-of-thousands-of-civilians-likely-killed-by-us-in-forever-wars/
14 https://www.nytimes.com/2021/12/13/us/politics/afghanistan-drone-strike.html

Chapter 11: The Final Airlift

1   https://news.sky.com/story/afghanistan-sky-reporter-feared-for-those-left-behind-as-he-departed-kabul-with-afghans-who-will-never-see-their-country-again-12391196

Chapter 12: The Aftermath

1 https://kabulfalling.com/episodes/still-falling-afghanistan-one-year-later/transcript/

2 https://www.npr.org/2021/12/31/1069428211/parents-selling-children-shows-desperation-in-afghanistan.

3 https://kabulfalling.com/episodes/still-falling-afghanistan-one-year-later/transcript/

4 https://holliesmckay.substack.com/p/dispatches-from-afghanistan-talking

5 https://www.hrw.org/news/2022/08/04/afghanistan-economic-crisis-underlies-mass-hunger

6 https://kabulfalling.com/episodes/still-falling-afghanistan-one-year-later/transcript/

7 https://www.hrw.org/news/2022/08/04/afghanistan-economic-crisis-underlies-mass-hunger

8 Ibid.

9 https://www.state.gov/the-united-states-and-partners-announce-establishment-of-fund-for-the-people-of-afghanistan/

10 https://kabulfalling.com/episodes/why-i-fight-a-taliban-fighter-speaks-from-afghanistan/transcript/

11 https://holliesmckay.substack.com/p/dispatches-from-afghanistan-talking

12 Ibid.

13 Ibid.

14 *Losing Afghanistan*, p. 147.

15 https://www.npr.org/2021/08/18/1028780816/transcript-taliban-spokesman-suhail-shaheen-interview

16 Ibid.

17 https://www.cnn.com/2021/09/19/asia/afghanistan-women-government-jobs-intl-hnk/index.html

18 https://www.nytimes.com/2022/09/30/world/asia/afghanistan-bombing-girls-education.html

19 https://www.aljazeera.com/news/2022/10/3/afghan-women-protest-against-recent-attack-on-kabul-school

20 https://www.nytimes.com/2022/09/30/world/asia/afghanistan-bombing-girls-education.html

21 *Losing Afghanistan*, p. 204.

22 https://www.bbc.com/news/uk-60613554
23 Ibid.
24 https://kabulfalling.com/episodes/still-falling-afghanistan-one-year
    -later/transcript/
25 https://www.axios.com/2021/08/24/afghan-refugees-conditions
    -qatar
26 https://kabulfalling.com/episodes/still-falling-afghanistan-one-year
    -later/transcript/
27 Ibid.
28 Ibid.
29 https://moralinjuryproject.syr.edu/about-moral-injury/

Index